THE BEST
AMERICAN
MAGAZINE
WRITING

2016

THE BEST
AMERICAN
MAGAZINE
WRITING
2016

**Edited by
Sid Holt for the
American Society
of Magazine
Editors**

Columbia University Press   New York

Columbia University Press
Publishers Since 1893
New York   Chichester, West Sussex
cup.columbia.edu
Copyright © 2016 American Society of Magazine Editors
All rights reserved

Library of Congress Cataloging-in-Publication Data
ISSN 1541-0978
ISBN 978-0231-18155-6 (pbk.)

Columbia University Press books are printed on permanent and durable
acid-free paper.
This book is printed on paper with recycled content.
Printed in the United States of America

p 10 9 8 7 6 5 4 3 2 1

Cover Design: Nancy Rouemy

Contents

Roger Hodge

Introduction: Going Native: An Eight-Minute Read

Every year hundreds of magazine editors congregate in one or another New York City conference center to pass judgment on thousands of stories, essays, columns, special issues, photo essays, videos, punning headlines, and gorgeously produced service packages. Each editor arrives at the National Magazine Awards judging session with a singular set of prejudices, biases, grudges, and agendas—we're only humans, after all—but also hoping to discover new stories, new magazines, and perhaps some subtle indication of how our own entries might be faring in the room next door. Over the last several years, as the American Society of Magazine Editors has moved to embrace new platforms and modes of publishing, the digital transformation of the industry has been much on our minds. This year the separate print and digital categories were almost but not entirely eliminated.

Despite years of moans and lamentations about the state of the magazine industry, anxiety over job security, dwindling fees, vanishing expense accounts, and the ever-encroaching menace of Facebook, writers once again, even in 2016, somehow found the resources to report and write; editors managed to edit amid the cacophony of open-plan offices; and all the other indispensable players in the quality-lit game—designers, photo editors, fact-checkers, copy editors, researchers, publicists, interns, and ad salespeople—got their jobs done as well. And by some miracle we managed to find a readership for our more ambitious articles even though people insist on reading our products on their smartphones.

I have a confession. This year I, too, did most of my magazine reading on a screen, often a small handheld one, lost in the digital garden of forking paths, moving from one link to another, and occasionally finding myself back at *The Intercept*, the website where I spend the labor of my days. Most of my newspaper reading occurred on a screen as well, and who really can distinguish newspapers from magazines anymore? A good chunk of my book reading also scrolled by on a (slightly larger) screen, so I suppose I've gone fully native. Back in the old days, which weren't so very long ago, during the first round of judging, ASME used to send us a large box of magazines to review. Some of those issues—like a special painted box-head containing unbound *McSweeny's* articles—are still collecting dust somewhere in my house, perched atop back issues of the *Oxford American* and *Lapham's Quarterly*. Then came the flash drive stuffed with entries that arrived in a FedEx envelope. Now we simply receive a login for a (somewhat slow) server loaded with PDFs. No iPad, laptop, or phone can compete with the pure tactile pleasure of flipping through the September issue of a glossy fashion magazine, however, and when we convened at Columbia University this year for judging, we all enthusiastically indulged our sadly neglected paper fetishes.

Like many other editors and literary types I used to fret over the fate of what we now call "longform," deeply reported narrative features and investigative reports that resist screen-friendly surgical-strike word counts. Yet this year I happily read on my phone Kathryn Shultz's "The Really Big One," a wonderfully scary 6,000-word feature on the coming destruction of the Pacific Northwest by earthquake, while standing on a Q train to Manhattan, trying not to think about how vulnerable my own city is to natural disasters. Instapaper informed me that it was a twenty-five-minute read, which perfectly matched my typical commute. I shuddered in amazement as I read on my two-inch screen about Goldfinger the seismologist watching on *his* two-inch screen the Tohoku tsunami roll in, and then I wondered how anyone could possibly remain living in the Cascadia inundation zone after reading Shultz's article. But then, I thought, where would those millions of people go?

It's kind of like the situation facing millions of undocumented immigrants in the United States who live under a constant threat of deportation. Not under the hypothetical threat of a President Trump but in the here and now, from a liberal Democratic president who has presided over the most efficient deportation regime in American history. I missed Luke Mogelson's "The Deported" when it first appeared in the *New York Times Magazine*, so when I saw it on the projected table of contents for *Best American Magazine Writing 2016* I pulled it up on my phone; it was a thirty-four-minute read. I had just edited a similar piece, one about refugees from gang violence in El Salvador who would surely be murdered if they were denied asylum and sent back but who almost certainly will be so denied. In his story, Mogelson follows a man who was denied asylum and deported to Honduras and who now must live separated from his children. In Honduras, Mogelson meets others, also deported, who have no choice but to risk once again the perilous journey north, where the odds of even making the passage through Mexico have grown ever longer. One man, named Abraham, said he had been deported *from Mexico* seven times on his way to the United States, imprisoned by the Zetas cartel, threatened with castration and death, enslaved for eight months. Yet he said he had no choice; he would eventually brave the trains once again.

People who have no choice simply do what they must. The migrant workers in *BuzzFeed*'s "The New American Slavery" thought they were avoiding the dangers of illegal immigration when they signed up for a guest-worker program, entering the United States on H-2 visas. They didn't want to end up as anonymous crosses on a map, data points among the thousands who have died in the Chihuahua and Sonora deserts of the American Southwest. Instead, as Jessica Garrison, Ken Bensinger, and Jeremy Singer-Vine document in their powerful investigation, they found themselves enslaved and abused in southern Louisiana. That was a thirty-five-minute read.

Other characters who appear in this volume, more fortunate by an accident of birth or geography, face conflicts and challenges that are no less mortal, and take significant actions that when rendered into prose yield writing of the highest caliber. I'm thinking particularly of "The Friend," by Matthew Teague, a story of uncommon devotion and extraordinary suffering. I don't recommend reading "The Friend" on the subway or in a cafe if you'd rather not be seen weeping in public.

"How it Feels," by Jenny Zhang, is a seventeen-minute read that feels like a nail in the skull, a punch in the solar plexus, a shot in the heart. Read that powerful essay about depression and then read "An Unbelievable Story of Rape," about a young woman who some policemen bullied into recanting her statement that she'd been raped at knifepoint. She was then prosecuted for the crime of making a false statement to police. Then maybe read *Cosmopolitan*'s disturbing seventeen-minute report on the anti-abortion clinics, a.k.a. pregnancy centers, that are popping up all over the country and Joshua Hammer's thirty-six-minute story about Ebola in Sierra Leone. These are extraordinary, powerful works of journalism, and now you hold them all in your hand, lucky reader, whether on paper or projected on glass and conjured out of photons, in this remarkably useful example of reading technology known as a book.

Not everything in this collection is so deadly serious; we magazine types like to laugh as well as cry and tear our hair in righteous anger at the injustices of the world. Barrett Brown's three essays, published in *The Intercept*, proceed from personal injustice and arrive at a kind of sublime universal comedy that is very rare indeed. I read each of those ten-minute essays aloud to my wife as I cried with laughter shortly after they arrived in my office—handwritten, on paper, from Barrett's prison cell in Texas, where he's serving time as a political prisoner on trumped up federal charges because the FBI and the DOJ didn't like his journalism. Those who have no choice simply do what they must.

One of the more irritating factoids of our digital age is the idea that no one will read longish, deeply reported articles on the Internet, much less on their phones. Of course, there's no question that short, clicky posts are more likely to go viral and generate huge traffic numbers, but there's also good evidence that readers engage more substantively with longer pieces, even on mobile. In May, for example, the Pew Research Center released a study finding that readers spend twice as much time with longer articles than with shorter ones, 123 seconds compared with 57 seconds. That doesn't sound like a long time, I admit, but wait! The report was based on Parse.ly data, which measure engagement based on screen movements in 5.5 second intervals, and the study's authors have good reasons for concluding that the actual time readers spend with articles is probably much longer.

The data on reader engagement are still pretty crude, despite the ubiquity of digital surveillance. The main point is that readers spend significantly more time with longer pieces—more than twice as much!—which is good news for editors and writers who are committed to producing groundbreaking investigations and telling complex stories.

One thing that the Parse.ly data do not capture is the use of "Read Later" apps such as Instapaper and Pocket. Personally, I almost always save longer articles to Instapaper, and I did so with every single article that appears in this book. I made a folder called ASME and filed them all away to read at my leisure. Sometimes that meant I gave up some cool graphics and illustrations, but in the case of Paul Ford's magisterial 131-minute, 35,000-word, issue-long "What Is Code?" article from *Bloomberg Businessweek*, easily the single most awesome piece of magazine journalism that appeared in 2015, I did occasionally pop back into Chrome on my laptop so I could enjoy the original as it was intended, gifs and all. By the way, I subscribe to the paper magazine, and that piece was better on a screen.

Unsurprisingly, in the inane controversies over longform and digital reading and so forth, it helps to take the long view, as the novelist Paul La Farge pointed out recently in a thoughtful eleven-minute essay in *Nautilus*, "The Deep Space of Digital Reading." People haven't always read in the same way, and every new "platform," from papyrus to illuminated manuscript to printed folio to mass-market paperback, has elicited almost verbatim alarums. La Farge didn't mention it in his essay, but the highly literate slave owners of ancient Athens typically enjoyed their scrolls as they were read aloud by slaves, and Plato's Socrates more than once pretends to worry that the habit of writing would ruin people's memories because they were no longer required to memorize the epic poems of the Homeric tradition. (Plato, the greatest prose writer of antiquity, is probably engaging in a bit of satire there, by the way.) St. Augustine famously reports, in his *Confessions*, that he was stunned to see his teacher Ambrose reading silently in 384 AD, without moving his lips, and reading remained an oral activity well into the medieval period and beyond. Reading silently, according to historians and cognitive scientists, set off a transformation of human consciousness. As La Farge puts it, "When the reading brain becomes able to process written symbols automatically, the thinking brain, the I, has time to go beyond those symbols, to develop itself and the culture in which it lives." As a highly sophisticated reader and writer, La Farge isn't terribly impressed with the legions of pessimists who see in our latest technological revolution the advent of a permanent shallowing of culture as the "endless, mesmerizing buzz" of the Internet renders us all into irredeemable idiots.

No uncritical digital cheerleader, La Farge recognizes the downsides of digital culture as well as anyone, but he's skeptical of claims that we've expelled ourselves from a readerly paradise. He observes, for instance, that the studies showing people are less able to comprehend material they've read on a screen are quite likely cultural artifacts rather than brute facts. We're in the midst of a big transition, after all, and though it's undeniably irritating to see phone drones rudely stumbling around ignoring their children and blocking the aisles of grocery stores, *at least they're reading something.* Social mores just haven't caught up yet, and pretty soon the good old-fashioned cultural mechanism known as shame will kick in and people will learn to mind their manners again. Then our publishing Cassandras can be counted upon to lament the decline in digital reading, but until then, thanks for all the page views!

Sid Holt

Acknowledgments

For nearly two decades, *Best American Magazine Writing* has been bringing together some of the best journalism of the previous year as chosen by the judges of the National Magazine Awards. (Not all the best journalism, of course, if for no other reason than the winner of, say, the Video award is impossible to translate into print—more's the pity, since this year's winner, *Vice News*'s "Selfie Soldiers: Russia's Army Checks In to Ukraine" is the best kind of magazine journalism— informative, entertaining, and surprising all at once.)

This edition of *BAMW* is, however, unlike any other. Seven of the seventeen pieces in this anthology first appeared online, and several of the others were parts of multiplatform packages. In fact, six of the twenty-one National Magazine Award winners this year were originally published online. In one of the oldest categories—Public Interest—four of the five finalists were digital only, and the fifth combined one print piece and two online pieces (that print piece—Meaghan Winters's *Cosmopolitan* story " 'Pregnant? Scared? Need Options? Too Bad' "—is included here).

You may think this means . . . wait for it . . . print is dead. Which somehow means that magazines are dead. Far from it. The business of magazines is changing as it has been changing since long before the first National Magazine Award winner,

Look, vanished in 1971, but as the pieces in this anthology demonstrate, magazine journalism has never been stronger. And whether it appears in print or online, as video or social media, magazine journalism plays an increasingly important role in American society, explaining us to ourselves as no other medium can.

The names, of course, are changing as well—and always will. Back in 1971, as *Look* teetered on the brink, a four-year-old magazine called *Rolling Stone* won its first National Magazine Award for its coverage of the Altamont festival and the Manson family. The four other winners that year were, however, titles as familiar today as they were then: *The Atlantic, Esquire, The Nation*, and *Vogue*. So, too, this edition of *BAMW* includes articles from *The New Yorker, Esquire*, and *ESPN the Magazine* alongside pieces from *BuzzFeed, Matter*, and *The Intercept*.

Even the way we talk about the awards is changing. We now call them the National Magazine Awards for Print and Digital Media and often refer to them as the Ellies, for the bronze replica of the Alexander Calder stabile *Elephant* that is given to each winner (the original has its own office at ASME headquarters in New York). But in many other ways the awards remain the same. They are still chosen by leading editors, graphic designers, and photo editors; still presented at an annual gala attended by hundreds of editors and publishers; still celebrate stories that are vigorously reported, elegantly written, lavishly illustrated.

This year 282 media organizations participated in the Ellies, submitting 1,590 print and digital entries, far more than any comparable competition. In January of this year 299 magazine journalists and educators—many of them traveling on their own dime—gathered at Columbia University in the City of New York to choose the finalists and winners. Each of the judges arrived at Columbia after spending the previous weeks reading or viewing entries in one of the twenty-one categories, sometimes interrupting holiday celebrations to ensure that each entry received the attention it deserved.

The judges chose five finalists in each category except Reporting and Feature Writing, two categories in which the number of entries well exceeds one hundred. Sequestered together for two days, the judges then chose the winners. Ten days later the judges' decisions were ratified by the National Magazine Awards Board, a committee composed of veteran judges and other magazine-industry leaders. One week later the finalists were announced in what has become an annual rite of its own—the Ellies Twittercast. (Follow @asme1963 if you want to be part of the, er, fun in 2017.)

Only three weeks later the winners were announced at "the magazine Oscars," the annual Ellies gala, hosted by Tamron Hall, national correspondent for NBC News and day-side anchor for MSNBC. Some of the finalists and winners had been published only weeks before being honored at the gala—testament in its own way to the timeliness that distinguishes magazine journalism.

The 2016 gala also included the presentation of the Magazine Editors' Hall of Fame Award to Gayle Goodson Butler, the former editor in chief of one of the most widely read magazines in America, *Better Homes and Gardens*. In receiving this recognition from her colleagues, Butler joined a distinguished group of editors that already includes *Vanity Fair*'s Graydon Carter, *Vogue*'s Anna Wintour, and Martha Stewart, as well as such legendary figures as Helen Gurley Brown, Clay Felker, and Richard B. Stolley.

The members of ASME owe both Tamron Hall and Gayle Butler our thanks for joining us at the 2016 gala, but there are hundreds of others who also deserve our gratitude for making the Ellies a success. All of the judges should be acknowledged for taking time away from their increasingly complex responsibilities as editorial leaders to ensure that the best magazine work published in America receives the recognition it rightfully is owed. A complete list of the judges and judging leaders is posted on the ASME website.

Also deserving of thanks is the ASME board of directors, especially the 2014–2016 president of ASME, Mark Jannot, who, when he was not supervising the running of the Ellies, served as vice president of content for the National Audubon Society. Each of the sixteen board members not only shares responsibility for overseeing the administration and presentation of the Ellies but also joins in fiercely protecting the integrity of the awards.

For the last fifty years, ASME has cosponsored the Ellies with the Columbia Journalism School. ASME thanks Steve Coll, the Pulitzer Prize–winning reporter who now serves as dean of the journalism school and Henry R. Luce Professor, for his passionate support of the awards. ASME also thanks Abi Wright, the executive director of the Alfred I. DuPont–Columbia University Awards, for her help organizing the judging of the Ellies and for her service as a member of the National Magazine Awards Board.

On behalf of ASME, I especially want to thank Roger Hodge, national editor of *The Intercept*, for writing the introduction of the 2016 edition of *Best American Magazine Writing*. Roger's work at *The Intercept* was, of course, recognized by the 2016 Ellie for Columns and Commentary awarded to the highly original— and deeply amusing—Barrett Brown pieces included in this anthology. Not to be overlooked, however, is Roger's contribution as the former editor in chief of *Oxford American* to the Ellie for General Excellence won by that magazine this year.

David McCormick of McCormick Literary has represented ASME as its book agent for more than a decade. The members of ASME are grateful for his work on our behalf. Philip Leventhal and Michael Haskell of Columbia University Press deserve special thanks for their commitment to *BAMW*. Year after year their enthusiasm and skill guarantee the success of each new anthology, and I have long come to depend on their kindness and patience as collaborators.

ASME works closely throughout the year with the members and staff of MPA, the Association of Magazine Media. I want to thank the chair of the MPA board of directors, Steve Lacy of Meredith Corporation, and Linda Thomas Brooks, the president and CEO of MPA, for their steadfast support. As always, thanks are due to my ASME associate, Nina Fortuna, for all she does to make the Ellies a success. I know every member of ASME joins me in considering her the eighth wonder of the world.

Of course, our biggest debt of gratitude belongs to the journalists whose writing and editing the Ellies celebrate, especially those who graciously permit ASME to print their work in *Best American Magazine Writing*. At a time of startling change, their labors on our behalf—on behalf of all readers—guarantees the future success of magazine journalism.

For more information about the National Magazine Awards, including a searchable database of winners and finalists, go to http://www.magazine.org/asme. To view the presentation of the 2016 Ellies, visit the ASME YouTube Channel.

THE BEST
AMERICAN
MAGAZINE
WRITING

2016

Vice

Q&As are pretty standard magazine fare. Q&As with the president of the United States are not—especially when the Q&A occurred during the first visit by a sitting president to a federal prison. President Obama was interviewed by Shane Smith, the cofounder and CEO of Vice Media, for Vice*'s October 2015 "Prison Issue," part of the organization's multiplatform investigation of mass incarceration in the United States. The Ellie judges who nominated "The Prison Issue" for the National Magazine Award for Single-Topic Issue described the interview as "historic" and praised the magazine for having "the confidence, generosity and imagination to turn over its pages to the 2.2 million Americans whom we always hear about but rarely hear from." Since 2012, Vice Media has received six Ellie nominations, including three in 2016, and won two Video awards.*

Shane Smith

Fixing the System

An Interview with President Obama on Prison Reform

This past July, *Vice* accompanied President Barack Obama to the Federal Correctional Institution in El Reno, Oklahoma, to film a special episode about the U.S. criminal justice system for our show on HBO. It was the first time a sitting president has visited a federal prison. Below are excerpts, slightly edited for length and clarity, from a sit-down interview during the episode, which aired Sunday, September 27, on HBO.

SHANE SMITH: *This is the first time in history a sitting president has visited a federal prison. Why now? Why is it important?*
PRESIDENT BARACK OBAMA: Over the last twenty years, we've seen a shift in incarceration rates that is really unprecedented. We've seen a doubling of the prison population. A large percentage of that is for nonviolent drug offenses.

There are twenty-one times the number of federal drug offenders now than there were in the eighties; there are more federal incarcerations for drug offenses than there are for homicide, aggravated assault, kidnapping, robbery, weapons, immigration, arson, sex offenses, extortion, bribery, etcetera, etcetera, combined.* How did that happen?

---

* While the majority of federal prisoners are indeed drug offenders, the majority of inmates overall are in state prisons on violent offenses.

I think there was a lot of fear. The War on Drugs, the crack epidemic, it became, I think, a bipartisan cause to get tough on crime. Incarceration became an easy, simple recipe in the minds of a lot of folks. Nobody ever lost an election because they were too tough on crime.

And so nobody stepped back and asked, is it really appropriate for somebody who's engaged in a serious but nonviolent drug offense to get more time than a rapist?

What's been interesting is that violent crime rates have consistently declined, and the costs of incarceration obviously have skyrocketed.

The stats are staggering: One in seventeen white men have the chance they will go to prison in their lifetime, compared with one in three black men. Is the criminal justice system in America racist?

I think the criminal justice system interacts with broader patterns of society in a way that results in injustice and unfairness. The system, every study has shown, is biased somewhere institutionally in such a way where an African American youth is more likely to be suspended from school than a white youth for engaging in the same disruptive behavior. More likely to be arrested, more likely to be charged, more likely to be prosecuted aggressively, more likely to get a stiffer sentence.

The system tilts in a direction that is unjust. And particularly when you think about nonviolent drug offenses. This is an area where the statistics are so skewed, you have to question whether we have become numb to the costs that it has on these communities, whether we think it's somehow normal for black youth or Latino youth to be going through the system in this way. It's not normal. And it has to be addressed from soup to nuts in order for us to get some better outcomes.

You've done drugs. And you said today, "Look, I've made bad decisions when I was young." Pretty much everybody does. "But you know, I was in a community or I had the ability to not have as harsh ramifications for my mistakes." Is one of the reasons why you're here today because, perhaps, you're the first president to feel empathy for the people who are here?

Well, I'd like to think other presidents feel the same way, but I can tell you I feel it acutely.

When I moved to Chicago and I started doing community organizing in low-income neighborhoods, one of the most powerful thoughts that I had was driving by street corners with kids who at that stage—I was in my early twenties—really weren't that far off from where I was, and knowing that the mistakes they made would land them potentially in prison, in ways that just were not true for me growing up in Hawaii. The notion that you or I couldn't have easily been drawn into that, that somehow we wouldn't have fallen prey to the temptations of the streets, I think, that doesn't feel right to me. That doesn't feel true.

You've said—a lot of other people have said, as well—the War on Drugs is a failure; the criminal justice system has problems. That's bipartisan now. Both sides of the aisle are saying, "Yes, we realize there are problems." This has become a big issue for you. Can it be fixed?

There's a whole bunch of front-end investments that we can make: If we focus on intervening with young people early; if we focus on the schools and making sure that black boys and Latino boys aren't suspended at higher rates.

If we're really investing in their education and they're reading at a third-grade level when they are in third grade, then we know they are less likely to get into the criminal-justice system in the first place. If we invest in education programs in prisons— you heard those guys talking about how much of a difference it made for them. Substance-abuse programs and education programs.

Vocational programs.

Vocational programs, so that we recognize you've got to prepare them for a better way when they get of here. Because most of them are going to get out of here eventually.

If we can make progress on this subset of the problem, which is nonviolent drug offenses, we can actually get a working majority around this issue.

Nothing's easy. Most people aren't interacting with the criminal justice system, and they don't see the impact that it's having on their communities. And part of our job is just to shine a spotlight. I think there's enough empathy among people of goodwill across the political spectrum that we may be able to pull this off.

Bloomberg Businessweek

WINNER—SINGLE-TOPIC ISSUE

Front to back, the entire June 15–28, 2015, issue of Bloomberg Businessweek *was devoted to the publication of "Code: An Essay." In a note introducing the article, Josh Tyrangiel, then the editor of* Bloomberg Businessweek, *explained the importance of the piece: "Now that software lives in our pockets, runs our cars and homes, and dominates our waking lives, ignorance is no longer acceptable. The world belongs to people who code. Those who don't understand will be left behind." Written by Paul Ford, who is both a programmer and an essayist (he has a book coming soon from FSG), "Code" is filled with real-world insight and regular-guy charm. Which is a good thing, because the story that won the Ellie for Single-Topic Issue was originally 38,000 words in length. This version is a mere 16,500.*

Paul Ford

What Is Code?

If You Don't Know,
You Need to Read This

1. The Man in the Taupe Blazer

You are an educated, successful person capable of abstract thought. A VP doing an SVP's job. Your office, appointed with decent furniture and a healthy amount of natural light filtered through vertical blinds, is commensurate with nearly two decades of service to the craft of management.

Copper plaques on the wall attest to your various leadership abilities inside and outside the organization: One, the Partner in Innovation Banquet Award 2011, is from the sales team for your support of its eighteen-month effort to reduce cycle friction—net sales increased 6.5 percent; another, the Civic Guidelight 2008, is for overseeing a volunteer team that repainted a troubled public school top to bottom.

You have a reputation throughout the organization as a careful person, bordering on penny-pinching. The way you'd put it is, you are loath to pay for things that can't be explained. You expect your staff to speak in plain language. This policy has served you well in many facets of operations, but it hasn't worked at all when it comes to overseeing software development.

For your entire working memory, *some Internet thing* has come along every two years and suddenly hundreds of thousands of dollars (inevitably millions) must be poured into amorphous projects with variable deadlines. Content management projects, customer relationship management integration projects, mobile apps, paperless office things, global enterprise resource planning initiatives—no matter how tightly you clutch the purse strings, software finds a way to pry open your fingers.

Here we go again. On the other side of your (well-organized) desk sits *this guy* in his mid-thirties with a computer in his lap. He's wearing a taupe blazer. He's come to discuss spending large sums to create intangible abstractions on a "website re-architecture project." He needs money, support for his team, new hires, external resources. It's preordained that you'll give these things to him, because the CEO signed off on the initiative—and yet should it all go pear-shaped, you will be responsible. Coders are insanely expensive, and projects that start with uncomfortably large budgets have an ugly tendency to grow from there. You need to understand where the hours will go.

He says: "We're basically at the limits with WordPress."

Who wears a taupe blazer?

The CTO was fired six months ago. That CTO has three kids in college and a mustache. It was a bad exit. The man in the taupe blazer (TMitTB) works for the new CTO. She comes from Adobe and has short hair and no mustache.

Here is what you've been told: All of the computer code that keeps the website running must be replaced. At one time, it was very valuable and was keeping the company running, but the new CTO thinks it's garbage. She tells you the old code is spaghetti and your systems are straining as a result. That the third-party services you use, and pay for monthly, are old and busted. Your competitor has an animated shopping cart that drives across the top of the screen at checkout. That cart remembers everything customers have ever purchased and generates invoices on demand. Your cart has no memory at all.

Salespeople stomp around your office, sighing like theater students, telling you how embarrassed they are by the site. Nothing

11

What Is Code? If You Don't Know, You Need to Read This

works right on mobile. Orders are cutting off halfway. People are logged out with no warning. Something must be done.

Which is why TMitTB is here.

Who's he, anyway? Webmaster? IT? No, he's a "Scrum Master."

"My people are split on platform," he continues. "Some want to use Drupal 7 and make it work with Magento—which is still PHP." He frowns. "The other option is just doing the back end in Node.js with Backbone in front."

You've furrowed your brow; he eyes you sympathetically and explains: "With that option it's all JavaScript, front and back."

Those are all terms you've heard. You've read the first parts of the Wikipedia pages and a book on software project estimation. It made some sense at the time.

You ask the universal framing question: "Did you cost these options?"

He gives you a number and a date. You know in your soul that the number is half of what it should be and that the project will go a year over schedule. He promises long-term efficiencies: The $85,000 in Oracle licenses will no longer be needed; engineering is moving to a free, open-sourced database. "We probably should have done that back when we did the Magento migration," he says. Meaning, of course, that his predecessor probably should have done that.

You consult a spreadsheet and remind him that the Oracle contract was renewed a few months ago. So, no, actually, at least for now, you'll keep eating that cost. Sigh.

This man makes a third less than you, and his education ended with a BS from a large, perfectly fine state university. But he has 500+ connections on LinkedIn. That plus sign after the "500" bothers you. How many more than 500 people does he know? Five? Five thousand?

In some mysterious way, he outranks you. Not within the company, not in restaurant reservations, not around lawyers.

Still: He strokes his short beard; his hands are tanned; he hikes; his socks are embroidered with little ninja.

"Don't forget," he says, "we've got to budget for apps."

This is real. A Scrum Master in ninja socks has come into your office and said, "We've got to budget for apps." Should it all go pear-shaped, his career will be just fine.

You keep your work in perspective by thinking about barrels of cash. You once heard that a U.S. dry barrel can hold about $100,000 worth of singles. Next year, you'll burn a little under a barrel of cash on Oracle. One barrel isn't that bad. But it's never one barrel. Is this a five-barrel project or a ten-barreler? More? Too soon to tell. But you can definitely smell money burning.

At this stage in the meeting, you like to look supplicants in the eye and say, *OK, you've given me a date and a budget.* But when will it be done? Really, truly, top-line-revenue-reporting finished? Come to confession; unburden your soul.

This time you stop yourself. You don't want your inquiry to be met by a patronizing sigh of impatience or another explanation about ship dates, Agile cycles, and continuous delivery. Better for now to hide your ignorance. *When will it be done?* You are learning to accept that the answer for software projects is *never*.

1.1. Why Are We Here?

We are here because the editor of this magazine asked me, "Can you tell me what code is?"

"No," I said. "First of all, I'm not good at the math. I'm a programmer, yes, but I'm an East Coast programmer, not one of these serious platform people from the Bay Area."

I began to program nearly twenty years ago, learning via `oraperl`, a special version of the Perl language modified to work with the Oracle database. A month into the work, I damaged the accounts of 30,000 fantasy basketball players. They sent some angry e-mails. After that, I decided to get better.

13

What Is Code? If You Don't Know, You Need to Read This

Which is to say I'm not a natural. I love computers, but they never made any sense to me. And yet, after two decades of jamming information into my code-resistant brain, I've amassed enough knowledge that the computer has revealed itself. Its magic has been stripped away. I can talk to someone who used to work at Amazon.com or Microsoft about his or her work without feeling a burning shame. I'd happily talk to people from Google and Apple, too, but they so rarely reenter the general population.

The World Wide Web is what I know best (I've coded for money in the programming languages Java, JavaScript, Python, Perl, PHP, Clojure, and XSLT), but the Web is only one small part of the larger world of software development. There are 11 million professional software developers on earth, according to the research firm IDC. (An additional 7 million are hobbyists.) That's roughly the population of the greater Los Angeles metro area. Imagine all of L.A. programming. East Hollywood would be for Mac programmers, West L.A. for mobile, Beverly Hills for finance programmers, and all of Orange County for Windows.

There are lots of other neighborhoods, too: There are people who write code for embedded computers smaller than your thumb. There are people who write the code that runs your TV. There are programmers for everything. They have different cultures, different tribal folklores, that they use to organize their working life. If you told me a systems administrator was taking a juggling class, that would make sense, and I'd expect a product manager to take a trapeze class. I've met information architects who list and rank their friendships in spreadsheets. Security research specialists love to party.

What I'm saying is, I'm one of 18 million. So that's what I'm writing: my view of software development, as an individual among millions. Code has been my life, and it has been your life, too. It is time to understand how it all works.

Every month it becomes easier to do things that have never been done before, to create new kinds of chaos and find new kinds of order. Even though my math skills will never catch up, I love the work. Every month, code changes the world in some interesting, wonderful, or disturbing way.

2. Let's Begin

A computer is a clock with benefits. They all work the same, doing second-grade math, one step at a time: Tick, take a number and put it in box one. Tick, take another number, put it in box two. Tick, *operate* (an operation might be addition or subtraction) on those two numbers and put the resulting number in box one. Tick, check if the result is zero, and if it is, go to some other box and follow a new set of instructions.

You, using a pen and paper, can do anything a computer can; you just can't do those things billions of times per second. And those billions of tiny operations add up. They can cause a phone to boop, elevate an elevator, or redirect a missile. That raw speed makes it possible to pull off not one but multiple sleights of hand, card tricks on top of card tricks. Take a bunch of pulses of light reflected from an optical disc, apply some math to unsqueeze them, and copy the resulting pile of expanded impulses into some memory cells—then read from those cells to paint light on the screen. Millions of pulses, sixty times a second. That's how you make the rubes believe they're watching a movie.

Apple has always made computers; Microsoft used to make only software (and occasional accessory hardware, such as mice and keyboards), but now it's in the hardware business, with Xbox game consoles, Surface tablets, and Lumia phones. Facebook assembles its own computers for its massive data centers.

So many things are computers, or will be. That includes watches, cameras, air conditioners, cash registers, toilets, toys, airplanes, and movie projectors. Samsung makes computers that look like TVs, and Tesla makes computers with wheels and engines. Some

15

What Is Code? If You Don't Know, You Need to Read This

things that aren't yet computers—dental floss, flashlights—will fall eventually.

When you "batch" process a thousand images in Photoshop or sum numbers in Excel, you're programming, at least a little. When you use computers too much—which is to say a typical amount—they start to change you. I've had Photoshop dreams, Visio dreams, spreadsheet dreams, and web-browser dreams. The dreamscape becomes fluid and can be sorted and restructured. I've had programming dreams where I move text around the screen.

You can make computers do wonderful things, but you need to understand their limits. They're not all-powerful, not conscious in the least. They're fast, but some parts—the processor, the RAM—are faster than others—like the hard drive or the network connection. Making them seem infinite takes a great deal of work from a lot of programmers and a lot of marketers.

The turn-of-last-century British artist William Morris once said you can't have art without resistance in the materials. The computer and its multifarious peripherals are the materials. The code is the art.

2.1. How Do You Type an "A"?

Consider what happens when you strike a key on your keyboard. Say a lowercase "a." The keyboard is waiting for you to press a key or release one; it's constantly scanning to see what keys are pressed down. Hitting the key sends a scancode.

Just as the keyboard is waiting for a key to be pressed, the computer is waiting for a signal from the keyboard. When one comes down the pike, the computer interprets it and passes it farther into its own interior. "Here's what the keyboard just received—do with this what you will."

It's simple now, right? The computer just goes to some table, figures out that the signal corresponds to the letter "a," and puts it on screen. Of course not—too easy. Computers are machines. They don't know what a screen or an "a" are. To put the "a" on the screen, your computer has to pull the image of the "a" out of its memory as part of a font, an "a" made up of lines and circles. It has to take these lines and circles and render them in a little box of pixels in the part of its memory that manages the screen. So far we have at least three representations of one letter: the signal from the keyboard; the version in memory; and the lines-and-circles version sketched on the screen. We haven't even considered how to store it or what happens to the letters to the left and the right when you insert an "a" in the middle of a sentence. Or what "lines and circles" mean when reduced to binary data. There are surprisingly many ways to represent a simple "a." It's amazing any of it works at all.

Coders are people who are willing to work backward to that key press. It takes a certain temperament to page through standards documents, manuals, and documentation and read things like "data fields are transmitted least significant bit first" in the interest of understanding why, when you expected "ü," you keep getting "�."

2.2. From Hardware to Software

Hardware is a tricky business. For decades the work of integrating, building, and shipping computers was a way to build fortunes. But margins tightened. Look at Dell, now back in private hands, or Gateway, acquired by Acer. Dell and Gateway, two world-beating companies, stayed out of software, typically building PCs that came preinstalled with Microsoft Windows—plus various subscription-based services to increase profits.

This led to much cursing from individuals who'd spent $1,000 or more on a computer and now had to figure out how to stop the antivirus software from nagging them to pay up.

Years ago, when Microsoft was king, Steve Ballmer, sweating through his blue button-down, jumped up and down in front of

17

What Is Code? If You Don't Know, You Need to Read This

a stadium full of people and chanted, "Developers! Developers! Developers! Developers!"

He yelled until he was hoarse: "I love this company!" Of course he did. If you can sell the software, if you can light up the screen, you're selling infinitely reproducible nothings. The margins on nothing are great—until other people start selling even cheaper nothings or giving them away. Which is what happened, as free software-based systems such as Linux began to nibble, then devour, the server market, and free-to-use web-based applications such as Google Apps began to serve as viable replacements for desktop software.

Expectations around software have changed over time. IBM unbundled software from hardware in the 1960s and got to charge more; Microsoft rebundled Internet Explorer with Windows in 1998 and got sued; Apple initially refused anyone else the ability to write software for the iPhone when it came out in 2007, and then opened the App Store, which expanded into a vast commercial territory—and soon the world had Angry Birds. Today, much hardware comes with some software—a PC comes with an operating system, for example, and that OS includes hundreds of subprograms, from mail apps to solitaire. Then you download or buy more.

There have been countless attempts to make software easier to write, promising that you could code in plain English, or manipulate a set of icons, or make a list of rules—software development so simple that a bright senior executive or an average child could do it. Decades of efforts have gone into helping civilians write code as they might use a calculator or write an e-mail. Nothing yet has done away with *developers, developers, developers, developers.*

Thus a craft, and a professional class that lives that craft, emerged. Beginning in the 1950s, but catching fire in the 1980s, a proportionally small number of people became adept at inventing ways to satisfy basic human desires (know the time, schedule a flight, send a letter, kill a zombie) by controlling the machine. Coders, starting with concepts such as "signals from a keyboard" and "numbers in memory," created infinitely reproducible units of digital execution that we call software, hoping to meet the needs of the marketplace. Man, did they. The systems they built are used to manage the global economic infrastructure. If coders don't run the world, they run the things that run the world.

Most programmers aren't working on building a widely recognized application like Microsoft Word. Software is everywhere. It's gone from a craft of fragile, built-from-scratch custom projects to an industry of standardized parts, where coders absorb and improve upon the labors of their forebears (even if those forebears are one cubicle over). Software is there when you switch channels and your cable box shows you what else is on. You get money from an ATM—software. An elevator takes you up five stories—the same. Facebook releases software every day to something like a billion people, and that software runs inside web browsers and mobile applications. Facebook looks like it's just pictures of your mom's crocuses or your son's school play—but no, it's software.

2.3. How Does Code Become Software?

We know that a computer is a clock with benefits, and that software starts as code, but how?

We know that someone, somehow, enters a program into the computer and the program is made of code. In the old days, that meant putting holes in punch cards. Then you'd put the cards into a box and give them to an operator who would load them, and the computer would flip through the cards, identify where the holes were, and update parts of its memory, and then it would—OK, that's a little too far back. Let's talk about modern typing-into-a-keyboard code. It might look like this:

19

What Is Code? If You Don't Know, You Need to Read This

```
ispal: {x~|x}
```

That's in a language called, simply, K, famous for its brevity. That code will test if something is a palindrome. If you next typed in `ispal "able was i ere i saw elba"`, K will confirm that yes, this is a palindrome.

Coding is a broad human activity, like sport or writing. When software developers think of coding, most of them are thinking about lines of code in files. They're handed a problem, think about the problem, write code that will solve the problem, and then expect the computer to turn word into deed.

Code is inert. How do you make it ert? You run software that transforms it into machine language. The word "language" is a little ambitious here, given that you can make a computing device with wood and marbles. Your goal is to turn your code into an explicit list of instructions that can be carried out by interconnected logic gates, thus turning your code into something that can be executed—software.

Computing treats human language as an arbitrary set of symbols in sequences. It treats music, imagery, and film that way, too. It's a good and healthy exercise to ponder what your computer is doing right now. Maybe you're reading this on a laptop: What are the steps and layers between what you're doing and the Lilliputian mechanisms within? When you double-click an icon to open a program such as a word processor, the computer must know where that program is on the disk. It has some sort of accounting process to do that. And then it loads that program into its memory—which means that it loads an enormous to-do list into its memory and starts to step through it. What does that list look like?

Maybe you're reading this in print. No shame in that. In fact, thank you. The paper is the artifact of digital processes. Remember how we put that "a" on screen? See if you can get from some sleepy writer typing that letter on a keyboard in Brooklyn, N.Y., to the paper under your thumb. What framed that fearful symmetry?

Thinking this way will teach you two things about computers: One, there's no magic, no matter how much it looks like there is. There's just work to make things look like magic. And two, it's crazy in there.

2.4. What Is an Algorithm?

"Algorithm" is a word writers invoke to sound smart about technology. Journalists tend to talk about "Facebook's algorithm" or a "Google algorithm," which is usually inaccurate. They mean "software."

Algorithms don't require computers any more than geometry does. An algorithm solves a problem, and a great algorithm gets a name. *Euclid's algorithm*, for example, is the go-to specimen that shows up whenever anyone wants to wax on about algorithms, so why buck the trend? It's a simple way of determining the greatest common divisor for two numbers. Take two numbers, like 16 and 12. Divide the first by the second. If there's a remainder (in this case there is, 4), divide the smaller number, 12, by that remainder, 4, which gives you 3 and no remainder, so we're done— and 4 is the greatest common divisor. (Now translate that into machine code, and we can get out of here.)

A programming language is a system for encoding, naming, and organizing algorithms for reuse and application. It's an algorithm-management system. This is why, despite the hype, it's silly to say Facebook has an algorithm. An algorithm can be translated into a function, and that function can be called (run) when software is executed. There are algorithms that relate to image processing and for storing data efficiently and for rapidly running through the elements of a list. Most algorithms come for free, already built into a programming language, or are available, organized into libraries, for download from the Internet in a mo-

21

What Is Code? If You Don't Know, You Need to Read This

ment. You can do a ton of programming without actually thinking about algorithms—you can save something into a database or print a webpage by cutting and pasting code. But if you want the computer to, say, identify whether it's reading Spanish or Italian, you'll need to write a language-matching function. So in that sense, algorithms can be pure, mathematical entities as well as practical expressions of ideas on which you can place your grubby hands.

One thing that took me forever to understand is that computers aren't actually "good at math." They can be programmed to execute certain operations to certain degrees of precision, so much so that it looks like "doing math" to humans. A huge part of computer science is about understanding the efficiency of algorithms—how long they will take to run. Computers are fast, but they can get bogged down—for example, when trying to find the shortest path between two points on a large map. Companies such as Google, Facebook, and Twitter are built on top of fundamental computer science and pay great attention to efficiency because their users do things (searches, status updates, tweets) an extraordinary number of times. Thus it's absolutely worth their time to find excellent computer scientists, many with doctorates, who know where all the efficiencies are buried.

It takes a good mathematician to be a computer scientist, but a middling one to be an effective programmer. Until you start dealing with millions of people on a network or you need to blur or sharpen a million photos quickly, you can just use the work of other people. When it gets real, break out the comp sci. When you're doing anything a hundred trillion times, nanosecond delays add up. Systems slow down, users get cranky, money burns by the barrel.

The hardest work in programming is getting around things that aren't computable, in finding ways to break impossible tasks into small, possible components, and then creating the impression that the computer is doing something it actually isn't, like having a human conversation. This used to be known as "artificial intelligence research," but now it's more likely to go under the name "machine learning" or "data mining." When you speak to Siri or Cortana and they respond, it's not because these services understand you; they convert your words into text, break that text into symbols, then match those symbols against the symbols in their database of terms, and produce an answer. Tons of algorithms, bundled up and applied, mean that computers can fake listening.

A programming language has at least two jobs, then. It needs to wrap up lots of algorithms so they can be reused. Then you don't need to go looking for a square-root algorithm (or a genius programmer) every time you need a square root. And it has to make it easy for programmers to wrap up new algorithms and routines into functions for reuse. The DRY principle, for Don't Repeat Yourself, is one of the colloquial tenets of programming. That is, you should name things once, do things once, create a function once, and let the computer repeat itself. This doesn't always work. Programmers repeat themselves constantly. I've written certain kinds of code a hundred times. This is why DRY is a principle.

Enough talk. Let's code!

2.5. The Sprint

After a few months the budget is freed up, and the web re-architecture project is under way. They give it a name: Project Excelsior. Fine. TMitTB (who, to be fair, has other clothes and often dresses like he's in Weezer) checks in with you every week.

He brings documents. Every document has its own name. The functional specification is a set of at least a thousand statements about users clicking buttons. "Upon accessing the webpage the user if logged in will be identified by name and welcomed and if not logged in will be encouraged to log in or create an account. (See user registration workflow.)"

23

What Is Code? If You Don't Know, You Need to Read This

God have mercy on our souls. From there it lists various error messages. It's a sort of blueprint in that it describes—in words, with occasional diagrams—a program that doesn't exist.

Some parts of the functional specification refer to "user stories," tiny hypothetical narratives about people using the site, e.g., "As a visitor to the website, I want to search for products so I can quickly purchase what I want."

Then there's something TMitTB calls wireframe mock-ups, which are pictures of how the website will look, created in a program that makes everything seem as if it were sketched by hand, all a little squiggly—even though it was produced on a computer. This is so no one gets the wrong idea about these ideas-in-progress and takes them too seriously. Patronizing, but point taken.

You rarely see TMitTB in person, because he's often at conferences where he presents on panels. He then tweets about the panels and notes them on his well-populated LinkedIn page. Often he takes a picture of the audience from the stage, and what you see is an assembly of mostly men, many with beards, the majority of whom seem to be peering into their laptop instead of up at the stage. Nonetheless the tweet that accompanies that photo says something like, "AMAZING audience! @ the panel on #microservice architecture at #ArchiCon2015."

He often tells you just how important this panel-speaking is for purposes of recruiting. Who's to say he is wrong? It costs as much to hire a senior programmer as it does to hire a midlevel executive, so maybe going to conferences is his job, and in the two months he's been here he's hired four people. His two most recent hires have been in Boston and Hungary, neither of which is a place where you have an office.

But what does it matter? Every day he does a fifteen-minute "standup" meeting via something called Slack, which is essentially like Google Chat but with some sort of plaid visual theme, and the programmers seem to agree that this is a wonderful and fruitful way to work.

"I watch the commits," TMitTB says. Meaning that every day he reviews the code that his team writes to make sure that it's well-organized. "No one is pushing to production without the tests passing. We're good."

Your meetings, by comparison, go for hours, with people arranged around a table—sitting down. You wonder how he gets his programmers to stand up, but then some of them already use standing desks. Perhaps that's the ticket.

Honestly, you would like to go to conferences sometimes and be on panels. You could drink bottled water and hold forth just fine.

3. Why Are Programmers So Intense About Languages?

Many conferences are organized around specific programming languages or specific communities (PyCon for Python programmers; the Strata conference for big data; Oscon for open-source coders); these are ritual events for the people in those communities. Attendees gather, talk, and post the videos on YouTube. Language matters.

Programmers track the success of computer languages the way other people track sports rankings, commenting on web forums such as Reddit (where many languages get their own "subreddit," and reddit.com/r/programming currently has 620,202 readers), or *Hacker News*, run by the venture capital firm Y Combinator (a company named after a special kind of function that operates on other functions), or *Lambda the Ultimate* (named after a series of papers written mostly in the 1970s about the influential programming language Scheme—the more inside-baseball the name, the nerdier the subject matter).

There are hundreds of programming blogs. Many large corporations let their engineers blog (a generous gift, given how many recruiters are hovering). Discussions about programming go on

25

What Is Code? If You Don't Know, You Need to Read This

everywhere, in public, at all times, about hundreds of languages. There is a keen sense of what's coming up and what's fading out.

It's not simply fashion; one's career as a programmer depends on demonstrating capacity in one or more languages. So there are rankings, frequently updated, rarely shocking. As of April 15, the world's most-used computer languages, according to the Tiobe index (which uses a variety of indicators to generate a single ranking for the world of programming), are Java, C, C++, Objective-C, and C#, followed by JavaScript, PHP, and Python. The rankings are necessarily inexact; another list, by a consulting firm called RedMonk, gives JavaScript the top spot, followed by Java. There are many possible conclusions here, but the obvious one is that, all things being equal, a very good Java programmer who performs well in interviews will have more career options than a similar candidate using a more obscure language.

If you code, by the time a language breaks through to the top ten or twenty, you've heard of it, read blog posts about it, heard people lament how terrible or wonderful or misguided it is, possibly watched a few video tutorials, or played with it a little. Taking new languages out for a spin is a good thing for a programmer to do. Often all you have to do is download some files and write a couple lines of code, then decide if you want to go further. Most languages are free to download and use.

Why do people construct and then give away free languages? Well, the creation of a good computer language is the work of an apex programmer. To have produced a successful language is acknowledged as a monumental effort, akin to publishing a multivolume history of a war, or fighting in one. The reward is glory.

Changing a language is like fighting that war all over again, and some languages have at times been trapped in a liminal state between their old, busted selves, and their new, promised version. Perl 5, released in the mid-1990s, was a language uniquely suited to the World Wide Web, and it grew as the Web grew; Perl

6 was supposed to be better in every way, and a redesign began with grand pronouncements in 2000. But after fifteen years of people working continually and often for free on a project they consider in the public interest, there's still no official Perl 6. (Latest ETA: Christmas 2015.)

The Python language community, keenly aware of the Perl community's problems, decided to make necessary but difficult changes to the language as part of the transition from Version 2 to Version 3. They would modernize, clean up rough edges—but avoid grand reinventions. Development of Python 3.0 started in 2006; the first working version came out in 2008; and in 2015, the transition is ongoing.

Making a new language is hard. Making a popular language is much harder still and requires the smile of fortune. And changing the way a popular language works appears to be one of the most difficult things humans can do, requiring years of coordination to make the standards align. Languages are large, complex, dynamic expressions of human culture.

3.1. The Beauty of the Standard Library

The true measure of a language isn't how it uses semicolons; it's the *standard library* of each language. A language is software for making software. The standard library is a set of premade software that you can reuse and reapply.

Take Python, which is "batteries included," meaning that it comes with tons of preexisting code, organized into "modules," that you can reuse. Its standard library has functions that let you copy webpages or replace words in a document.

What does that mean, to process text? Well, you might have a string of text (The Quick Brown Fox) and save it in a variable called `my_string`. So now you can call standard methods on that string. You can say `my_string.lower()`, and it will make all the words lowercase, producing "the quick brown fox."

27

What Is Code? If You Don't Know, You Need to Read This

Truly understanding a language's standard library is one of the ways one becomes proficient in that language. Typically you just visit webpages or read a book.

But the standard library is only the beginning. For many languages—and Python is exemplary—there's an enormous library of prewritten modules available for nearly instantaneous download, using "package manager" software. A module (or library or package) is code that is intended to extend a language's capabilities.

Let's say you work for an advertising agency and need to process through 100,000 pictures and scale and sharpen them.

You type one command: `sudo pip install Pillow`, and the Pillow module is downloaded, compiled automatically, and placed into the correct directory for later reuse. You have to know, of course, that most modern languages have modules for image processing; you also need to know that Pillow is the most commonly used image-processing toolkit. Knowing how to find that out is part of the job of coding. You might learn it by Googling. You might ask a friend. You might get that information out of a book, or a website like The Hitchhiker's Guide to Python.

A coder needs to be able to quickly examine and identify which giant, complex library is the one that's the most recently and actively updated and the best match for his or her current needs. A coder needs to be a good listener.

But what a payoff! Now that Pillow is installed, you have, at your typing fingertips, dozens of routines and functions related to image processing that you can use in your code: change colors, rotate by a number of degrees, scale, convert GIF images to JPEGs, and so forth. Or if you need to do very complex numerical analysis and statistics work, you can download NumPy, and suddenly an enormous range of mathematical algorithms are available to you, hundreds of years of science and research boiled down. Audio processing, interacting with peculiar hardware, speaking to databases—there are packages for all of these things. But you need to know how to find them, what they are called. Code isn't just obscure commands in a file. It requires you to have a map in your head, to know where the good libraries, the best documentation, and the most helpful message boards are located. If you don't know where those things are, you will spend all of your time searching, instead of building cool new things.

3.3. The Importance of C

C is as big a deal as you can get in computing. Created by Dennis Ritchie starting in the late 1960s at Bell Labs, it's the principal development language of the UNIX operating system. Unix (lowercased now, to refer to the idea of Unix instead of the branded version) is a simple operating system—basically it's a kernel that manages memory and runs software, a large collection of very small utility programs, and a "shell" that helps you knit programs into "shell scripts." If you couldn't do what you needed with shell scripts, you might write a new utility in C and add it to the utility library. This was a nice and practical way of working, and it coincided with the rise of various kinds of networks that today we refer to collectively as the Internet. So Unix spread from Bell Labs to academia, to large industrial systems, and eventually leached into the water supply of computing until it was everywhere. And everywhere that Unix went, C was sure to go.

C is a simple language, simple like a shotgun that can blow off your foot. It allows you to manage every last part of a computer—the memory, files, a hard drive—which is great if you're meticulous and dangerous if you're sloppy. Software made in C is known for being fast. When you compile C, it doesn't simply become a bunch of machine language in one go; there are many steps to making it really, ridiculously fast. These are called optimizations, and they are to programming what loopholes are to taxes.

29

What Is Code? If You Don't Know, You Need to Read This

Think of C as sort of a plain-spoken grandfather who grew up trapping beavers and served in several wars but can still do fifty pull-ups.

C's legendary, lucid manual and specification, *The C Programming Language*, written by Ritchie and Brian Kernighan (known by its nickname, K&R), is a quick and simple read—physically light in comparison with modern, heavy-stock guides to programming on bookstore shelves. This recommended text was published in 1978, when personal computing barely existed, back when a computer was a large piece of industrial equipment used to control a refrigeration system or calculate actuarial tables. It was in K&R that "Hello, world!" became the canonical example program for any language. By convention, almost every introduction to any programming language since then starts with a variation on "Hello, world!"

The Linux kernel is written in C. The software that connects your printer to your computer could be in C. The web servers that serve up your webpages are often written in C. It's also a good language for writing other languages—Python, PHP, and Perl are written in C, as are many others. C is a language you use for building systems; it has the same role in computing that Latin did among Renaissance academics. You won't often meet a serious practitioner of the digital arts who doesn't have at least a passing familiarity. The more serious scholars are pretty fluent.

But remember that list of popular languages? C++? Objective-C? C#? Java? What many people code daily is not actually C, but one of the many Vulgates. Advocates of these languages make various arguments in their favor; they are better for large groups, for "programming in the large." These languages, they say, organize code into libraries that are shareable, reusable, and less likely to cause pain and suffering. These are object-oriented adaptations of C.

3.4. The Corporate Object Revolution

If you're going to understand how code works in a corporate environment, you need to understand what object-oriented programming is.

There are many definitions. I'll wade in and provide my own and face the consequences. Object-oriented programming is, at its essence, a filing system for code. As anyone who's ever shared a networked folder—or organized a physical filing cabinet—knows, without a good shared filing system your office will implode. C, people said in the 1980s and '90s, is a great language! An excellent language! But it doesn't really let you organize things. You end up with all these functions. It's a mess. I mean, we have this data structure for our customers (name, address, and so forth), and we have all these functions for manipulating that data (`update_address`, `send_bill`, `delete_account`), but the thing is, those functions aren't related to the data except by the naming convention. C doesn't have a consistent way to name things. Which means it's hard to find them later. Object-oriented programming gave programmers a great way to name things—a means of building up a library. I could call (run) `update_address` on a picture of a dog or an Internet address. That approach is sloppy and dangerous and leads to bugs (our forebears reasoned, and not without precedent), and it makes it hard to program with big teams and keep track of everything.

So what if, whaaaat if, we made a little box called Customer (call it a "class," as in the taxonomical sense, like a Customer is a subclass of the species human, which is a subclass of mammal, etc.), and we put the data and methods relating to customers into that box. (And by box, it's literally just "`public class Customer {}`" and anything inside the {} relates to that particular class.)

31

What Is Code? If You Don't Know, You Need to Read This

I mean, you wouldn't even need to look inside the box. You'd just download a large set of classes, all nested inside one another, study the available, public methods and the expected data, and start programming. Hey, you'd say, let's put some data into our object, take some data out. Every time we have a new customer we make a new instance of our class. Code can be a black box, with tentacles and wires sticking out, and you don't need to—don't want to—look inside the box. You can just put a couple of boxes next to each other, touch their tentacles together, and watch their eldritch mating.

This works out very well, in theory.

4. Why Are Coders Angry?

There's a website dedicated to language benchmarks, to measuring how fast certain languages run compared with others, and it includes this preface to stave off riots: "These are not the only compilers and interpreters. These are not the only programs that could be written. These are not the only tasks that could be solved. These are just 10 tiny examples."

It sometimes appears that everyone in coding has a beef. You can feel it coming off the webpages. There are a lot of defensive postscripts added in response to outrage. "People have reacted strongly to this post," they'll read. "I did not mean to imply that Java sucks."

Languages have agendas. People glom onto them. Blunt talk is seen as a good quality in a developer, a sign of an "engineering mindset"—spit out every opinion as quickly as possible, the sooner to reach a technical consensus. Expect to be told you're wrong; expect to tell other people they're wrong. (Masculine anger, bluntly expressed, is part of the industry.)

Coding is a culture of blurters. This can yield fast decisions, but it penalizes people who need to quietly compose their thoughts, rewarding fast-twitch thinkers who harrumph efficiently. Programmer job interviews, which often include abstract and meaningless questions that must be answered immediately on a whiteboard, typify this culture. Regular meetings can become sniping matches about things that don't matter. The shorthand term for that is "bikeshedding." (Who cares what color the bike shed is painted? Well . . .)

Code culture is very, very broad, but the geographic and cultural core is the Silicon Valley engine of progress. The Valley mythologizes young geniuses with vast sums. To its credit, this culture works; to its shame, it doesn't work for everyone.

At any moment some new thing could catch fire and disrupt the tribal ebb and flow. Instagram was written in Python and sold for $700 million, so Python had a moment of glory. The next mind-blowing app could show up, written in some new language—and start everyone taking that more seriously. Within eighteen months your skills could be, if not quite valueless, suspect.

I was in a meeting once where someone said, "How long will it take to fix that?" One person, who'd been at the company for years, said, "Three months." A new person, who'd just come from a world of rapidly provisioned cloud microservices, said, "Three minutes." They were both correct. That's how change enters into this world. Slowly at first, then on the front page of Hacker News.

Programmers carve out a sliver of cognitive territory for themselves and go to conferences, and yet they know their position is vulnerable. They get defensive when they hear someone suggest that Python is better than Ruby, because [insert 500-comment message thread here]. Is the next great wave swelling somewhere, and will it wash away Java when it comes? Will Go conquer Python? Do I need to learn JavaScript to remain profitable? Programmers are often angry because they're often scared. We are, most of us, stumbling around with only a few candles to guide the way. We can't always see the whole system, so we need to puzzle it out, bit by bit, in the dark.

33

What Is Code? If You Don't Know, You Need to Read This

4.2. The Thing About Real Artists Is That They—

As a class, programmers are easily bored, love novelty, and are obsessed with various forms of productivity enhancement. God help you if you're ever caught in the middle of a conversation about nutrition; standing desks; the best keyboards; the optimal screen position and distance; whether to use a plain text editor or a large, complex development environment; chair placement; the best music to code to; the best headphones; whether headphone amplifiers actually enhance listening; whether open-plan offices are better than individual or shared offices; the best bug-tracking software; the best programming methodology; the right way to indent code and the proper placement of semicolons; or, of course, which language is better. And whatever you do, never, ever ask a developer about productivity software.

Meanwhile, the executives who run large programming teams have to actually ship software. "Ship" is a cult word. If they don't ship on time, managers could get a lower rating on their performance reviews and end up making only inordinate, as opposed to obscene, amounts of money. Wine cellars are at risk, not to mention alimony payments. As managers, their job—along with all the trust falls and consensus-building and active listening—is to reduce ship risk, which comes in many forms: bad bugs; features that were promised to bosses or clients that distract from boring, utterly necessary features; or test servers that crash at night.

One of the greatest ship risks is anything shiny. This is where languages are particularly risky. An experienced and talented programmer can learn a language in a week, but a middling one is going to take much longer. Meanwhile, exciting, interesting programming languages always come with a list of benisons, promises of speed or productivity or just happiness. No, really. Happiness is a serious selling point for languages, and people have written blog posts where they analyze how people discuss code. According to an analysis by GitHub user Tobias Hermann, PHP coders are far more likely to use the word "hate" in their Reddit comments than Clojure programmers; Clojure programmers are far more likely to use the word "cool" than PHP programmers.

There are many blog posts on how to persuade your manager to switch to a new language. Experienced managers, who bear scars and were often coders themselves, become practiced at squinting and coughing and saying things like, "No, the switching cost is just too high right now," or, "Maybe we could do a two-week trial project when we build the analytics reporting engine."

Then the programmers shuffle back to their standing desks and complain until the product is shipped. Or else they just quit, because Lord knows there are jobs out there. For programmers, particularly the young ones, there are jobs everywhere.

Managers and old coders have fewer options. It's often better to just keep working and shipping, even if the code starts to look ugly, even if there are nominally better solutions, even as the technical debt accrues around you because in a few years everything will change. Maybe you'll get promoted and the new manager will have the will and motive to tear up everything you did, cursing, and start again (perhaps using a new language) with the goal of making something much simpler. Or the entire industry will spasm and everything you've done will need to be thrown away and rebuilt along new lines anyway. (From desktop to web, from web to mobile, from mobile to . . . quantum? Who knows. But there's always something.)

Some code is beautiful and you want to read it, reuse it, and take it into your program and your heart. Some code is annoying and pretentious, and some code looks good at first and turns out to be kind of mean. Estimating code quality is a big part of programming. Go on—judge.

35

What Is Code? If You Don't Know, You Need to Read This

Somehow it keeps working out. The industry is always promising to eat itself, to come up with a paradigm so perfect that we can all stop wasting our time and enter a world of pure digital thought. It never happens.

4.3 We Still Need to Choose . . .

Nine weeks into the re-architecture, you have asked TMitTB to come by the office and talk next steps.

You've noticed that his team has started to dress like him. One of the women is in tall boots and has done something complex with her hair. She's wearing a black leather jacket. Nothing ostentatious, just cooler. She was previously all Patagonia. Is this how programmers dress? How did they get their own executive style?

"PHP," he says, "well—it is what it is. The team had a good time at PHP[world]. But I think the thing we might have learned . . ."

He doesn't pronounce the brackets, of course, but you approved the expense, and that's how they write it, bracketed. It's good they had a good time, because it cost you $25,000 to send them to that conference and put them in hotels and feed them, and you have no idea whether that was money well spent or not.

". . . is that we really need to move off of PHP."

Oh. Well. There's your answer.

"We're all agreed that PHP isn't the language for our next five years."

"Which one would you say is?"

"Ay, there's the rub," he says, and you have to remind yourself to not show him your real face right now. If he quotes *Hamlet* again, though . . .

"Well," you ask, "which language do you want to use?"

He looks confused. "I mean, it doesn't matter," he says. "I don't write the code."

Then who does? And you realize, right now, the answer is no one.

5.1 What Is the Relationship Between Code and Data?

Data comes from everywhere. Sometimes it comes from third parties—Spotify imports big piles of music files from record labels. Sometimes data is user-created, like e-mails and tweets and Facebook posts and Word documents. Sometimes the machines themselves create data, as with a Fitbit exercise tracker or a Nest thermostat. When you work as a coder, you talk about data all the time. When you create websites, you need to get data out of a database and put them into a webpage. If you're Twitter, tweets are data. If you're the IRS, tax returns are data, broken into fields.

Data management is the problem that programming is supposed to solve. But of course now that we have computers everywhere, we keep generating more data, which requires more programming, and so forth. It's a hell of a problem with no end in sight. This is why people in technology make so much money. Not only do they sell infinitely reproducible nothings, but they sell so many of them that they actually have to come up with new categories of infinitely reproducible nothings just to handle what happened with the last batch. That's how we ended up with "big data." I've been to big-data conferences and they are packed.

5.2 Where Does Data Live?

It's rare that a large task is ever very far from a database. Amazon, Google, Yahoo!, Netflix, Spotify—all have huge, powerful databases.

The most prevalent is the relational database, using a language called SQL, for Structured Query Language. Relational databases represent the world using tables, which have rows and columns. SQL looks like this:

37

What Is Code? If You Don't Know, You Need to Read This

```
SELECT * FROM BOOKS WHERE ID = 294;
```

Implying that there's a table called BOOKS and a row in that table, where a book resides with an ID of 294. IDs are important in databases. Imagine a bookstore database. It has a customer table that lists customers. It has a books table that lists books. And it has a clever in-between table of purchases with a row for every time a customer bought a book.

Congratulations! You just built Amazon! Of course, while we were trying to build a bookstore, we actually built the death of bookstores—that seems to happen a lot in the business. You set out to do something cool and end up destroying lots of things that came before.

Relational databases showed up in the 1970s and never left. There's Oracle, of course. Microsoft has SQL Server; IBM has DB2. They all speak SQL and work in a similar manner, with just enough differences to make it costly to switch.

Oracle makes you pay thousands of dollars to use its commercial enterprise database, but more and more of the world runs on free software databases such as PostgreSQL and MySQL. There's even a tiny little database called SQLite that's so small, so well-behaved, and so permissively licensed that it's now in basically every smartphone, available to apps to help them save and load data. You probably have a powerful SQL-driven database in your pocket right now.

5.3. The Language of White Collars

If you walk up to some programmers and say, "Big corporate programming," they'll think of Java.

Java is a programming language that was born at Sun Microsystems (RIP), the product of a team led by a well-regarded programmer named James Gosling. It's object-oriented, but it also looks a lot like C and C++, so for people who understood those languages, it was fairly easy to pick up. It was conceived in 1991, eventually floating onto the Internet on a massive cloud of marketing in 1995, proclaimed as the answer to every woe that had ever beset programmers. Java ran on every computer! Java would run right inside your web browser, in "applets" (soon called "crapplets"), and would probably take over the Web in time. Java! It ran very slowly compared with more traditional languages such as C. What was it for? Java! They also had network-connected computer terminals called JavaStations. Java! Kleiner Perkins Caufield & Byers even announced a $100 million Java fund in 1996. But after all that excitement, Java sort of . . . hung out for a while. The future didn't look like Sun said it would.

Java running "inside" a web browser, as a plug-in, never worked well. It was slow and clunky, and when it loaded it felt like you were teetering on the edge of disaster, a paranoia that was frequently validated when your browser froze up and crashed. Java-enabled jewelry, meant to serve as a kind of digital key/credit card/ ID card, also had a low success rate. But Java was free to download and designed to be useful for small and large teams alike.

Here are some facts about Java to help you understand how it slowly took over the world by the sheer power of being pretty good.

It was a big language. It came with a ton of code already there, the "class library," which had all the classes and methods you'd need to talk to a database, deal with complex documents, do mathematics, and talk to various network services. There were a ton of classes in that library waiting to be turned into objects and brought to life.

It automatically generated documentation. This was huge. Everyone says code deserves excellent documentation and documentation truly matters, but this is a principle mostly proven in the breach. Now you could run a tool called `javadoc`, and it would make you webpages that listed all the classes and methods. It was lousy documentation, but better than nothing and

39

What Is Code? If You Don't Know, You Need to Read This

pretty easy to enhance if you took the time to clean up your code.

There were a lot of Java manuals, workshops and training seminars, and certifications. Programmers can take classes and tests to be officially certified in many technologies. Java programmers had an especially wide range to choose from.

It ran on a "virtual" machine, which meant that Java "ran everywhere," which meant that you could run it on Windows, Mac, or Unix machines and it would behave the same. It was an exceptionally well-engineered compromise. Which made it perfect for big companies. As the 2000s kept going, Java became more popular for application servers. Creating a content management system for a nongovernmental organization with 2,000 employees? Java's fine. Connecting tens of thousands of people in a company to one another? Java. Need to help one bank talk to another bank every day at 5:01 p.m.? Java. Charts and diagrams, big stacks of paper, five-year projects? Java. Not exciting, hardly wearable, but very predictable. A language for building great big things for great big places with great big teams.

People complain, but it works.

5.5. Liquid Infrastructure

"Enterprise" is a feared word among programmers because enterprise programming is a lot of work without much to show for it. Remember healthcare.gov, the first version that was a total disaster? Perfect example of enterprise coding. At the same time, programmers respect big systems—when they work. We respect the ambition of huge heavy machines running big blobs of code. We grew up reading about supercomputers. Big iron is cool, even if the future seems to be huge cloud platforms hosting with tons of cheap computers.

But Java is also in wide use at Google. It's a language for places such as General Electric and Accenture. These aren't startups, but if their product schedules slip, so does their revenue, and they are beholden to the public markets. Gigantic data-driven organizations are structured around code, around getting software made. But that doesn't mean their teams are huge—Amazon, for example, is famous for its two-pizza rule: "Never have a meeting where two pizzas couldn't feed the entire group."

These companies have cultures that know how to make software. They have whole departments dedicated to testing. The process is important because there are so many moving pieces, many of them invisible.

Academic researchers often produce things that basically work but don't have interfaces. They need to prove their theses, publish, and move on to the next thing. People in the free-software community often code to scratch an itch and release that code into the digital commons so that other people can modify and manipulate it. While more often than not this process goes nowhere, over time some projects capture the imagination of others and become part of the infrastructure of the world.

Java, interestingly, profits from all this. It's designed for big corporate projects and has the infrastructure to support them. It's also a useful language for midsize tasks. So the libraries that you need to do things—image processing, logging on to files, full-text search—keep appearing at a steady clip, improving on the standard libraries or supplanting them entirely.

Eventually, people realized that if they didn't like the Java language, they could write other languages that compile to Java "bytecode" and run on the Java virtual machine (JVM). So there are now many languages that run on top of Java. Some are versions of well-known languages, such as Jython and JRuby. Others are totally new, like Scala, which is one of the languages that Twitter began to use when it outgrew Ruby.

The point is that things are fluid in the world of programming, fluid in a way that other industries don't seem to be. Languages are liquid infrastructure. You download a few programs and,

41

What Is Code? If You Don't Know, You Need to Read This

whoa, suddenly you have a working Clojure environment. Which is actually the Java Runtime Environment. You grab an old PC that's outlived its usefulness, put Linux on it, and suddenly you have a powerful web server. Now you can participate in whole new cultures. There are meetups, gatherings, conferences, blogs, and people chatting on Twitter. And you are welcomed. They are glad for the new blood.

Java was supposed to supplant C and run on smart jewelry. Now it runs application servers, hosts Lisplike languages, and is the core language of the Android operating system. It runs on billions of things. It won. C and C++, which it was designed to supplant, also won. A lot of things keep winning because computers keep getting more plentiful. It's weird.

5.7. What About JavaScript?

Remember Netscape, the first huge commercial web browser? In 1995, as Java was blooming, Netscape was resolving a problem. It displayed webpages that were not very lively. You could have a nice cartoon of a monkey on the webpage, but there was no way to make the monkey dance when you moved over it with your mouse. Figuring out how to make that happen was the job of a language developer named Brendan Eich. He sat down and in a few weeks created a language called JavaScript.

JavaScript's relationship with Java is tenuous; the strongest bond between the languages is the marketing linkage of their names. And the early history of JavaScript was uninspiring. So the monkey could now dance. You could do things to the cursor, make things blink when a mouse touched them.

But as browsers proliferated and the Web grew from a document-delivery platform into a software-delivery platform, JavaScript became, arguably, the most widely deployed language runtime in the world. If you wrote some JavaScript code, you could run it wherever the Web was—everywhere.

JavaScript puttered around for years in the wilderness, as Java did, too. But without the resolute support of a corporate entity like Sun.

Then, about a decade ago people began to talk about Ajax—the idea that you could build real software into a webpage, not just a document, but a program that could do real work.

Things could respond and change according to inputs. You could distribute your software to hundreds of millions of people this way, and JavaScript would work for them. It wasn't as controlled as Java, it was much slower than natively compiled C, and it had a terrible lack of niceties. And yet: Gmail, Google Maps, Flickr, Twitter, and Facebook. Every single pixel on a webpage can be manipulated now; the type can be changed, the words can move around; buttons can be pressed.

As with any celebrity, there's a whole industry dedicated to spackling up its deficiencies and making it look good. There are books about the "good parts" of JavaScript; there are libraries that make it easier and more consistent to program, too, such as jQuery, which can turn the many lines of code necessary to make a paragraph disappear into a single `$("p.optional")
.hide();`.

Back in the era of the iPod and candy-colored Macintoshes, Apple took the code of an open-source web browser called Konqueror and modified it to create Safari, its own web browser to compete with Microsoft's Internet Explorer. Then in 2008 Google started to make its own modifications to the web engine underneath Safari, called Webkit, and made its own version called Chrome with a spanking-fast JavaScript engine called V8. They made JavaScript fast. "Devs still approach performance of JS code as if they are riding a horse cart," tweeted one developer, "but the horse had long been replaced with fusion reactor." Google does better when JavaScript is fast.

In 2009 a developer named Ryan Dahl modified the V8 engine, which was free software, and made it run outside the browser.

43

What Is Code? If You Don't Know, You Need to Read This

There had been freestanding versions of JavaScript before (including some that ran inside Java, natch), but none so fast. He called this further fork Node.js, and it just took off. One day, JavaScript ran inside webpages. Then it broke out of its browser prison. Now it could operate anywhere. It could touch your hard drive, send e-mail, erase all your files. It was a real programming language now. And the client . . . had become the server.

Here's some JavaScript, squaring some numbers for you:

```
function squares(count) {
var x = [];
for (var i=1;i<count+1;i++) {
x.push(i*i);
}
console.log(x.join(" "));
}
squares(10);
```

In a great and sudden wave, thousands of developers began to use Node.js and create modular libraries. If you knew how JavaScript worked on a webpage, then you could make it work on a server. And a few interesting characteristics of the language made it good for writing software that handles lots of simultaneous users. JavaScript listened for lots of things at once in a web browser: A mouse moves; a key is typed; some information comes in from the network. On a server it could listen to dozens or hundreds of people all at once and give them the information they requested.

Soon the community developed a huge library of packages—bits of software that do specific things, such as reading files, or chattering with databases, or talking to Amazon's web services tools. At this writing, npmjs.com has 150,000 packages, and more than a billion copies of various packages have been downloaded in the past month.

NPM stands for Node Package Manager. It's software that helps you install packages and ... well, it's unwieldy, honestly, because many of those 150,000 packages are just not that great. It's a lot of searching and testing and sighing. But when you have this much stuff to pick from, for free, you shouldn't complain. JavaScript is a hodgepodge designed in a hurry, and it runs on, well, who knows, but let's say a billion-plus devices, so you might as well get with the program. Your customers may not have iPhones, but they probably have some way of running JavaScript.

So you might use JavaScript to make a more interesting webpage. You might use it to make the client side of a full-fledged application, like Google Docs, that runs in the browser. You might use it to make a web server that talks to a web browser. Or you might use it to make an API that serves up data to a "client," and sure, that client could be a laptop web browser. But it's 2015, and that client is quite probably an app on a smartphone.

6. How Are Apps Made?

One of the privileges of owning a Mac is that you can download a program by Apple called Xcode. This is an IDE, an Integrated Development Environment.

It's an enormous download, more than 2 gigabytes, or roughly the size of an hour of DVD-quality video. Xcode is the heart of Apple. It's not only how the company writes software, it's the tool for everyone who wants to write software for the Mac or iPhone.

Within Xcode are whole worlds to explore. For example, one component is the iOS SDK (software development kit). You use that to make iPhone and iPad apps. That SDK is made up of dozens and dozens of APIs (application programming interfaces). There's an API for keeping track of a user's location, one for animating pictures, one for playing sounds, and several for rendering text on the screen and collecting information from users. And so forth.

45

What Is Code? If You Don't Know, You Need to Read This

There are other ways of working—I tend to do most of my code in a text editor with a black background, far less to see at first glance, though actually just as complex—but this right here is some serious code life. You fill out some fields, wire some things together (really, sometimes it's done by connecting virtual wires into virtual holes), and start coding.

When someone from Apple stands onstage and announces some new thing that ends with "Kit," such as ResearchKit or HealthKit—or WatchKit, the set of routines specifically for the Apple Watch—Xcode is where those kits will land, fully documented, to be used to make software.

Some functions are reserved for the manufacturer. You know how Apple is touting that you can track someone's heartbeat using an Apple Watch? Apple hasn't documented how to do it yet, not for the world. Maybe the company is worried that you'll misuse it somehow. Perhaps heartbeat monitoring requires careful battery management, and because the watch already has battery issues, Apple wants to avoid making things worse by letting anyone in there. It's likely that people are trying to figure out how to access that heartbeat API right now, though. That's just the way people are.

Apple is really good at all of this. It publishes interface guidelines and gives people tools for arranging app interfaces in predictable ways that end users will find familiar. It sets the flow with which to go.

Let's say you're making a podcasting application, and playing an audio file is a key feature. Great. Create an object of class AVAudioPlayer, and add a button to the screen, then connect that button to the code so that when clicked, the button sends the message "play."

There's a lot going on at once, so you want to leave it to the operating system to keep track of where windows are. It's up to an IDE to help you connect your ideas into this massive, massive world with tens of thousands of methods so you can play a song, rewind a song, keep track of when the song was played (meaning you also need to be aware of the time zones), or keep track of the title of the song (which means you need to be aware of the language of the song's title—and know if it displays left-to-right or right-to-left).

You should also know the length of the song, which means you need a mechanism for extracting durations from music files. Once you have that—say, it's in milliseconds—you need to divide it by 1,000, then 60, to get minutes. But what if the song is a podcast and ninety minutes long? Do you want to divide further to get hours? So many variables. Gah!

I guess you have problems to solve after all. The IDE doesn't do everything for you.

The greatest commercial insight of the technology industry is that if you control a computing environment, you can move the market. You can change the way people do things, the way they listen to music, watch videos, and respond to advertising. People who work at technology companies are supposed to take an idea and multiply it by a few million people, yielding a few billion dollars.

A great way to do that is to wrap up your intentions in APIs and SDKs and IDEs. That's why so much software to make software is free: It stimulates the development of even more software.

Sometimes this is the result of corporate ambition: Java was very much a Sun product, down to the class library; the same is true of C# for Microsoft. But much of the code in the world is freely available, created by generous volunteers over decades to serve their own needs. The give-and-take between corporations and programming languages is complex. Some language developers are hired to work on their open-sourced languages; Go and Python have been funded, to varying degrees, by Google; and the creator of PHP works at Etsy.

47

What Is Code? If You Don't Know, You Need to Read This

Apple and Microsoft, Amazon and Google: factory factories. Their APIs are the products of many thousands of hours of labor from many programmers. Think of the work involved. Someone needs to manage the SDK. Hundreds of programmers need to write the code for it. People need to write the documentation and organize the demos. Someone needs to fight for a feature to get funded and finished. Someone needs to make sure the translation into German is completed and that there aren't any embarrassing mistakes that go viral on Twitter. Someone needs to actually write the software that goes into making the IDE work.

The modern OS is a feast of wonders: fast video, music players, buckets of buttons. Apple may be the best imaginary button maker in history. Just the bezels are a work to behold. Today there are fifteen bezel styles, from NSThickSquareBezelStyle to NSSmallSquareBezelStyle. Freedom. (Sort of. They're still just bezels.) Things that used to require labor and care—showing a map, rotating a giant 3D landscape—can now be done with a few lines of code.

When everyone goes to Apple's annual Worldwide Developers Conference in San Francisco and they stare rapturously as some man in an untucked, expensive shirt talks about "core data," this is the context. Onstage, presenting its Kits, Apple is rearranging abstractions, saying: Look at the new reality we've defined, the way that difficult things are now easy and drab things can be colorful. Your trust in our platform and your dedication of thousands of hours of time have not been misplaced.

They've pitched variations on this annually for thirty years.

In Xcode you can compile everything with one command, and up pops your software for testing. You can see the button you made. You need to click on it. It yearns for clicks. It cries out in a shrill signaling voice like a nano cat on a microfence. Everything inside a computer beseeches everything else. It's a racket. You click your mouse, and the button cat is finally satisfied. Now the computer can increase the volume, change the color, or bring out the talking paper clip. Destiny fulfilled and, after many rounds of this, test complete.

When your app is done, you may sell it in an app store. And if users are excited to use your app, they'll be motivated to buy more apps. Loops upon loops, feeding into one another, capital accruing to the coffers of the patient software giants. An ecosystem. "Ecosystem" is another debased word, especially given what we keep doing to the real, physical one around us. But if a few hundred thousand people are raising their kids and making things for 100 million people, that's what they call it.

7. The Triumph of Middle Management

"I mean, this company will do everything imaginable to slow down shipping," TMitTB says as the CTO winces. That's fine; you expected this to be a stressful meeting. "First, I needed to pass everything through the security team, which was five months of review," TMitTB says, "and then it took me weeks to get a working development environment, so I had my developers sneaking out to Starbucks to check in their code . . ."

You listen, the same way you listened to people criticize the re-architecture project. But these people promised new, exciting ways of working that would cut through the problems experienced by failed technology initiatives of yore. They would be agile; they would use new tools; they would attract talent; and they would ship code. They knew this was a big company, not a startup, when they signed on. And the re-architecture is, to any casual observer, a failure.

TMitTB has, you noticed, gained weight. The CTO, who has several projects on roughly the same footing scattered across the organization, has lost weight.

"I was told I could, that I should do this right," TMitTB says. "So that it wouldn't need to be done again eighteen months later." He

49

What Is Code? If You Don't Know, You Need to Read This

sits back in his chair, but it's a shallow visitor chair with a lightly padded back, so any intended dramatic effect is diminished.

One of the lessons that TMitTB has tried to get across to you, the big message that matters most to him, is that code is never done; after shipping the new platform (no longer a website, this is a platform), with all its interlocking components, he and his team will continue to work on it forever. There will always be new bugs, new features, new needs. Such things are the side effects of any growth at all, and this platform is, he insists, designed to scale.

What no one in engineering can understand is that what they perceive as static, slow-moving, exhausting, the enemy of progress—the corporate world that surrounds them, the world in which they work—is not static. Slow-moving, yes, but so are battleships when they leave port. What the coders aren't seeing, you have come to believe, is that the staid enterprise world that they fear isn't the consequence of dead-eyed apathy but rather détente.

They can't see how hard-fought that stability is. Where they see obstacles and intransigence, you see a huge, complex, dynamic system through which flows a river of money and where people are deeply afraid to move anything that would dam that river.

You feel some pity for the coders now. Obviously, they will inherit the earth. But in their race to the summit, they missed a lot of memos.

"I just want to ship," TMITTB says. By which he means: "I just want to do what I was asked to do." But so much of the company hears that as, "I just want to destroy everything I touch. For I am Kali, destroyer of best practices."

"OK," you say. "I understand that. Here's what you are going to do for me." You look at the CTO and she nods. "First, no more conferences."

His mouth opens, then shuts.

He's afraid, you realize, that you can't understand the work he's doing, that you see software as a thing and not a golden braid forever weaving.

But you've been coming around. Finding your way to some programmer meetings. It's like your smartphone and its constant updates. Nothing is ever done. That's fine.

"You have to let me help with optics," you continue. "I need you here every day walking the halls with a big smile on your face. Giving high-fives. Looking sleepy. Second, I need a release date, a real one."

"Next month."

The CTO says his name, shakes her head.

"We'll work on it," you say. "For now, no more conferences. And don't talk about sprints. Don't talk about milestones and re-leases. Talk to people as if this platform exists, as if it's been work-ing for months. Ask them if they updated their product listings."

The time is up. The CTO asks TMitTB, "We're clear?"

"Yes," TMitTB says. He's not, but the fact that he doesn't ask any more questions indicates he might be learning. He's done a lot of work, and now it's time for him to get corporate and pre-tend to work.

"And can you pick a language?" you ask. This is for you.

"We did," TMitTB says. "We're using Node.js. With the Express framework."

"Great," you say. "Can't wait to see the code."

7.1. How Do You Pick a Programming Language?

Beware of arguments related to programming speed. All things being equal, faster is better. But all things are never equal. Do you need the kind of speed that lets you get a website up and running quickly? Or the kind that allows you to rotate a few thousand polygons in 3D in real time? Do you need to convert 10,000 PDFs into text per hour? Or 10 million PDFs into text once? These are different problems. What do we need to do, how many times do we need to do it, and what existing code can we use to help us do it that many times? Ask those questions.

51

What Is Code? If You Don't Know, You Need to Read This

It's possible to spend productive months preparing for a project without deciding on a language. It may be the sign of a fine manager, someone who assumes his people can learn new things, someone who's built an agile team capable of experimenting with new technologies and getting ideas into production. It could also be that this person is totally useless. You'll find out!

Let's say your programmers are developing a huge website that serves 5 million people who each visit five times a month. Do you use Python, which is slower, or Go, which is fast, or Node.js, which is something in between? Trick question! Twenty-five million webpage visits isn't that big a deal, unless they involve some deep wizardry or complex database queries that are very different for each page (good example: Facebook).

Now, that number isn't trivial; if it takes a minute to make a page, you'd need forty-eight years to make that many, which is way too slow. If it takes a second to make a page, that's still too slow—there are only 2.6 million seconds in a month. So you need to figure out how to serve about ten pages per second. You'll probably want more than one computer, a little redundancy, some good server setup. It will take some doing and planning. But it can be done in any language.

What if you are going to serve only a few hundred thousand pages a month? Then you've got tremendous breathing room. You don't need too many engineers to create the system architecture. You still need to plan, but in general you can read some blog posts and follow along with what others have done. You can be pretty sloppy, to be honest. Again, any language will do.

What if you want to include a live, person-to-person chat on those pages, and you expect thousands of people to use that chat at once, all speaking to each other? Now you're dipping your hand into that godforsaken river. But that is exactly the problem that Go was designed to solve. It's a language for creating highly available servers that use as much of the computer's processor as possible. It has other features as well, but this is where Go shines.

Actually, Node.js works pretty well for that sort of server, too, and Clojure certainly has the capacity. Oh, right, Java works, too. If you really needed to, you could even do it in PHP.

This is why the choice is so hard. Everything can do everything, and people will tell you that you should use everything to do everything. So you need to figure out for yourself what kind of team you have, what kind of frameworks you like using, where people can be most productive, so they will stick around through the completion of the project. This is hard. Most places can't do this. So they go with the lowest common denominator—Java, PHP—because they know that when people leave, they'll be able to get more of them.

And that's OK. The vast majority of technology projects don't require original research, nor do they require amazing technological discoveries. All the languages under discussion work just fine. There are great coders in all of them.

But the choice of a main programming language is the most important signaling behavior that a technology company can engage in. Tell me that you program in Java, and I believe you to be either serious or boring. In Ruby, and you are interested in building things quickly. In Clojure, and I think you are smart but wonder if you ship. In Python, and I trust you implicitly. In PHP, and we sigh together. In C++ or C, and I nod humbly. In C#, and I smile and assume we have nothing in common. In Fortran, and I ask to see your security clearance. These languages contain entire civilizations.

You can tell how well code is organized from across the room. Or by squinting or zooming out. The shape of code from twenty feet away is incredibly informative. Clean code is idiomatic, as brief as possible, obvious even if it's not heavily documented. Colloquial and friendly. As was written in *Structure and Interpretation of Computer Programs* (a.k.a. SICP), the seminal textbook of programming taught for years at MIT, "A computer language is not just a way of getting a computer to perform operations . . . it is

53

What Is Code? If You Don't Know, You Need to Read This

a novel formal medium for expressing ideas about methodology. Thus, programs must be written for people to read, and only incidentally for machines to execute." A great program is a letter from current you to future you or to the person who inherits your code. A generous humanistic document.

Of course all of this is nice and flowery; it needs to work, too.

7.3. Managing Programmers

On the Wikipedia page for "*Software development process*," there's a list of links to pages: "TDD BDD FDD DDD MDD"—"test-driven development," "behavior-driven development," "feature-driven development," "domain-driven design," and "model-driven development." Each one has its advocates and its critics. I include these only for your amusement. If you want to go deeper on management methodologies, have at it.

The management of programmers is a discipline unto itself. There are subdisciplines that deal with how coders communicate. The most prominent is the "Agile methodology," which calls for regular coordination among programmers, providing a set of rituals and norms they can follow to make their programs work with the programs of others.

The Agile Manifesto (yep, manifesto) reads as follows:

- Individuals and interactions over processes and tools
- Working software over comprehensive documentation
- Customer collaboration over contract negotiation
- Responding to change over following a plan

There are seventeen signatories. And there are as many variations of Agile. I've had terrible meetings in my life when I sat between two teams and one of them explained, at length, why Agile with Kanban was better than Agile with Scrum. You could smell the money burning.

Here is Agile, as I've seen it done: You break down your product into a set of simple-to-understand user stories about who needs what. You file those stories into an issue-tracking system, often a commercial product such as JIRA.

You divide work into sprints of a week, two weeks, or whatever suits your management style, and you give each sprint a name and a goal (implement search, user registration), then the programmers take stories to go off and make them happen.

Every day your team checks in and tries to unblock one another—if you are working on the tool that sends e-mail and the e-mail server isn't working, you tell everyone. Then someone else steps up to help, or you stick with that story and do the best you can, but everyone needs to be working toward the sprint goal, trying to release some software. And once the sprint is done, you deliver something that actually, really works and move on to the next thing, slowly bringing a large, complex system into operation.

That's an ideal case. Done well, it avoids magical thinking ("It will all work when we get everything done and wired together"). It has its critics and can seem to have as many branches (c.f. Scrum, Kanban, and "Agile with Discipline") as Protestantism.

Programmers are forever searching for a silver bullet and, worse, they always think they've found it. Which is why Frederick Brooks, the most famous of the early software methodologists, wrote a paper called "No Silver Bullet—Essence and Accident in Software Engineering." He wrote it in 1986. He was very hopeful, back then, that object-oriented programming would help fix things.

7.4 ."We Are Going to Ship"

Into your office comes TMitTB. He holds a large bottle of some sort and a laptop, and he looks sleepy. You tell him so, with a smile.

"We got to a release," he says. "Ran a little into last night."

55

What Is Code? If You Don't Know, You Need to Read This

He opens the laptop and brings up a secret website that, he assures you, can be seen only within the confines of the office's network, or via the virtual private network.

It's a plain and homely thing, the new website. Squares bumping into squares. The catalog and the items in the catalog are up on the screen, but there are no images. The text has all sorts of weird characters in it, strange bugs. There are products with the names "fake product" and "not real product" and "I hate all products."

There are no "related items" to purchase, even though that's a critical feature and one of the major revenue drivers on the current site. You suppress the question. It will be there.

There is, however, a way to log in with a username and password. TMitTB has done you the favor of creating, for you, an account. You are, he says, the first nonengineering person to test the site.

"This is real?" you ask.

"Yes. This is software. It speaks to the database. This is what we'll release."

"Does it speak to customer service?"

He squints for a second.

"In July," he says.

My God, a date. You've extracted a month, something positively deadline-ish.

He did as you asked. He managed outward, and he began to gum up the works in familiar ways. He started demanding documents of people who immediately began not providing them. He asked relative strangers for their insights and suggestions, and they gave them willingly. They asked for the logo to be bigger. They asked for games that could be played inside the app. He listened to them all. He hasn't been to a conference in months.

"So this is the real, actual website."

"Yes," he says, taking a sip from a complicated, fermented beverage with a health-food-store mandala-style label. A sticker on the bottle says, "$3.99."

"Now we do the next sprint," he says. "We push for July. And we release mid-August."

He looks tired, this man. But he also looks proud. The things on the screen—his team put them there, and they used good, modern tools to do so. That is their craft and their pleasure, and TMitTB has made it possible for them to do their work. "We," he finally says, "are going to ship."

They will do their standups. And after the standups, they will go off and work in the integrated development environments and write their server-side JavaScript and their client-side JavaScript. Then they will run some tests and check their code into the source code repository, and the continuous integration server will perform tests and checks, and if all goes well, it will deploy the code—perhaps even in August, in some cloud or another. They insist that they'll do this every day, continuous releases.

Then will come reports. Revenue reports, analytics, lists of new markets to conquer, all manner of new customer data that will be yours to parcel out and distribute. That will be your role, as the owner of the global database of customer intent. Thousands, then millions, of new facts that can help the company plan its sales and product-development cycles. A good thing. And, you hope, the new site will generate more revenue, being faster, better, API-driven, and deployed across platforms to Web, mobile Web, and multiple apps.

You decided to cut BlackBerry support. It stung, but there are three BlackBerrys in your desk drawer at home and none in your pocket. Life moves on.

When the site is introduced, you'll buy the coders a cake and send them to the JavaScript conference of their choice. You've learned that the only appropriate reward for people who write JavaScript is more JavaScript. TMitTB will get his bonus. The CTO is already considering him for new things. You like the CTO. She has become a friend of sorts.

57

What Is Code? If You Don't Know, You Need to Read This

You can feel it, the S, off in the distance, coming toward you. It will arrive in due time, and you will stick it to the front of the VP in your title and all will be well. The coders all smile at you in the hall now that you've sat in on code reviews and feature discussions and stood quietly in the middle of standups. You know some of their names, even if you could do a better job of pronouncing them.

Perhaps you have a future in software after all.

7.5. Should You Learn to Code?

I spoke with some friends in their forties who had spent careers in technology. I was complaining. I said, "I mentor some millennials, and my God. Every job is a contract position. Nothing comes with health care. They carry so much debt." They looked at me with perplexity. It took a moment, and then one of them said: "Not if they can code."

You probably already do code. You do it in Excel or Google Spreadsheets. You run little processes in a sequence or do a series of find-and-replace routines in a big document.

Programming as a career can lead to a rewarding, solidly middle-class existence. If you are inclined and enjoy the work, it's a good way to spend time, and if you work for and with good people, it can be very fun—even the dry parts have something to teach you. Of course this is true of any place where smart people work. If your situation is lousy, you can probably find another job more easily than, say, a writer.

The industry twists and turns so often, though, that who knows what the next ten or twenty years will bring? The iPhone, and mobile in general, created a brief renaissance for people who could program using lower-level languages such as Objective-C, people who could worry about a computer's memory. Perhaps the Internet of Things will turn everything into a sensor. (Already you wander Disney World with a wristband, and it watches and tracks you; the whole place is a computer.) This will require yet more low-level thinking. And then there will be websites to make, apps to build, and on and on.

There's likely to be work. But it's a global industry, and there are thousands of people in India with great degrees. Some used to work at Microsoft, Google, and IBM. The same things that made programming a massive world-spanning superstructure— that you can ship nothing and charge for it—make it the perfect globalized industry. There's simply no reason, aside from preju- dice, to think that Mumbai or Seoul can't make big, complex things as well as Palo Alto or Seattle.

You might learn to program because there's a new economy as irrational, weird, and painful as the old one. Books and songs are now rows in databases, and whole films are made on CPUs, without a real ray of light penetrating a lens. Maybe learning to code will give you a decoder ring for the future. Disruption is just optimization by another name. SDKs are just culture encoded and made reproducible, and to an entire generation, they're re- ceived as rapturously as Beatles albums were decades ago. The coder-turned-venture-capitalist-turned-Twitter-public-intellec- tual Marc Andreessen wrote that software is eating the world. If that's true, you should at least know why it's so hungry.

I've been the man in the taupe blazer, for sure, the person who brings the digital where it's not welcome and is certain that his way is better. It took me a long time to learn why this might not be welcomed—why an executive, an editor, or a librarian might not enjoy hearing about his entire world being upended because someone has a new toy in his pocket. I didn't put the toy in any- one's pocket, and you shouldn't kill the messenger. But messen- gers aren't blameless, either.

Aside from serious fevers and the occasional trip to the woods, I've used a computer every day for twenty-eight years. I learn about the world through software. I learned about publishing by

59

What Is Code? If You Don't Know, You Need to Read This

using the desktop publishing system QuarkXPress, and I learned about color and art by using a program called Deluxe Paint. Software taught me math and basic statistics. It taught me how to calculate great circle distance, estimating the distance between two points on a globe. I learned about the Internet by creating webpages, and I learned about music through MIDI. And most of all, software taught me about software.

I like cheap old computers more than new ones, and my laptop creaks when it opens. My house is filled with books and soft, non-digital things. But my first thought when I have to accomplish some personal or professional task is, What code can I use? What software will teach me what I need to know? When I want to learn something and no software exists, the vacuum bugs me—why isn't someone on this?

This is what Silicon Valley must be thinking, too, as it optimizes the hell out of every industry it can, making software (and the keepers of that software) the middleman. The Valley has the world in its sights. Government, industry, social services, human sexuality, agriculture: they want to get in there and influence the whole shebang.

Code has atomized entire categories of existence that previously appeared whole. Skilled practitioners have turned this explosive ability to their near total benefit. Bookstores exist now in opposition to Amazon, and Amazon's interpretation of an electronic book is the reference point for the world. For its part, Amazon is not really a bookseller as much as a set of optimization problems around digital and physical distribution. Microsoft Office defined what it was to work, leading to a multidecade deluge of PowerPoint. Uber seeks to recast transportation in its own image, and thousands more startups exist with stars in their eyes and the feverish will to disrupt, disrupt, disrupt, disrupt.

I'm happy to have lived through the greatest capital expansion in history, an era in which the entirety of our species began to speak, awkwardly, in digital abstractions, as venture capitalists waddle around like mama birds, dropping blog posts and seed rounds into the mouths of waiting baby bird developers, all of them certain they will grow up to be billionaires. It's a comedy of ego, made possible by logic gates. I am not smart enough to be rich, but I'm always entertained. I hope you will be, too. Hello, world!

BuzzFeed News

WINNER—PUBLIC INTEREST

Every year, more than 100,000 laborers arrive in the United States to work low-skilled jobs as part of the H-2 visa program, which permits employers to hire temporary foreign workers. "The New American Slavery" documents the state-sanctioned abuse of these especially vulnerable workers. After the publication of this story, BuzzFeed News *continued its reporting on the H-2 visa program with "All You Americans Are Fired." The judges who awarded* BuzzFeed News *the National Magazine Award for Public Interest praised both articles as belonging to the finest tradition of investigative journalism. Since the appointment of Ben Smith as editor in chief in 2011,* BuzzFeed News *has become known as much for its magazine-quality long-form reporting as for its pop-culture bravado. This was not only* BuzzFeed*'s first Ellie but also the first for an online-only publication in Public Interest.*

Jessica Garrison,
Ken Bensinger, and
Jeremy Singer-Vine

The New American Slavery *and* "All You Americans Are Fired"

The New American Slavery

Mamou, Louisiana—Travis Manuel and his twin brother, Trey, were shopping at Walmart near this rural town when they met two Mexican women who struck them as sweet. Using a few words of Spanish he had picked up from his navy days, Travis asked the two women out on a double date.

Around midnight the following Saturday, when they finished their shift at a seafood-processing plant, Marisela Valdez and Isy Gonzalez waited for their dates at the remote compound where they lived and worked.

As soon as they got in the Manuel brothers' car, the women began saying something about "*patrón* angry," Travis recalled. While he was trying to puzzle out what they meant, his brother, who was driving, interrupted: "Dude," Trey said. "There's someone following us."

Trey began to take sudden turns on the country roads threading through the rice paddies that dot the area, trying to lose the pickup truck behind them. Finally, they saw a police car.

"I said, we're gonna flag down this cop" for help, Travis recalled. "But the cop pulled us over, lights on, and told us not to get out of the vehicle," Trey added, noting that the pickup pulled up and the driver began conferring with the police.

An officer asked Trey and his brother for ID. From the backseat, their dates began to cry.

Travis tried to reassure them. They weren't doing anything wrong, he said, and they were in the United States. "I was like, 'There's no way they are going to take you away.'"

He was wrong.

The man in the truck was the women's boss, Craig West, a prominent farmer in the heart of Cajun country. As Sgt. Robert McGee later wrote in a police report, West said that Valdez and Gonzalez were "two of his girls," and he asked the cops to haul the women in and "scare the girls."

The police brought the women, who were both in their twenties, to the station house. McGee told them they couldn't leave West's farm without permission, warning that they could wind up dead. To drive home the point, an officer later testified, McGee stood over Valdez and Gonzalez and pantomimed cutting his throat. He also brandished a Taser at them and said they could be deported if they ever left West's property without his permission.

A little after two in the morning, they released the women to West for the fifteen-minute drive through the steamy night to his compound—a place where, the women and the Mexican government say, workers were stripped of their passports and assigned to sleep in a filthy, foul-smelling trailer infested with insects and mice. Valdez and Gonzalez also claimed that they and other women were imprisoned, forced to work for little pay, and frequently harassed by West, who demanded to see their breasts and insisted that having sex with him was their only way out of poverty.

•   •   •

These women were not undocumented immigrants working off the books. They were in the United States legally, as part of a government program that allows employers to import foreign labor for jobs they say Americans won't take—but that also allows those companies to control almost every aspect of their employees' lives.

Each year, more than 100,000 people from countries such as Mexico, Guatemala, the Philippines, and South Africa come to America on what is known as an H-2 visa to perform all kinds of menial labor across a wide spectrum of industries: cleaning rooms at luxury resorts and national parks, picking fruit, cutting lawns and manicuring golf courses, setting up carnival rides, trimming and planting trees, herding sheep, or, in the case of Valdez, Gonzalez, and about twenty other Mexican women in 2011, peeling crawfish at L.T. West Inc.

A *BuzzFeed News* investigation—based on government databases and investigative files obtained through the Freedom of Information Act, thousands of court documents, as well as more than eighty interviews with workers and employers—shows that the program condemns thousands of employees each year to exploitation and mistreatment, often in plain view of government officials charged with protecting them. All across America, H-2 guest workers complain that they have been cheated out of their wages, threatened with guns, beaten, raped, starved, and imprisoned. Some have even died on the job. Yet employers rarely face any significant consequences.

Many of those employers have since been approved to bring in more guest workers. Some have even been rewarded with lucrative government contracts. Almost none have ever been charged with a crime.

In interview after interview, current and former guest workers—often on the verge of tears—used the same word to describe their experiences: slavery.

"We live where we work, and we can't leave," said Olivia Guzman Garfias, who has been coming to Louisiana as a guest worker from her small town in Mexico since 1997. "We are tied to the company. Our visas are in the company's name. If the pay and working conditions aren't as we wish, who can we complain to? We are like modern-day slaves."

In a statement, the Department of Labor, which is charged with protecting workers and vetting employers seeking visas, said that the H-2 programs "are part of a wider immigration system that is widely acknowledged to be broken, contributing to an uneven playing field where employers who exploit vulnerable workers undermine those who do the right thing."

The number of H-2 visas issued has grown by more than 50 percent over the past five years. Unlike the better-known H-1B visa program, which brings skilled workers such as computer programmers into America's high-tech industries, the H-2 program is for the economy's bottom rung, designed to make it easier for employers to fill temporary, unskilled positions. Proponents argue that it gives foreigners a chance to work here legally, send home much-needed dollars, and return to their families when the job is over.

In March, the U.S. Chamber of Commerce defended the guest-worker program before a Senate committee, noting that such "temporary workers are needed in lesser-skilled occupations that are both seasonal and year round," and that aspects of the program are "critical" to "American workers, the local community, and companies that provide goods and services to these seasonal businesses."

Tens of thousands of companies, ranging from family businesses to huge corporations, have participated in the program since it took its modern form in 1986. Employers pledge to pay their workers a set rate, which can range from the federal minimum wage to a higher "prevailing wage" that varies from state to state and job to job. As for the employees, they can only work for the company that sponsored their visa. They are legally barred from seeking other employment and must leave the country when the job ends.

For some people, such as the hundreds of soccer coaches whom youth sports camps bring in every year from the United Kingdom and elsewhere, an H-2 visa offers an opportunity to make some money while spending time in another country. Many companies treat their H-2 employees well, and many guest workers interviewed for this article said they are grateful for the program.

But public records and interviews reveal how easy it is for companies that sponsor H-2 visas to abuse their employees.

Many companies pay their guest workers less than the law mandates. Others pay them for fewer hours than they actually work or force them to work extremely long hours without overtime. Some, on the other hand, offer them far less work than promised, at times leaving workers without enough money to buy food. Employers also whittle away at wages by imposing an array of prohibited fees—starting with bribes to get the jobs in the first place, which can leave workers so deep in debt that they are effectively indentured servants.

Guest workers often toil in conditions that are unsafe, inhumane, or simply exhausting, wielding dangerous machinery beneath a scorching sun or standing for hours on end in sweltering factories. And at the end of their shift, many workers retire to grim, squalid quarters that might be little more than a grimy mattress on the floor of a crowded, vermin-infested trailer. For such housing, some employers charge workers extortionate rent.

Though it is against the law, employers often exert additional control over guest workers by confiscating their passports, without which many foreign workers, fearful of being deported, feel unsafe leaving the worksite. Some employers extend their influence over workers to extremes, screening their mail, preventing them from receiving visitors, banning radios and newspapers, or even coercing them to attend religious services they don't believe in. Some foremen sexually harass female workers, who live in constant fear of losing their jobs and being deported.

The world has become accustomed in recent years to hearing of guest-worker abuse in countries such as Qatar or Thailand. But this is happening in the United States. And the problem is not just a few unscrupulous employers. The very structure of the visa program enables widespread abuse and exploitation.

The way H-2 visas shackle workers to a single employer leaves them almost no leverage to demand better treatment. The rules also make it easy to banish a worker to her home country at the boss's whim. And guest workers tend to be so poor—and, often, so indebted from the recruitment fees they paid to get the job in the first place—that they feel they have no choice but to endure even the worst abuses.

Court documents and interviews revealed numerous cases where workers who tried to speak out said they received threats to their lives. Many others claimed they were blacklisted by employers, losing the opportunity to get jobs that, however miserable, give them more money than they could earn in their own countries.

The government has been warned repeatedly over almost two decades that the guest-worker program is deeply troubled, with more than a dozen official reports excoriating it for everything from widespread visa fraud to rampant worker abuse, and even calling for its elimination. Since 2005, Labor Department investigation records show, at least 800 employers have subjected more than 23,000 H-2 guest workers to violations of the federal laws designed to protect them from exploitation, including more than 16,000 instances of H-2 workers being paid less than the promised wage.

Those numbers almost certainly understate the problem, as the federal government doesn't check up on the vast majority of companies that bring guest workers into this country. The Labor Department noted in its statement that it has limited resources, with only about 1,000 investigators to enforce protections for all 135 million workers in the United States. Still, it said, it recovered more than $2.6 million in back wages owed to roughly 4,500 H-2 workers in the 2014 fiscal year. In that year, the agency said, it found violations in 82 percent of the H-2 visa cases it investigated.

Kalen Fraser, a former investigator for the Labor Department's Wage and Hour Division who specialized in H-2 visa cases, said that while some companies stumble over complex rules, a substantial portion "maliciously" violate worker-protection laws. "There's a big power imbalance there, and the worst guys get away with everything."

• • •

Route 95 between Chataignier and Mamou, Louisiana, winds through endless acres of rice paddies that teem with crawfish after the grain is reaped. The country is dead flat, and stretching to the horizon there's little but lush fields of green, dotted with glassy brown pools beneath a heavy sky. Near a bend in the two-lane highway sits the L.T. West crawfish plant.

It was there that Valdez, Gonzalez, and the other women, tired and stiff from a crowded, 1,500-mile ride up from Mexico, stepped out into the dark, wet heat on the night of April 9, 2011.

Valdez said it was need that had brought her there—need and principle. "I wanted to work and make money and do it in a legal way," she said in a recent interview, "so I didn't have to cross the border illegally or undocumented."

She had left behind her five-year-old son and her eight-year-old daughter, along with her mother, who was taking care of the children, and her dream—at least for a time—of finishing her college degree. She was twenty-six. It was her first time away from home.

She landed in one of America's most distinctive and insular regions. Acadiana stretches from the bayous near the Gulf of Mexico up through Lafayette and into the Cajun Prairie north of Interstate 10. It is a place where Spanish moss drips so thick off trees they can hardly be discerned, French is still many people's first language, zydeco music blares from the radio, and social life for generations has centered around great feasts of boiled crab, shrimp, and crawfish.

Valdez and Gonzalez claim they were assigned, along with three other of the youngest women, to an isolated trailer that lacked safe drinking water. Valdez was terrified—of the dark, of the sounds of animals in the brush, of snakes. The women talked that first night about their goals and what their families would do with the money they earned.

"I felt very strange," she said. "Being with all these people I didn't know, having to leave behind my life, my family, my things, in a country I had never been in before. I felt very sad. I felt sad, but the truth is the need we had at that moment was so great that we had to do it, we had to be there."

Valdez lay awake, she said, "thinking about where I was, how did I get there, why I was in this position." A few hours later, the women were rousted and sent to peel crawfish.

After hatching and maturing in the shallow ponds that spool over the landscape, the crustaceans—rusty brown and squirming—are plucked from baited traps. The "mudbugs" are stuffed in mesh sacks, heaved into the back of pickup trucks, then cooked in steel baths until they are bright red.

Then the women go to work. Still steaming, the crawfish are dumped by the basketful onto long metal tables. The workers crowd in, standing shoulder to shoulder or perching on stools. Hour after hour, they pull the heads off and extract the tail meat.

The hot crawfish "would hurt your fingers," Valdez said. But the worst thing was the smell. "It stung your nostrils," she said. "The smell stuck to everything. We carried it home with us."

In its application for H-2 visas, filed in November 2010, L.T. West committed to pay the workers $9.10 an hour, plus overtime. The company also promised the Labor Department it would issue detailed pay statements.

The women soon learned, however, that they would sometimes be paid for each pound of crawfish tails they peeled. Federal law allows guest workers to be paid a piece rate, but only if the employer makes up any difference between that and the promised hourly wage.

L.T. West did not backfill their wages, according to the women's complaint. Some weeks, they said, their piece-rate wages amounted to the equivalent of less than four dollars an hour. Sometimes they were given only about fifteen hours of work per week.

Craig West denies that he shorted the women. But notes from a Labor Department investigation show that he did not keep proper pay records, making it impossible to verify that assertion.

The women also said West forbade them from leaving his plant and ordered one of his employees to confiscate their passports and visas—their only proof, in a region that takes border enforcement seriously, that they were in the United States legally. On numerous occasions, they said, West threatened to call police or immigration authorities.

A few days after the disastrous double date, two of the women claimed, West pointed a gun at Valdez, the red beam of his laser scope directly on her face, and told her never to leave the work camp.

West, a solidly built man with a honey drawl, vehemently denied that he mistreated his workers, taking particular umbrage at the allegation involving the gun. He is a hunting instructor and runs the church skeet shoot, he said in an interview outside his home in June, and would never recklessly point a weapon at anyone.

The real story, West said, is that Valdez, Gonzalez, and some of the other women in their trailer were "wild," partying and arranging to have cases of beer dropped off at his property. In a sworn deposition, one L.T. West employee said the women went out often and sometimes came back after "having been drinking." Another said that West did not get angry if they went out without his permission.

West also denied trying to use the Mamou police to intimidate the women. He called them, he said, because some of the workers had expressed fears that a rapist would sneak onto the property.

Police officers, however, tell a different story. Two testified that when West arrived at the station that night, he was in a state of fury. In a sworn deposition in 2012, Mamou Police sergeant Lucas Lavergne described West's behavior this way: "He said— like looking toward the girls, he said, 'Mucho fuck you. Mucho kill you.'"

What happened that night, Travis said, was "nuts" and "wrong." Reflecting on West's and the police's attitude toward the women, he said, "It seemed like we had messed with his property, like we had stolen a horse or did damage to his property."

His brother Trey added, "Shortest date ever."

By scouring legal and administrative documents, *BuzzFeed News* identified more than 800 workers over the last ten years who complained to authorities that they had their passports confiscated, were held against their will, were physically attacked, or were threatened with harm for trying to leave their housing or job sites. The number who experienced these abuses but did not speak out may be much higher.

In January 2013, a group of Mexican forestry workers said that they had been held at gunpoint in the mountains north of Sacramento and forced to work thirteen hours a day and handle chemicals that made them vomit and peeled their skin, according to a search warrant affidavit filed in federal court last year by a Department of Homeland Security investigator.

Their employer, a small forestry contractor out of Idaho called Pure Forest, had also illegally charged the workers about $2,000 apiece for their visas, paid for out of deductions from their paychecks, the workers said. After additional fees were levied for food, they said, they were sometimes left with less than $100 for two weeks of grueling work. In one case, a worker said he was charged $100 for a pair of used shoes held together with nails.

"Two of Pure Forest's foremen . . . reportedly carried firearms and threatened to shoot workers in the head and leave them in the woods if they did not work harder," the DHS special agent, Eugene Kizenko, wrote. He added that "multiple workers heard these threats."

Five workers who escaped sued Pure Forest in federal court last year. They filed the suit, which is ongoing, using pseudonyms; the complaint states that the workers fear "retaliation due to threats of bodily injury or death made by defendants."

Pure Forest denied the allegations in court papers and in an interview. "Completely false," Owen Wadsworth said by phone. His father, Jeff, owns the company, and Owen was also named in the workers' suit. "We've had nothing but good working relationships with all our employees," he said. The H-2 program "seems more set up to put the company, the owner or the employer, in a bad situation," he added, "and whatever allegations or negative that come up, it's treated almost like it's true, and they'll assume that you're the bad guy."

·   ·   ·

A particularly effective force to keep workers in line is debt.

Interviews and court records reviewed by *BuzzFeed News* turned up hundreds of workers who claimed they were forced to pay for their visas. That's illegal; companies are responsible for making sure their labor brokers don't charge bribes. But diplomats from the United States and Mexico say such bribes are rampant. In cables released by WikiLeaks, U.S. consular officials in Mexico, Jamaica, Guatemala, and the Dominican Republic describe reports of recruiters demanding fees for visas and also committing fraud in order to get visas approved.

Jacob Joseph Kadakkarappally was eager to come from India to the United States to work as a welder at the Pascagoula, Mississippi, shipyard of Signal International in late 2006. But he didn't have the approximately $14,500 recruiters demanded for the visa and other fees, so first he pawned the gold bangles his wife wore every day on her wrist. Then he hocked a gold chain that, he later testified, "is considered to be holy, a symbol of wedding."

Other Signal workers from India, who had been misled into thinking they would get green cards, went deeply into debt or sold property to pay fees. Once the workers arrived in the United States, Signal housed them in a labor camp, up to twenty-four men to a trailer, for which Signal charged them each $1,050 a month.

After Kadakkarappally and others began asking for better working and housing conditions, security guards raided his trailer early one morning and managers told him he was fired.

"I almost lost my breath," Kadakkarappally testified. He pleaded with managers, he said, recounting his huge debts and telling them "that I would not be able to support my family." A fellow worker slit his wrist in a failed suicide attempt.

Kadakkarappally and four other welders eventually sued Signal, and in February a federal jury in New Orleans awarded them $14 million. This month, the Southern Poverty Law Center announced that Signal had agreed to a $20 million settlement that resolves those claims and those of 200 additional Indian welders in 11 related lawsuits. Signal, which filed for bankruptcy to carry out the settlement, also agreed to apologize to its guest workers. Signal did not respond to requests for comment.

Such a victory is extremely rare. Very few H-2 workers have the resources or support to file a lawsuit. Many workers become prisoners of their debt. The best way to pay it off is with a job in the United States—and the only job H-2 workers can legally get is the one with the company that sponsors their visas.

"In so many cases, these workers end up being abused," said Jennifer Gordon, a law professor at Fordham University and a former MacArthur Fellow who has conducted research into the discrimination against and mistreatment of immigrant workers. "In routine ways, all the time, the workers pay fees, they are threatened, their families are threatened. And the employer knows that if you get workers through that program, they're not going to complain."

•　　•　　•

That stark power imbalance can be downright dangerous, contributing to on-the-job injuries and even deaths.

Leonardo Espinabarro Telles entered the country on an H-2 visa in April 2011, to work for Crystal Rock Amusements as it moved from Pennsylvania to Vermont and back, staging that most American of pastimes: county fairs. The Mexico native had been on the job about three months, living in a crowded converted horse trailer without a working bathroom, when the crew of seventeen guest workers arrived in northern Vermont for the Lamoille County Field Days.

A little before three in the afternoon on Tuesday, July 19, Espinabarro went to retrieve electrical connectors from a trailer housing the hulking Caterpillar generator that powered the carnival rides.

Inside, two feet separated the trailer wall from the generator's massive spinning fan blades. The protective guard over the blades had either broken or been removed. At ankle level, pulleys and fan belts were also exposed.

Espinabarro was alone, so no one witnessed what happened, but coworkers heard cries for help. One man rushed to the trailer to see Espinabarro standing upright, then watched him collapse and fall out of the trailer. His clothing had gotten tangled in the machinery, and the fan blades had ripped through his body. From neck to waist, his back was carved open, his organs spilling out. He was dead by the time he reached the hospital.

Inspectors from the Vermont Occupational Safety and Health Administration found that Crystal Rock management knew the fan blades were unguarded at the time of the accident but had not told the workers. No one had posted proper warning signs. Nor had they delivered safety training in any language.

Vermont OSHA levied $114,550 in fines. The case is still open, because Crystal Rock has not paid.

Asked whether he had ever trained his guest workers how to be safe around heavy equipment, Crystal Rock's owner, Arthur Gillette, told an inspector: "How can you train these guys?" adding, "Do you train someone to eat a hot dog?"

Gillette, whose company has been certified for at least 358 visas since 2002, added that Mexican workers were "mechanically inclined and would figure things out" and that if the investigator had ever been to the country she would understand that. He explained: "The streets of Mexico, cars were stolen and disassembled with just the frames left on the street."

The Labor Department conducted its own investigation following the accident, finding that Gillette routinely underpaid workers and owed more than $60,000 in back wages. This month, the Maine state fire marshal criminally charged Gillette with falsifying physical evidence after an accident on a roller coaster injured three children at a carnival in Waterville in June.

Gillette, reached by phone, said the criminal charges in Maine were "unjust" and denied tampering with evidence.

He said both the Labor Department and Vermont OSHA investigations of Crystal Rock, which is now out of business, were unfair. "I've worked dozens of carnivals and dealt with hundreds of foreign employees," he added. "The vast majority of the guys that worked for me said I am more than fair. That I owe them nothing. That we are square."

Guest workers in other industries have died after being run over in grisly accidents, or collapsing for unknown reasons. They've had limbs amputated and suffered other catastrophic injuries.

On-the-job injuries happen to all kinds of employees, of course, but employers' virtually unchecked sway over H-2 workers—as well as some employers' attitudes about foreigners—can foster a cavalier attitude toward workplace dangers. It can also keep workers from pointing out safety violations or even reporting injuries.

In a 2012 report from the Labor Occupational Health Program at the University of California, Berkeley, researchers surveyed 150 forestry workers in Oregon, about a third of them on H-2 visas, and found that more than 40 percent had been injured on the job in the previous twelve months. Fifteen of the workers had suffered broken bones, and another eighteen had dislocated one or more bones. And yet workers kept quiet about many of their injuries—including more than a quarter of the broken bones and nearly half of the dislocated ones.

The report concluded: "They were afraid they would be fired, and they were afraid of otherwise getting in trouble."

·　　·　　·

Topolobampo occupies a peninsula at the mouth of a bay off the Sea of Cortez in violence-ravaged Sinaloa, the home state of the infamous drug lord Joaquín "El Chapo" Guzmán. The sparkling sea along the *malecón* belies a deep listlessness, more stifling than the tropical heat, that has settled over the town. The seafood plant along the waterfront closed down years ago. Mangy dogs range along barely maintained streets, while a few tiny restaurants with cement floors have almost nothing on the menu. Decent jobs—outside of the drug trade—are hard to find.

As much as a third of the population of 6,500 travels to the swamps and prairies of Louisiana every year to catch and process seafood, according to local recruiters. Those who make the trek are colloquially known as "Louisianeros." The rewards of their work are easy to see: solidly built houses, clean tile floors, modern appliances, and framed degrees from private schools. Less visible are the costs: children who grow up in someone else's family because their own parents are working "on the other side."

Fernanda Padilla was just three when her mother, Guadalupe, started coming to Louisiana for ten months a year to process shellfish. "I couldn't understand," said Padilla. "I used to tell her, 'I don't care. I'll eat rice and beans every day, but be here with me.'"

But at seventeen, Padilla dropped out of school and decided to follow in her mother's footsteps to make money. She secured an H-2 visa and arrived at her new job at Bayou Shrimp in April 2009. She was pregnant, but her pay stubs show she worked more than sixty hours some weeks. Forty days after her daughter was born, Padilla was back at work at the plant, leaving her baby with a friend.

Padilla, who has since had a second child, worked in the Louisiana shrimp industry for five seasons before losing her job last year. She said she used to worry that, like her own mother, she was abandoning her children in order to provide for them.

"Five years working there seemed like no time had passed at all, and my daughter had already grown up and I didn't even realize it," Padilla said, adding that she is now cobbling together a living with odd jobs.

North of the border, H-2 visas are also important to the economy.

Louisiana is the nation's second-largest seafood-producing state, and its crawfish industry used to rely on local labor. But competition from cheap Asian imports, along with the demand by huge retailers such as Wal-Mart for ever lower prices, have squeezed profit margins and put downward pressure on wages—below the point, producers say, where people in America will take the jobs on a seasonal basis. In the 1990s, processors including Craig West hoped that machines could be built to take over the repetitive task of extracting the tail meat from the crustaceans. But eventually crawfish farmers discovered that the best and cheapest option is a Mexican on an H-2 visa.

The visa comes in two types: H-2A for agricultural workers and H-2B for nonagricultural unskilled workers, with varying rules and provisions. While many workers say that regulators don't do enough to protect them, their employers generally have the opposite complaint. They say they are burdened by endless bureaucratic hurdles and inspectors who ding them for tiny infractions of incomprehensible rules.

Ben LeGrange, the general manager of Atchafalaya Crawfish Processing, in Henderson, Louisiana, said most crawfish processors treat their workers well, and "isolated incidents" shouldn't taint the whole industry. He said he tries to treat guest workers "as an extension of someone in my family" and that without them the whole company, which also employs six American workers, would be in jeopardy.

•   •   •

Standing on his expansive lawn beside a riding mower, West, who co-owns the crawfish producer L.T. West with his brother, said he treats his workers well. "My wife got holy water for them," he said, adding that when they were not working he and his wife, Cathy, drove workers to Walmart or church, and sometimes invited them to relax in the shade of a tree that protects his house from the sun.

But seven of his workers, including Valdez and Gonzalez, claim West took a different kind of interest in some of them.

Some of their allegations include that he took to bursting into their trailer unexpectedly, even when they were dressing, and called them his "property" and his "Mexican ladies," according to their complaint. Some of the women recall him saying things such as "mucho booby" and "mexicanas mucho booby," gesturing for them to lift up their shirts. He instructed one of his other workers to tell the women in Spanish that the only way they could get out of poverty was to accept his propositions, which included requests that they come to his house when his wife was away. In the suit, the women did not allege he actually had sex with them.

West, with his wife looking on, flatly denied the allegations, saying the women had made them up.

Cut off from their families, often unable to speak English, and beholden to their employers, women with H-2 visas are among the most vulnerable workers in America. Advocates and law enforcement officials say they have logged numerous reports of guest workers being coerced into having sex with their employers or being sexually harassed. Over and over, that abuse involves the threat of deportation—and the loss of desperately needed income.

Under such threats, workers describe attempts to control deeply private aspects of their lives, even their religious identity. When they worked at Harvest Time Seafood in Abbeville, Louisiana, Manuela Ruiz and her sister Yadira said workers were compelled to attend an evangelical church with their boss, Kevin Dartez, and his wife. Those who didn't—even those who said they were Roman Catholic—were threatened with fewer hours, the sisters claimed in interviews. Employees were also ordered to keep their heads down while working, they said, and were forbidden to make eye contact with anyone of the opposite gender.

"We couldn't talk to any men because we were told it's disrespectful to their religion," said Manuela, who worked at Harvest Time from 2007 to 2009 and is now back home in Sinaloa, Mexico. "A lot of workers got baptized in their church to ensure they got a visa for the following year," she added. "It's ugly to work like that."

They said they never complained to outside authorities about being coerced to change their faith or about their bosses confiscating their passports or even about the seeping lesions that formed on their arms and legs that they attributed to chemicals in the crab bath. What finally convinced the sisters to seek outside help was Harvest Time cutting back on the one thing that made the pain and humiliation bearable: their wages. Dartez instructed his foremen to squeeze crabmeat after it had been pulled from shells, Ruiz said, making the juice run out and the meat weigh less. For workers paid by the pound, this meant less money. Particularly galling, she said, was that when the crab was canned, the juice was poured back in.

A Labor Department investigation opened in 2011 found that Harvest Time owed workers more than $52,000 in back wages for 167 violations of worker-protection laws.

Dartez said he invited workers to his church but didn't coerce them to follow his religious practice. "We weren't choosing family or church or nothing," he said in an interview. He did not confiscate passports, he said, though "the problem with giving them their passports, they can skip out anytime they want."

As for crab squeezing, he said it was the only way to stop his workers from adding water to bloat their pay: "They didn't tell you that they patted their hand in the water bowl and dropped the water on the meat, did they?"

In an attempt to help workers who fall victim to abuses, U.S. consular officials hand out pamphlets to guest workers following their visa interviews. Among other information, that literature includes toll-free phone numbers they can call for help.

Belinda Flores Shinshillas, an employee of the Mexican Consulate in New Orleans whose job was to protect Mexicans in the United States, was on duty when a distress call came in from a worker at L.T. West.

Flores and a colleague made the four-hour drive to the compound that very day. Recalling her first glimpse of the trailer where Valdez, Gonzalez, and other women stayed, she shook her head. "They didn't have means to buy food. They didn't have water to drink," she said. "Based on the standards of today, those girls were slaves."

The women, Flores recalled, began to sob. "They didn't believe someone was there to help them," she said.

The Mexican government called a team of lawyers from Chicago, who came to Mamou and met with the women, taking statements and gathering evidence late at night to avoid detection. About a week later, the Mexican consul removed four women from L.T. West, including Valdez and Gonzalez, in another late-night operation. (Gonzalez couldn't be reached for comment.) Others escaped separately and called a human-trafficking hotline. The women together filed suit against L.T. West and the Mamou Police Department in federal district court in Lafayette.

Mexico has repeatedly appealed to the United States to do more to protect guest workers.

In 2003, 2005, and again in 2011, advocates petitioned the Mexican government to intervene on workers' behalf under the North American Free Trade Agreement. Mexico's Secretariat of Labor and Social Welfare forwarded the complaints to the U.S. Department of Labor but received little or no response. Mexico resubmitted the complaints in 2012, making clear that it considers mistreatment of H-2 workers to be a grave human rights abuse. "The 13th Amendment of the Constitution prohibits all forms of slavery or involuntary servitude, regardless of nationality, and therefore it protects H-2A and H-2B workers," the Mexican government wrote.

It is the job of the U.S. government, the report continued, "to make sure workers are not intimidated, threatened or held against their will."

In response, the Labor Department said, it has taken steps to educate employers of their responsibilities and workers of their rights. Late in 2014 and early this year, it held a series of outreach events for guest workers in fifteen states. At some of those events, a spokeswoman said, officials learned of sixteen cases that may merit further investigation.

• • •

If a United States citizen were threatened on the job by a supervisor holding a gun or cornered by her boss while she was getting dressed, she might well go to the police. But H-2 visa holders rarely choose that option.

"These are people that work ten to fourteen hours a day," said Doug Molloy, a former assistant U.S. attorney in Florida who now works as a criminal defense attorney in Fort Myers, Florida. "People that wouldn't know how to even call the police for help."

But another factor may also be at work: the close relationship that their employers have with local authorities.

Even before Star One Staffing, a Miami labor-staffing company, brought Filipino workers to the United States to clean hotel rooms, its owners informed those workers that the company had tight connections with politicians and police.

The company squeezed numerous unpermitted fees from its workers, at times reducing their net pay to less than one dollar per hour, employees alleged. They also feared being deported, especially because the company was connected to "powerful people" such as Florida criminal judge Andrew Hague, who is married to the company's president and who met the workers in the Philippines. In addition, workers said a police officer frequently visited the house where they slept, and they were brought to meet to a staffer for a U.S. congressman. Reached by phone, Judge Hague said he could not comment on the matter, and his wife, Mary Jane Hague, did not respond to requests seeking comment.

If workers ever tried to complain or leave, Star One managers "would have our visas revoked or deport us and we could never work in the U.S. again," Robert Bautista, who shared a house with forty other workers, said in a sworn declaration. "They were very powerful people and we all knew this."

In Mamou, West told his workers he was friends with local police and made a point of inviting an officer into the trailer where they lived, according to the lawsuit.

When the Manuel brothers picked up Valdez and Gonzalez for their date, West called 911. "I asked [Sgt. McGee] why he brought the girls" to the station, Officer Brent Zackery said in a sworn deposition, "and he told me that Mr. West wanted him to scare them because they shouldn't go out late like they did."

It worked, especially when, Zackery testified, Sgt. McGee threatened that they could be deported and pulled out the Taser. "That really scared the mess out of them," Zackery said.

Zackery also testified that, after the women filed their lawsuit, some of the officers conspired to cover up the Taser incident: If discharge tests were ever administered, they agreed that they would swap out McGee's Taser with another one. Then they all went to Hooters for lunch. McGee is now Mamou's police chief. He did not return calls seeking comment.

·　　·　　·

Ten months after the women were detained, the Labor Department's Wage and Hour Division opened an investigation of L.T. West.

The probe, begun in March 2012, was supposed to audit the treatment and pay of H-2 employees at the plant dating back almost two years. Although case files show the department was aware of the women's lawsuit, the investigator waited until June to visit the plant—by which time crawfish season had ended, and almost all the workers had returned home. The inspector did not visit any worker housing at the crawfish plant.

As for Craig West, he told the investigator that he had not kept complete payroll records—not even a daily log of hours worked—and didn't have home addresses for his employees.

In the end, the Department of Labor fined L.T. West $7,200—not for underpaying or abusing its employees, but for keeping poor records.

BuzzFeed News reviewed more than three dozen investigations by the Department of Labor, the arm of the government that is supposed to ensure employers treat guest workers in accordance with the law. In most cases, inspectors interviewed few if any workers, showed up at workplaces only with advance warning, and accepted at face value the employer's version of events.

The Labor Department's Wage and Hour Division investigated the Arkansas-based Superior Forestry—the largest forestry contractor in the country, according to the department—at least fifteen times between 2000 and 2014. Few of those probes involved any worker interviews, records show. In one case, the inspector had not even been fully trained in applicable H-2 law.

In a 2011 probe, investigators did interview workers, but only after setting up a formal visit far in advance with a third-party labor broker that handles Superior's visa applications. The labor broker arranged for the interview to be conducted at a nearby motel rather than the job site, which inspectors did not visit. Still, they concluded that everything was in order, adding that the labor broker "makes sure all applicable laws are 'followed to a T.'"

None of the investigation reports mentioned that Superior had been sued in 2006 in Tennessee federal court by 2,200 H-2 workers who alleged the company did not pay them the promised wage or overtime or that those workers were subsequently threatened by Superior agents who said they would report the workers to immigration if they didn't drop the lawsuit or that even after the court issued a protective order, a Superior recruiter spooked workers back home in Oaxaca, Mexico, by attending a meeting where legal information was being shared.

"I can't honestly say we do everything right all the time, but we try to," said John Foley, an operations manager at the company, which has 25 full-time employees but brings in as many as 450 H-2 workers every year. "The laws are very confusing," he added in a phone interview. "It's telling that we have a full-time attorney."

The guest workers eventually won a $2.75 million settlement to resolve claims that they'd had millions in back wages stolen over a period of six years. But over the course of the Labor Department's fifteen investigations, the agency pinned only minor violations on the company, ordering Superior to repay its workers a total of just $12,652 in back wages over a dozen years.

For many companies, the financial incentive to underpay guest workers far outweighs the risk of getting caught, said Jacob Horwitz, an organizer for the National Guestworker Alliance in New Orleans. Stealing wages "is standard business practice," he said.

The Labor Department, in its statement, noted it has "finite resources" and "must be strategic" in how it deploys them for enforcement. It has sought greater powers to raise wages, prevent unlawful fees and retaliation against workers who speak out, and punish companies that break the law. However, it said, "these efforts have met with legal challenges and Congressional opposition."

In the case of the most egregious violations, the Department of Labor has the option of debarring a company—banning it for up to three years from bringing in guest workers. The department maintains a public list of companies under such censure; the current list has seventy-six names on it. Employers that do work for the federal government can also be debarred from future contracts.

That's how it works in theory. This March, however, the Government Accountability Office found that the Department of Labor's Wage and Hour Division failed to conclude more than half its investigations of H-2 employers within the two-year statute of limitations. And many companies that were repeatedly found to abuse workers were nevertheless granted more H-2 visas, lucrative federal contracts, and farm subsidies.

Over the previous five years, government investigations found at least twelve firms underpaid H-2 workers by more than $100,000. Yet only one of them was debarred. Five—including an onion producer that had more than 1,400 violations and owed its Mexican workers $2.3 million in back wages—have been certified for more than 2,000 additional visas this year alone. In short, even though the U.S. government determined that these companies stiffed guest workers on a grand scale, it granted them the right to bring in more.

Some companies the Labor Department moves to debar nonetheless continue to receive government contracts.

Garcia Forest Service was caught multiple times stealing thousands of dollars in wages from guest workers, misleading investigators, and doctoring time sheets to cover it up. "Some of these violations were innocent mistakes," Garcia's attorney, Ray Perez, said in an interview. "A lot of the times the investigators have it in their mind that they're going to nitpick you and get you."

The Labor Department didn't see it that way and debarred the company from receiving federal contracts for three years starting in March of last year. But so far, the ban has had little if any effect. The Rockingham, North Carolina, company appealed, and while awaiting a final ruling it has been awarded $715,082 in contracts from the U.S. Forest Service, including a $72,147 award early this month to spray herbicide on 529 acres of the Apalachicola National Forest in Florida.

During her four years auditing companies with H-2 visas, said Kalen Fraser, the former Wage and Hour Division investigator, she saw terrible abuses. She recalled the agricultural guest workers in western Colorado who slept four to a room in a filthy old roadside motel, cooking on hot plates on the floor and unable to drink the tap water because the plumbing was defective and actually issued electric shocks. "That was really an instance of you feeling horrible because people are just living in really bad conditions," said Fraser, who now helps employers comply with labor laws.

She fined their employer, but did not escalate the case or refer it to law enforcement. Indeed, Fraser said, despite seeing hundreds of serious violations, she never recommended a single case to the FBI, Immigration and Customs Enforcement, or her own inspector general, all of which can bring criminal actions. "We didn't do any criminal stuff," she said. "If you see a problem, you don't stomp out and say something." Instead, she said, she and other Labor Department inspectors would ask companies "to agree not to hold people's passports, not to deduct wages, etc. And hopefully they agree to that."

. . .

In January 2013, Valdez, Gonzalez, and the other women reached a final settlement in their lawsuit with L.T. West and the city of Mamou. The city paid Valdez and Gonzalez $20,000 each. L.T. West settled with all seven plaintiffs, but the amount is confidential.

Today, Valdez doesn't want to say where she is living. She declined to discuss the allegations in the lawsuit, or the settlement. She signed a confidentiality agreement. But looking back, she said that a big part of being a guest worker is feeling "vulnerable" and "like we're not worth anything."

"We make lots of plans; we think this is the thing that is going to change our lives for the better. We have so many illusions about what it's going to be like," she said. And then when it's not, "you get desperate. You feel like there won't be any more opportunities. You so badly want to go home but not like this, not like a failure. It's not just your dreams and your illusions. It's your mom and dad, your kids: 'Oh my mom is going to bring me this thing,'" but then "having to come back with empty hands."

She continued: "People have asked me whether they should go to the U.S." on an H-2 visa. "They say they want to go and ask if I can help. But, honestly," she said, "I just tell them I don't know anyone who can help."

"All You Americans Are Fired"

Moultrie, Georgia—"All you black American people, fuck you all . . . just go to the office and pick up your check," the supervisor at Hamilton Growers told workers during a mass layoff in June 2009.

The following season, according to a lawsuit filed by the Equal Employment Opportunity Commission, about eighty workers, many of them black, were simply told: "All you Americans are fired."

Year after year, Hamilton Growers, which has supplied squash, cucumbers, and other produce to Wal-Mart and the Green Giant brand, hired scores of Americans, only to cast off many of them within weeks, according to the U.S. government. And time after time, the grower filled the jobs with foreign guest workers instead.

Although Hamilton Growers eventually agreed to pay half a million dollars to settle the suit, company officials said the allegations are baseless. Mass firings never happened, they said, nor did anyone use racially inflammatory language. But workers tell a different story.

"We want to go to work and work all day," said Derrick Green, thirty-two, a father of six who said he was fired by Hamilton Growers in 2012 after only three weeks picking squash. "But they don't want that."

Last year, thousands of American companies won permission to bring a total of more than 150,000 people into the country as legal guest workers for unskilled jobs, under a federal program that grants them temporary work permits known as H-2 visas. Officially, the guest workers were invited here to fill positions no Americans want: The program is not supposed to deprive any American of a job, and before a company wins approval for a single H-2 visa, it must attest that it has already made every effort to hire domestically. Many companies abide by the law and make good-faith efforts to employ Americans.

Yet a *BuzzFeed News* investigation, based on Labor Department records, court filings, more than one hundred interviews, inspector general reports, and analyses of state and federal data, has found that many businesses go to extraordinary lengths to skirt the law, deliberately denying jobs to American workers so they can hire foreign workers on H-2 visas instead.

A previous *BuzzFeed News* report found that many of those foreign workers suffer a nightmare of abuse, deprived of their fair pay, imprisoned, starved, beaten, sexually assaulted, or threatened with deportation if they dare complain.

At the same time, companies across the country in a variety of industries have made it all but impossible for U.S. workers to learn about job openings that they are supposed to be given first crack at. When workers do find out, they are discouraged from applying. And if, against all odds, Americans actually get hired, they often are treated worse and paid less than foreign workers doing the same job, in order to drive the Americans to quit. Sometimes, as the government alleged happened at Hamilton Growers, employers comply with regulations by hiring Americans only to fire them en masse and hand over the work to foreign workers with H-2 visas.

What's more, companies often do this with the complicity of government officials, records show. State and federal authorities have allowed companies to violate the spirit—and often the letter—of the law with bogus recruitment efforts that are clearly designed to keep Americans off the payroll. And when regulators are alerted to potential problems, the response is often ineffectual.

Officials at the U.S. Department of Labor, which is charged with protecting workers and vetting employers seeking visas, said in a statement: "We acknowledge that the laws that authorize these programs are inadequate." But the department also said that despite limited resources, it "actively pursues measures to strengthen protections for foreign and U.S. workers."

The H-2 visa was created to address shortages in the American workforce. Although labor is indeed tight in some areas—such as North Dakota, where an oil boom has driven unemployment below 3 percent—there is little evidence of labor shortages in many industries that use the visas. In some cases, there is even a glut of available workers.

Landscaping companies, for example, were approved for more than 30,000 H-2 visas in the 2014 fiscal year. Yet Daniel Costa, a researcher at the Economic Policy Institute, which receives some funding from unions, found that over the same period, unemployment in landscaping was more than twice as high as the national average.

"The problem with the system is that the H-2 workers who are coming in are not tied to actual, demonstrated labor shortages," Costa said.

Companies that have difficulty finding American workers could attract more applicants by offering higher wages. But instead of encouraging or even subsidizing that, the government's H-2 program effectively subsidizes the opposite effort—helping companies find pliant foreign labor, often at the expense of American workers.

In the last five years, the number of H-2 visas issued by the State Department, which administers the program along with the Department of Homeland Security and the Labor Department, has surged by more than 50 percent.

Bills in Congress to expand the guest-worker program have won support from both Democrats and Republicans in recent years. Business groups such as the Chamber of Commerce have lobbied for as many as 400,000 additional H-2 visas per year. But the issue has been overshadowed by larger debates over the legal status of millions of undocumented immigrants.

Around the country, lawyers and labor brokers actively promote the H-2 program as a way to boost profit margins. Usafarmlabor, a labor broker serving the agricultural industry, until this month bluntly stated on its site: "Our workers actually save you money each month in a comparison with U.S. workers."

Employers who use the H-2 program note that it entails numerous added costs, including visa fees and transportation, as well as compliance with complex rules. It requires that most workers be paid above minimum wage, sometimes substantially so.

But the guest-worker program also offers numerous financial incentives. Agricultural employers are exempt from payroll and unemployment taxes on H-2 workers, for example; nonagricultural employers do not have to provide housing, but if they do they are allowed to charge their workers rent, which is sometimes extortionate.

Foreign laborers usually live at the job site, available to work at any time. They typically come alone, without families or other distractions that could cause them to miss work. The terms of their visas prohibit them from taking other jobs, so they have almost no leverage when it comes to wages or working conditions. And since they often come from abject poverty in their home countries, many visa holders put up with difficult or even back-breaking conditions without complaint to ensure they are invited to return the next year.

The visa program can be even more advantageous to the many employers that exploit their guest workers, making them work long hours without overtime pay, charging them illegal fees, or flat-out cheating them of their wages—all of which are against the law, regardless of whether workers are American or foreign.

Hamilton Growers has been cited, repeatedly, for its treatment of its mostly Mexican workforce. Even as the farm was accused of casting off American workers, government investigators found that it failed to pay foreign employees all they were owed and that it housed them in often deplorable conditions. Hamilton Growers vigorously denies that it mistreated workers.

Americans are far less isolated than foreigners on H-2 visas, many of whom cannot speak a word of English. U.S. workers often know at least some of their rights and how to complain about abuses. They frequently have family nearby whom they can turn to for support. And, perhaps most importantly, they can't be threatened with deportation. But the guest-worker program can still have a devastating impact on their jobs, their families, and their entire communities.

In house after house in Moultrie, American workers said they have been shut out of agriculture jobs that have been available in their community for generations. Older workers talked of becoming impoverished; younger ones said their chances of financial stability have been strangled, leaving them, in some cases, with little choice but to leave town.

"They got rid of us," said Mary Jo Fuller, referring to black workers. A field-worker on and off for most of her life, she said she was abruptly terminated from J&R Baker Farms, near Moultrie, as part of a mass firing in 2010. Unable to find other employment, the fifty-nine-year-old said she wound up homeless for more than a year. "We don't really have jobs no more."

Moultrie is "nowhere, really, for a young person trying to make it," added Green. "It just makes you angry, very angry," he said. "We right here in America, and you don't want us to work. You'd rather get foreigners."

For several years, Abrorkhodja Askarkhodjaev ran a temp firm based in Kansas City that relied on H-2 guest workers from the Philippines, Jamaica, and the Dominican Republic and that serviced large hotels and other businesses around the country.

"Foreign people will clean two rooms in one hour. The American will not even finish in one hour one room," he said speaking from the federal prison where he is serving a twelve-year term for crimes related to visa fraud.

"Foreigners are better," Askarkhodjaev added. "Of course I tried not to hire Americans."

Before a company can bring in any guest workers, it must clear a series of legal hurdles to prove to the government that it has tried but failed to recruit Americans for the job.

Companies that don't actually want Americans, however, have devised a whole set of creative tricks to get around these hurdles.

Step 1: Don't Let Them Know the Job Exists

To apply for the right to import foreign workers, a company must first post at least two newspaper job ads, including one on a Sunday, "in the area of intended employment."

Some employers have a very broad definition of "area of intended employment."

In January 2011, Talbott's Honey, a small honey producer, placed ads as required soliciting workers for jobs in Kimball, South Dakota. The ads, however, ran in Elkader, Iowa; Dalhart, Texas; and Hobbs, New Mexico—towns that are hundreds of miles from Kimball.

Talbott's then told the government there were no available American workers and got permission to import twelve foreign workers instead.

Reached by phone, the company declined to comment on the matter. But when asked why it hadn't run an ad somewhere in the actual vicinity of the job, Talbott's wrote that it had tried but the ad "somehow fell thru the cracks," according to Labor Department records.

Sometimes the government actually abets this tactic. In North Carolina's Blue Ridge Mountains, seasonal jobs cutting down Christmas trees in the frenzied weeks before the holiday pay well. But year after year, the state's online job board has incorrectly posted those jobs in the wrong counties, sometimes hundreds of miles from any pine forests. As a result, workers looking for Christmas-tree work close to home face a peculiar paradox: The only way to find the openings nearby is to search in a faraway corner of the state.

Lawyers at Legal Aid of North Carolina have been complaining to the state Department of Commerce about the Christmas tree job-posting discrepancies for years. Yet despite repeated promises by state regulators to fix it, the issue persists, the lawyers said.

Indeed, officials in the state at times seem to make it easy for employers to avoid hiring Americans. During the fiscal year that ended this July, the state's job bank tallied work orders seeking H-2 workers for 17,496 agricultural job openings, according to the North Carolina Department of Commerce. More than 7,000 U.S. farmworkers had registered with the agency actively seeking work—yet only 505 of them were referred to those jobs.

Kim Genardo, spokesperson for the department, wrote in an e-mail that the state's "Foreign Labor Certification program is absolutely in compliance with federal law."

Across the country, employers have run ads that failed to list any contact information, omitted the name of the company, or excluded relevant information such as what kind of job it was, where it was located, or how much it would pay, records show.

Some simply don't place ads at all.

For years, Linda White ran a business in Livingston, Louisiana, securing H-2 visas for hundreds of employers. Late last month, she was sentenced to eighteen months in federal prison for creating phony receipts in an attempt to convince regulators she had placed newspaper ads for dozens of clients when in fact she had not. During a three-year period reviewed by the Labor Department, her clients were approved for more than 8,000 visas, federal data show.

In an interview, White called the matter "a mistake," adding that "nobody was going to call for these jobs over dumb newspaper ads anyhow. When clients come to me, what they want is their Mexicans."

Step 2: Make the Job Sound So Awful No One Will Apply

The H-2 program dates all the way back to 1952, and employers have been coming up with ways to game the system for almost as long.

An information sheet from the Snake River Farmers Association in Idaho from the mid-1980s, obtained by a legal aid group representing farmworkers from Texas, offered a list of tips on how to write job postings so that they would deter American applicants.

"Irrigators or pipe movers is a great job description because no one wants to move pipe," the fact sheet said. "Ranch Hands," by contrast, is "a poor description," the memo noted, adding: "One might get some adventuresome young ladies from Cincinnati seeking the thrill of working on a western ranch. With numerous applications from such U.S. workers, the employer would never get around to recruiting aliens."

In response to a query from *BuzzFeed News*, Jeanne Malitz, a lawyer who represents the association, initially said it was "unaware of the source of this document, or whether it was published or ever disseminated" and disavowed its contents. Told of the document's origin, she declined to comment further.

Step 3: Convince Job Seekers That They Shouldn't Bother Applying

Despite all the obstacles, some U.S. workers do manage to find out about job openings at the companies that are seeking to hire abroad. But many of those companies set unusually stringent requirements—for their U.S. applicants, at least.

Even for entry-level jobs or tasks as simple as picking melons, some employers demand that American applicants have months or sometimes even years of experience, clean drug tests, high school diplomas, familiarity with botanical nomenclature, knowledge of diabetic cooking, multiple references, or commercial driver's permits.

Despite the H-2 program's focus on unskilled labor, employers seeking guest workers routinely demand previous work experience, further raising the bar for Americans. In recent years a full three-quarters of companies approved to bring in agricultural guest workers have listed such requirements, according to a *BuzzFeed News* analysis of federal data. In some states—as geographically diverse as New York, North Carolina, Montana, and Washington—virtually all agricultural employers demand prior experience.

Such requirements are a way to "filter out U.S. workers," said Lori Johnson, an attorney at Legal Aid of North Carolina. She noted that some fruit- and vegetable-picking jobs now require three months of experience. And, Johnson said, there is little evidence that such requirements are ever imposed on the foreign guest workers who ultimately get the jobs.

Some requirements also appear racially coded.

"I will keep my pants pulled up around my waist. I will wear pants and shirts that fit," reads a document that Hamilton Growers required its workers to sign in 2013. "If I have long hair or extensions in my hair, I will fix my hair in such a manner that it can be placed under a hair net."

Jon Schwalls, director of operations at the farm, said it was "ridiculous" to suggest that the language targeted black workers; those rules were about food and workplace safety, he said.

Step 4: Make Applicants Perform Extraordinary Feats

Early this year, the sign manufacturer Persona, of Watertown, South Dakota, obliged American applicants to take the Thurstone Test of Mental Alertness, which "helps measure an individual's ability to learn new skills quickly, adjust to new situations, understand complex or subtle relationships, and be flexible in thinking."

The twenty-minute exam is often deployed to assess computer programmers, accountants, bank managers, and commercial airline pilots, but Persona used it to evaluate—and reject—Americans applying for painting and welding jobs. A Labor Department official questioned whether the test "is going to be administered to foreign workers."

A Persona official declined to comment.

When American workers showed up to apply for a job at Pro Landscape, in Hillsboro, Oregon, they were told they would have to dig a trench four feet long, a foot and a half wide, and a foot and a half deep within five minutes to be considered for the position, according to Labor Department records.

Manuel Castaneda, the company's owner, called the task a "fair way" to see who was up to the job. But the Labor Department said the tests appeared "to not be normal" for the industry and to "be restrictive to U.S. workers." Indeed, Labor Department records show that only five of the eighteen applicants who attempted the tests passed. "The employer's tests," the department found, appear to have "discouraged U.S. workers."

Step 5: When the Perfectly Qualified U.S. Worker Does Present Herself, Ignore Her

When Nicole Burt applied for work as a stable attendant in Kentucky, she was sure her experience and skills were unimpeachable. As a teenager in Vermont she showed, trained, and groomed horses, and no sooner did she graduate high school than she moved to the Bluegrass State in order to be in what she dubbed "the horse capital of the world."

In early 2011, she applied to a dozen or so stables, she said, but none called her back. One of them was Three Chimneys Farm, a stately home for legendary thoroughbreds including the 1977 Triple Crown winner, Seattle Slew.

Three Chimneys, based in the town of Versailles, had told federal authorities it was "facing a distinct labor crisis and cannot locate or retain American workers" and that "all U.S. workers who express an interest in the employment opportunity will be interviewed for employment." But when Burt called to check on her application, she was told no jobs were available.

"Basically we never hire US workers who are applying," the farm's director of human resources, LaTerri Williams, told the Department of Labor in a signed statement. "I don't conduct interviews or take their applications. Basically I just tell them we have no openings."

Asked by regulators why it didn't give Burt a chance, as federal law required, the company stated that the single mother of three was better off unemployed than taking the $9.71-an-hour job. "Given the length of the commute, the cost of daycare, the loss of her eligibility for food stamps, it would cost Ms. Burt more to work for Three Chimneys than if she did not work at all," the company said.

Burt said she never found another job working with horses, and in the months she waited, holding out hope that she'd get a call, she lost both her cars and her house. Almost four years later, the Labor Department awarded her $16,313—the amount regulators calculated she would have earned at Three Chimneys had she been hired as the law required.

Three Chimneys did not respond to several requests for comment.

"I kept hearing the employers say that they couldn't find anybody. And I just want to smack them, because we're right here," said Burt. "I felt betrayed. I just felt like America had let Americans down."

Step 6: If Compelled to Interview Qualified American Workers, Lie

The Westin Kierland Resort and Spa in Scottsdale, Arizona, was approved for twenty-three foreign housekeepers in 2012, arguing that the golf and convention seasons created a need from October to May. As required by law, the sprawling luxury resort, part of the $12 billion Starwood chain, placed ads for American workers in the *Arizona Republic* newspaper—but it rejected all five applicants. The company told the Labor Department that some failed to meet a one-month experience requirement.

The following year, however, when government inspectors contacted some of those rejected workers, a different story emerged. One applicant "revealed that she had over 25 years of housekeeping experience" and "used to run her own motel in Colorado," investigation documents said.

The Labor Department ultimately ordered the Westin Kierland, which has a championship golf course, multiple pools, and a 900-foot "lazy river" spread over 262 acres, to pay a total of $13,500 in lost wages to two American workers it judged should have been hired. In a statement, Bruce Lange, Westin Kierland's managing director, said the resort disagreed with the Labor Department's findings but "chose to resolve the matter in order to focus our time and resources on caring for our associates and guests."

Throughout the Midwest, corn detasseling is a popular summertime gig. So when D&K Harvesting filed a job posting in April 2013—a step it had to take to win approval to import 120 H-2 workers—Katlyn Sanchez rushed to apply. The job, which involves removing the flower from cornstalks, typically draws high school kids and young adults.

But when the Kalamazoo, Michigan, teenager's mother spoke to a recruiter over the phone a few days later, she was warned that it was "not a good situation for a young female worker alone," according to a complaint later filed to regulators by Sanchez. "There will be all single men from Mexico" working alongside her, the recruiter later said, and her daughter "could get physically or sexually attacked."

The recruiter added that D&K "will not be responsible for anything that happens" to Sanchez in the fields. Employers do not have the right to absolve themselves of workplace dangers, nor to decide that they'd rather not hire women. But the recruiter's tactic worked: Sanchez's mother agreed not to let her take the job.

The recruiter offered her approval: "I think you've made a good choice."

D&K president Larry Marsh did not return several calls seeking comment.

Step 7: When Forced to Hire Americans, Get Rid of Them as Soon as Possible

Far off the interstate, perched under a big blue sky and surrounded by fields of fluffy cotton, Moultrie, population 14,000, feels frozen in time. Coffee can be found for less than a dollar. The charming central square is listed on the National Register of Historic Places. And the town's quiet old neighborhoods—some graceful, some ragged—are deeply segregated.

For many black men, job options are especially scarce. In the spring of 2012, Derrick Green, the father of six, had been unemployed and looking for work for several months, while his wife's uncle, Derek Davis, forty-two, had trouble landing a job because of a pair of old drug convictions. When the two friends went together to the Moultrie branch of the Georgia Department of Labor to review job listings, both said they were desperate for work.

They were referred to Hamilton Growers, one of the area's largest farms and one of the county's largest employers, which had posted the openings as part of three separate applications to import a total of 614 H-2 workers that year.

Along with roughly a dozen other folks, most of them black, Green and Davis submitted to drug tests and filled out applications. Picking squash under a relentless Georgia sun for $9.39 an hour is brutally hard and monotonous. But Green, who is athletic and slender, said he "learned to pick" as a child alongside his grandmother. Davis, a former U.S. Army mechanic, said he first toiled in the fields at fourteen.

It was June and already sweltering when they reported to work among lush crops rolling across the red clay. Rumbling old school buses transport workers to and from long rows where they stoop in the hot sun, picking squash, cucumber, and peppers.

Hamilton Growers is owned by the Hamilton family, which boasts that it has cultivated land in this area for six generations. The enterprise has grown into an agricultural behemoth, with more than half a dozen interconnected corporations and LLCs running each aspect of the business: While Hamilton Growers files H-2 visa requests to the Labor Department, Southern Valley Fruit and Vegetable sells produce grown on the land.

Beyond south Georgia, the farm also has operations in Tennessee and in 2003 went international, cultivating hundreds of acres in a remote section of Mexico's Yucatan Peninsula.

At the headquarters in Norman Park, a twenty-minute drive northeast of Moultrie, a prominent plaque proclaims that the farm commits to "feeding the nations and providing a source of income for those who labor here, as servants of our Lord for His glory." The chief executive, Kent Hamilton, is beloved by local youths for the zip line over his swimming hole. He is on the board of the nonprofit Georgia Fruit and Vegetable Foundation and has donated thousands of dollars to local elected officials, including former U.S. senator Saxby Chambliss, who lives in Moultrie and previously chaired the powerful agriculture committee.

Nearly two decades ago, Hamilton Growers began bringing in foreign guest workers. It's a transition increasing numbers of farmers have made in recent years—often, as in Hamilton's case, after complaining they had lost crops for want of people to pick them.

"You don't save any money" by using H-2 guest workers, said Matt Scaroni, whose family owns Fresh Harvest, a farm-labor contractor based in California that accounted for roughly one-fifth of all agricultural H-2 visas approved in the state last year.

By Scaroni's calculation, housing, transportation, and legal costs, not to mention state and federal inspections and regulations, cost upwards of $4,000 to $5,000 for each guest worker "before they pick one fruit."

In the past year, Scaroni said, Fresh Harvest has rented entire motels in Salinas to accommodate workers, along with apartments and traditional farmworker housing. The company has also been forced into once unthinkable expenditures, such as purchasing 3,000 new beds and launching a catering operation to provide meals, he said. In Salinas, he added, a paid cleaning service even visits many of the Fresh Harvest motels.

That's a very different standard of living from that of many guest workers at Hamilton Growers. Some of them live in concrete dorms, others in rotting old school buses on cinder blocks in a forest near the grower's packing operation, for which they say they must pay nearly $300 a month. In 2005, health inspectors told Hamilton Growers that its portable toilets couldn't simply "have a hole cut in the bottom and a pit dug for waste."

On a recent afternoon, some Mexican H-2 workers sat in the thick heat inside a dimly lit school bus and said that the company wasn't paying them for all the hours they worked. None agreed to be named. "People are scared," one of them said.

Their grievances echo those made by more than a dozen Mexican H-2 workers who sued Hamilton Growers and Southern Valley in federal court last year, alleging that the companies had engaged in intentional wage theft. American workers eventually joined the suit.

The companies deny the charge, but earlier this month they agreed to pay $485,000 to settle the lawsuit because, Schwalls said, doing so was less expensive than litigating it.

He said that the company pays its employees properly and that its housing "meets and exceeds" federal standards. All bedrooms have central heat and air conditioning even though it is not required, he said, and there are no pit toilets at the housing site.

He expressed shock when told that workers had a receipt showing they had paid the company's longtime foreman, who departed this summer, $296 a month to live in the school buses. "That is not our land," Schwalls said. "I can only speak to those workers who choose company housing, which is at no charge to the employees."

Hamilton Growers has consistently maintained that it uses foreign workers not because they are cheaper or more pliant but because there are simply not enough U.S. workers. "I would prefer to have an all-domestic workforce," Schwalls said. "We hire 100 percent of the American applications we receive."

But according to the Equal Employment Opportunity Commission, Hamilton Growers fired or pushed out "the overwhelming majority" of the 114 American field-workers it hired in 2009—but "few to none" of the 370 Mexican guest workers. In 2010, the company hired 233 American workers and got rid of "nearly all" of them, yet almost none of its 518 Mexican H-2 employees lost their jobs. The story was the same in 2011, the government charged in a rare lawsuit.

In late 2012, the company agreed to pay $500,000, without admitting guilt, and entered into a consent decree, pledging to be "a model employer in the area of anti-discrimination and equal employment opportunity."

Despite the settlement, Schwalls said the government's claims were "completely inaccurate and false" and that it was only poor record keeping that prevented Hamilton Growers from proving that workers had voluntarily abandoned their jobs. "It's just a family farm," he said. "There was no understanding of the need for documentation." Wal-Mart, which has been one of the farm's customers, declined to speak for this story, while Green Giant didn't respond to a request to comment.

By the time Derrick Green applied for the job at Hamilton Growers in 2012, he had heard rumors about troubles at the farm but was assured by staff at the local employment office that the company had mended its ways.

"They told me they was good now," Green recalled.

He lasted just three weeks, he said, before he and a dozen other Americans were abruptly fired for not meeting production targets.

The workers protested, demanding to see some kind of accounting of their performance, but the company refused to provide it, Green recalled. "We had a big argument in that office," he said. The dispute ended, he said, only after one manager pulled out a can of mace and another picked up the phone to summon the cops.

Schwalls said he could not comment on terminations of individual employees but insisted no one was ever threatened with mace.

This month, as part of their settlement of the suit brought by foreign guest workers, Hamilton Growers and Southern Valley agreed to pay thirteen American workers, including Green, $1,500 each for claims that they were wrongly fired.

After their time at Hamilton Growers, Green and Davis returned to the employment office and were referred to J&R Baker Farms, another big vegetable grower in the area that has come to rely heavily on guest workers. In 2012, the farm applied for 160 H-2 visas, arguing there were not enough Americans who wanted the job.

Davis and Green were both hired. For the first few days, they say, the company made it difficult for them to work—by not sending the bus that was supposed to transport them to the fields or by dismissing them after just a couple of hours. On Green's fourth day, the bus made an unscheduled stop at the front office, Green recalled, and a foreman told the Americans—but not the Mexican guest workers—to get off the bus. Nine Americans were fired that day, according to a lawsuit Green and others later filed against the company.

J&R Baker too has been repeatedly accused of mistreating both its American workers and guest workers. In 2010, the Department of Labor's Wage and Hour division fined the farm $136,500 and said it should pay $1.3 million in back wages. The farm eventually settled with the agency, agreeing to pay a fraction of those amounts.

In 2012, two dozen black workers sued J&R Baker, alleging that they were held to different production standards than H-2 workers and that many of them were unlawfully fired for not meeting quotas. The grower settled that case in February 2014, agreeing to pay up to $2,200 to each of the terminated employees.

Six months later, in a case similar to the one it filed against Hamilton Growers, the EEOC filed suit against J&R Baker in federal court, accusing the grower of giving American workers fewer hours than guest workers and then firing them.

Among the plaintiffs who received $2,200 in the 2012 case is Fuller, the woman who said she wound up homeless after being laid off. Fuller said her firing was particularly painful because of her long relationship with the Baker family. She grew up on the farm, she said, and her grandmother was a nanny for the family. She said she took care of Jerod and Rodney Baker, the two current owners, when they were kids.

Back then, she said, they were "sweet little boys." Sitting on a rickety lawn chair in front of her tiny home in Moultrie, Fuller frowned. "They grown now. They can do what they want." She paused. "They mean."

In an interview, Jerod Baker said his former workers' allegations were false. They weren't fired, he said—they quit.

"They'll say anything, believe me. Half of them was either on drugs or coming to work late or smelling like a brewery," he said. "They literally come out here with baggy pants, and they have to hold their pants up, and the other ones either have a cigarette in their mouth or a cell phone. How are they going to be able to work like that?" He added, "Eighty-five percent of them told me, 'Screw this, we'll keep getting our government check.'"

Baker vowed never to settle the lawsuit filed by the EEOC, even though, he said, fighting it is costing him a fortune. "The word on the street is go get a job with J&R Baker or Southern Valley, work for a few days, and quit—you can go sue them and then get you a check. That's exactly what's going on."

As for Fuller, he said the idea that she was his babysitter was "the craziest bull sense of crap I ever heard."

The heart of the issue, Baker said, is that domestic workers "can't keep up with the Mexican workers. It's just a disaster," he said. "We would much rather hire American people in our own country to work, but they will not work." Without legal guest workers or "illegal people" to work the fields, Americans are "either going to have to buy all our food from another country, or we're going to have to all starve to death."

. . .

The H-2 program often pits one vulnerable group against another.

Last year, the South Carolina watermelon and blueberry producer Coosaw Farms was sued in federal court by black workers who allege their bosses told them "colored people just don't work as fast as Mexicans." The suit charges that Coosaw officials called its American employees "niggers" and made it easier for Mexican workers to meet production quotas. The farm also gave its H-2 workers access to nicer bathrooms, letting them wash their hands before lunch, the lawsuit claims.

Angela O'Neal, who helps direct the H-2 program at the farm, said she could not comment on the litigation, which is still pending, but added, "I can say that we do not, nor would we ever, tolerate a work environment that is anything less than respectful toward each and every employee."

She added that "independent, third-party audits"—performed on behalf of buyers—"confirm that the company has a strong record of providing a positive and fair work environment for our employees, regardless of their nationality." She declined to provide the audits, saying, "We do not own them and do not have the legal authority to share them." In 2013, Labor Department investigators looked into a complaint that Coosaw had displaced domestic workers in favor of guest workers but found it was unsubstantiated.

Around Moultrie, the resentment goes both ways. Inside a sweltering school bus near the Hamilton Growers labor camp, Mexican workers complained that U.S. workers don't have to work as hard as they do, aren't required to work on Sundays, and often get released early—apparently unaware that the American workers want more hours, not fewer.

Many American workers, meanwhile, are resentful because they claim guest workers are stealing their jobs. But some Americans note that the workers who replace them get a raw deal too.

"It ain't hard to see. As long as they out there on that farm, they must work, and they never get to leave. I felt bad for them," Green said.

His uncle-in-law, Davis, said he feared that the lack of jobs might eventually force him to leave his home. Standing next to a trailer he is refurbishing on a family plot of land, Davis gestured out at the lawn and the quiet country roads slicing through green fields that stretch to the horizon.

"This is my country," he said, "and I can't get a break for nothing."

Cosmopolitan

FINALIST—PUBLIC
INTEREST

*The result of a year-long
investigation, " 'Pregnant? Scared?
Need Options? Too Bad' " was
one of three stories written by
Meaghan Winter and published by*
Cosmopolitan *that examined the
practices of crisis pregnancy
centers (the other stories—" 'Save
the Mother, Save the Baby' " and
" 'I Felt Set Up' "—are posted in the
Politics section of Cosmopolitan
.com). Often operated by religious
organizations opposed not only to
abortion but to any form of sexual
activity outside heterosexual
marriage, these centers are
frequently disguised as medical
clinics, largely unregulated, and
supported by a network of pro-life
donors, lobbyists, and legislators.
The Ellie judges described Winter's
reporting as "relentless" and her
discovery of federal and state
funding of crisis pregnancy
centers "troubling." This was*
Cosmopolitan's *sixth Ellie
nomination in the last three years
and its first for Public Interest.*

Meaghan Winter

"Pregnant? Scared? Need Options? Too Bad"

Three hundred fifty miles of cattle pasture and cornfields and single-stoplight towns separate Rapid City, near the western edge of South Dakota, from Sioux Falls, near its eastern border. That distance takes on new significance when a woman living in Rapid City needs an abortion.

The state's only abortion clinic is in Sioux Falls. In 2011, state lawmakers began requiring women to wait seventy-two hours between pre-abortion counseling and procedures. That means women who live in the state's western reaches must make four drives, totaling twenty-four hours, or be away from home for at least three days—weekends and holidays don't count toward the waiting period. Women pay for a hotel, miss school or work, find child care or bring kids. South Dakota doesn't have any doctors who do abortions; physicians fly in from surrounding states. With limited scheduling, the Sioux Falls Planned Parenthood is often booked weeks in advance.

In Rapid City one Thursday last summer, a twenty-six-year-old bartender and student I'll call Nicole—her middle name—had a positive pregnancy test. Usually even-keeled, almost unflappable, Nicole says that afternoon, "I was just bawling." But as soon as she "got over the initial shock," she knew she wanted an abortion. She was committed to finishing school, and her boyfriend had recently moved to another state.

Nicole drove to a childhood friend's apartment, where they began making phone calls. She knew her best option was the Sioux Falls clinic—the next-closest option was 400 miles away, in Colorado. It didn't have an appointment for three weeks. Nicole wasn't sure she could wait that long; she wanted to use the abortion pill, which can't be taken after nine weeks of pregnancy. She knew an ultrasound would reveal exactly how far along she was, but she got conflicting information on whether her insurance would cover it. Later that night, her friend sent her an instant message with a link to the website for a nearby Care Net center that advertised free ultrasounds alongside information on "emergency contraception" and "abortion education."

"Just to let you know, they're probably going to be pro-life," her friend typed.

The next morning, Nicole called Care Net. "I didn't have anywhere else to go," she explains. On Tuesday, Nicole drove alone down Main Street, to a one-story office in a shopping center with a credit union and a KFC.

Inside, a receptionist behind a counter instructed Nicole to provide a urine sample in the bathroom. Then a nurse and a younger woman, about Nicole's age, brought her to a small room with a couch. For forty-five minutes, they showed her Bible verses and pamphlets on adoption and an embryo's development. Nicole says, "The nurse really, really slowed down during the fetal pain part. She said, 'Here are the fingertips. The baby feels everything you're feeling.'" They told Nicole having an abortion might complicate future pregnancies and cause suicidal thoughts—both common myths. *This is BS*, Nicole kept thinking, *but you're trying to make me think it's true.*

During the ultrasound, the nurse said the images weren't clear and she needed to do a transvaginal scan. "She didn't explain anything or say, 'We're going to stick this cone inside you,'"

Nicole says, agitated. The nurse displayed the embryo on a screen, pointed to its features, and printed the images. The younger women prayed over Nicole and asked to be invited to her baby shower. The next week, ultrasound results in hand, Nicole drove more than six hours, following a two-lane highway across Wyoming and staying overnight in a hotel, to reach an abortion provider in Denver.

Stacey Wollman, CEO of the Care Net center in Rapid City, says all clients are informed that the center is a faith-based Christian ministry and can opt out of discussing faith, being prayed over, or receiving follow-up calls. She disputes that the staff would ever point out fingertips while explaining fetal development, discuss a baby feeling the sensations the mom feels, or ask to be invited to a shower.

Nicole says the nurse from Care Net called her every day for two weeks. Then once a month, she called from a restricted number and left messages saying, "I just want to chitchat." Annoyed, Nicole never answered or complained. The calls kept coming all the way until February—around when she would have delivered.

Every year, thousands of women like Nicole seek help at what appear to be secular medical clinics but are actually Christian antiabortion centers. Throughout the United States, there are at least 3,000 crisis pregnancy centers, many of which belong to two religious antiabortion organizations—Care Net and Heartbeat International. Some women arrive at those centers in search of Christian counseling or free diapers, but the vast majority are looking for professional advice to help them navigate unplanned pregnancies.

Increasingly, pregnancy centers are what's available. Around the country, access to abortion has eroded dramatically. As abortion regulations shutter medical clinics offering the full range of options, a woman facing an unplanned pregnancy finds herself in a very different landscape, one in which a pregnancy center is her most visible, most affordable—and sometimes the only—place to turn.

This isn't happening only in red states. Nationwide, anti-abortion centers now outnumber abortion clinics three to one. They're in all kinds of towns, from Beverly Hills, California, to Shreveport, Louisiana. You've seen their ads on highway billboards and online: "Pregnant? Scared? We offer confidential counseling." Search Google Maps for abortion help in almost any town and you'll find local centers with pro-choice-seeming names and websites that say, "Need someone to talk to about your options? Contact us," or, "We inform. You decide."

Centers increasingly look just like doctor's offices with ultrasound rooms and staff in scrubs. Yet they do not provide or refer for contraception or abortion. Many pregnancy-center counselors, even those who provide medical information, are not licensed. And even some workers who are licensed, such as nurses and ultrasound technicians, repeat myths about abortion and contraception. Last year, I attended Heartbeat International's annual conference, where nurses told me that birth control "introduces too many chemicals into your body" and that women "never recover" emotionally from abortion.

The antiabortion movement regularly presents pregnancy centers as a scattering of kindly women working with shoestring budgets. In the press or on websites, center directors use language about being small, humble grassroots organizations, without explaining national affiliations. Pro-life strategy documents reveal how, historically, the pregnancy-center movement "purposely remained underground, avoiding the limelight and the controversy of the pro-life political activism."

Many pregnancy centers are, in fact, run by religious women who want to help. But they also are an arm of a sophisticated political movement. A yearlong investigation of crisis pregnancy centers—including dozens of interviews with center staff and volunteers, antiabortion and reproductive-rights advocates, lobbyists, elected officials, and women who have visited centers across the country—reveals that behind the scenes, an orchestrated network of donors, lawyers, lobbyists, and state representatives supports the individual centers. The national organizations Care Net and Heartbeat International train thousands of center staff to attract and dissuade "abortion-minded women." Online for Life, a deep-pocketed tech nonprofit funded by Texas billionaire Farris Wilks, helps pregnancy centers market themselves to "abortion-determined women" searching online for abortion-related terms, according to an *Inside Philanthropy* report.

At the Heartbeat conference, pregnancy-center staff referred to centers as "ministries" and discussed their underlying goal—shepherding spiritually "broken" women toward Christ. The majority of pregnancy-center staff I've met are Evangelical Christians who say they're dedicated to helping women escape a cycle of premarital sex and spiritual pain. Yet at the conference, Heartbeat speakers coached center staff to scrub their websites of Christian references. Speakers also recommended pregnancy-center staff to discourage women and girls from not only abortion but also contraception by emphasizing disproven "negative consequences" and encouraging "sexual integrity," meaning sex only within heterosexual marriage.

All of this is supported by tens of millions of federal and state dollars. At least eleven states now directly fund pregnancy centers, according to state contracts and contractor websites. Many states refer low-income pregnant women to antiabortion centers on health department websites, as well as in "informed consent" materials that abortion providers distribute to patients.

Few states, however, have any laws regulating how pregnancy centers interact with women. Unlike other mental-health providers, center counselors are generally not bound by professional standards or malpractice laws. In many cases, the antiabortion organizations that run the centers—not state employees—monitor their own work.

South Dakota has gone the farthest. As part of its 2011 legislation, the state required all women seeking an abortion to first visit one of two state-approved antiabortion centers. One is the Care Net in Rapid City—the center that Nicole visited. The other is the Alpha Center in Sioux Falls, run by a longtime anticontraception and antiabortion activist. A district court has put the law on hold and is deciding whether the state has the right to force women to visit antiabortion centers. As the judge evaluates the arguments, women across the state—and country—walk into pregnancy centers in search of free medical services. Some, like Nicole, are savvy about the centers' true goals. They also know they have no better option.

"Empowering Women for Life"

In Philadelphia, Cathedral Basilica of Saints Peter and Paul, a huge pillared brownstone with a green copper dome, was built without first-floor windows—its nineteenth-century architects feared Protestant passersby would break the glass. As the decades passed and Catholic immigrants flocked to Pennsylvania, however, the church would grow to wield significant political power in the state.

Much of the public debate about abortion as we now recognize it began in Pennsylvania in the 1960s, when the Catholic Church lobbied hard to malign contraception and abortion. In her book, *Before Roe*, political historian Rosemary Nossiff describes how a lawyer for the Pennsylvania Catholic Conference, William Ball, pushed against the state's plan to counsel low-income couples on contraception by running full-page ads in fifty newspapers and testifying before legislators. On Sundays, priests sermonized against politicians who veered from the church's positions. Former representative Stephen Freind told me that Pennsylvania legislators and church lawyers worked side-by-side to draft the nation's strictest abortion laws, with hopes of overturning *Roe v. Wade*.

In 1989, Planned Parenthood sued the state—represented by its governor, Bob Casey, an antiabortion Democrat—arguing its restrictions violated women's constitutional right to abortion. It's well known that the antiabortion movement won its power when *Planned Parenthood v. Casey* reached the Supreme Court three years later. The court said states could write abortion laws as long as the restrictions don't put an "undue burden" on a woman seeking an abortion—a decision that opened the gates for laws now sweeping the country. Fewer people know that the same antiabortion campaigners behind *Casey* also lobbied for tax dollars for crisis pregnancy centers, paving the way for their current spread.

In the early 1990s, Pennsylvania set aside $1 million for privately run antiabortion centers. The state eventually tapped a nonprofit, Real Alternatives, and a lawyer, Kevin Bagatta, to run it. Before becoming president and CEO of Real Alternatives, Bagatta clerked for William Ball, the lawyer who in 1965 led the charge against the state's plan to counsel poor women on contraception, at Ball, Skelly, Murren and Connell. That's the same firm that represented the Pennsylvania Catholic Conference and sent lawyers to help legislators write abortion restrictions. Pennsylvania now pays Bagatta $223,075 per year.

Real Alternatives' slogan is "Empowering women for life." The organization holds itself out as a safety net for women so they don't "choose abortion out of a sense of helplessness, hopelessness, or being completely alone."

Between 2012 and 2017, Pennsylvania will give Real Alternatives more than $30 million in state and federal funding to support ninety-eight sites, including pregnancy centers, social-service agencies, maternity residences, and three adoption agencies. Real Alternatives reimburses centers for services they provide women (similar to how insurance companies reimburse doctors). Real Alternatives says its sites give pregnant women comprehensive support if they want to parent. And I spoke with women who arrived at centers happily pregnant and appreciated staff's parenting advice and gifts.

But a close look at Pennsylvania's pregnancy-center program shows the government money is not going toward the things expectant women need: accurate health information, medical care, and long-term support in raising children. According to Real Alternatives' contract with the state, it reimburses a center just two dollars each time a woman receives food, clothing, or furniture—a maximum of four times. That's a twenty-four-dollar cap for an individual pregnant woman's material needs. Centers may dispense more through donations. Still, the government program gives them the incentive to spend more time providing ideologically driven counseling, which is reimbursed at more than one dollar per minute, than they spend providing direct services.

In order for a woman to receive any material support, the program requires that she receive at least twenty minutes of counseling from staff, usually after taking a pregnancy test. Real Alternatives' contract with the state relies on debunked studies that imply abortion leads to breast cancer and clinical depression. Centers are not allowed to advocate for birth control, much less dispense it. The contract's directives advise pregnancy-center staff to make an "assessment of the client's spiritual needs" by asking questions like, "How does your faith impact the choices you make?" (One quarterly report from a center to Real Alternatives refers to clients with the aliases "Mary" and "Joseph.")

Some Real Alternatives centers market themselves as secular medical clinics, following the strategies Care Net and Heartbeat outline in their training. On its website, Morning Star Pregnancy Services, for example, offers "ultrasound before abortion" at its three locations in the Harrisburg area. Morning Star and about two dozen other Real Alternatives centers turned down my requests to visit. Kevin Bagatta and his staff declined multiple calls over several months. Real Alternatives is helping spread tax-funded antiabortion centers throughout the country. The organization advised Florida, Minnesota, Nebraska, and North Dakota in establishing state-financed antiabortion centers, and it helped establish Texas's multi-million-dollar program, which runs on the same model. In 2014, Real Alternatives won a no-bid contract to operate Michigan's burgeoning program.

"They Know It's a Baby."

Last spring, I drove across Arkansas and saw ads promising free pregnancy tests in empty downtowns and busy strip malls. Roadside crosses marked the miles, and I visited one center near a cluster of wooden shanties. Arkansas and Mississippi, two of the country's poorest states, each have more than forty pregnancy centers and only one surgical abortion provider. Walmart's cheapest pregnancy test costs about nine dollars—the same amount as its cashiers' hourly wage—so it's not hard to imagine why a working woman might pull over for a free test.

In a corporate park in Little Rock, Arkansas, Pregnancy Resource Center shares a secluded cul-de-sac with the state's only surgical abortion provider. A few years ago, when a doctor who performs abortions moved across town to join the clinic's staff, the antiabortion center followed. One Saturday, I watched about thirty protestors—mostly white men in T-shirts and shorts—stand on the lawn of the crisis pregnancy center screaming, "You're killing your baby!"

Every weekend, protestors block the clinic's driveway, and on some weekends, the police are called, clinic workers and escorts told me. The pregnancy center allows the protestors to stay, and protestors sometimes redirect women into the center. A physician at the clinic told me that patients periodically arrive for their abortion appointments late, after mistakenly first going to the pregnancy center across the cul-de-sac. That Saturday, women entering the clinic looked over their shoulders, then at the ground, some with tears in their eyes.

About thirty miles north of Little Rock, a billboard displayed between exits ("Pregnant? Need options?") advertised A Woman's Place, a pregnancy center in the small town of Cabot that has since been renamed Options Pregnancy Center. Cabot feels neither down-and-out nor especially fancy: Tidy homes and churches fade into a strip of chain stores like Kmart and Popeyes. Down the road, Options Pregnancy Center occupies a brick building beside a salon. Its website and ad in the high-school paper offer "options counseling." It has an ultrasound machine. The needlepoint sampler in its bathroom says, "You will live with the guilt for the rest of your life knowing you made the choice to kill the precious life God placed in your womb for you to love."

I first met Options Pregnancy Center's director, Vikki Parker, at the 2014 Heartbeat conference. In Cabot, Parker and I sit in a meeting room in the center, describing how she started it after her daughter became pregnant at fifteen. "I did my very best as a Christian mom, trying to raise her right, but [unplanned pregnancy] came knocking at my door. When it did, I was devastated," she tells me. When her grandson was eight months old, she went to her pastor and said she'd heard about crisis pregnancy centers and wanted to start one. "I didn't know she was sexually active . . . I was thinking these kids have got to have a safe haven where they're not going to be judged."

I see why a girl who's afraid to talk to her mother about sex might confide in Parker, who exudes warmth and concern. Parker says she doesn't have to talk girls into continuing their pregnancy, explaining, "They know it's a baby. They know the part they played in it when they had sex." Options Pregnancy Center doesn't provide or refer for contraception because Parker believes the Bible forbids premarital sex and she doesn't think condoms are effective. She says she does not believe public schools should teach students how to access birth control. (Still, when I ask her whether the young women who arrive at the center generally use contraception, she tells me, "Honestly, I don't know why they don't. I mean, it's so readily available. It's not like they can't get it.")

In 2013, the U.S. Department of Health and Human Services awarded the center a federal grant of $352,125 to teach abstinence education in public schools. Over the years, government funding for abstinence programs has aided the mushrooming of pregnancy centers. Despite proposals by the Obama administration to reduce funding, Congress has continued and even increased it in recent years, explains Monica Rodriguez, president of the non-profit Sexuality Information and Education Council of the United States. This spring, Congress has already set aside $75 million for the latest abstinence-only-until-marriage program—an increase of 50 percent. The House budget proposed in June would double the program that funds Options Pregnancy Center, while eliminating all funding for health centers that provide birth control.

Options Pregnancy Center hired pastors to lead its public-school lessons. I spoke with two of those pastors and read their curriculum, which only discusses contraceptives in terms of failure rates and emphasizes the "negative emotional consequences" of premarital sex. One of the pastors, Daniel Tyler, told me he teaches the idea that "if you start having sex, you can't grow emotionally." He adds, "The stuff we're saying is stereotypical, like guys thinking about sex all the time . . . We teach that even the way a girl dresses can draw a guy to think about [sex]. There's a whole chapter on that."

The year Options Pregnancy Center won its federal grant, Arkansas had one of the nation's highest teen birth rates. And those pregnancies "disproportionately impact teen girls" because they "end up doing an overwhelming majority of the child rearing," according to a 2014 report by Kristen Jozkowski, Ph.D., assistant professor of community health at the University of Arkansas. Less than 2 percent of teen mothers will graduate college by the age of thirty. Yet the federal government invests in programs that specifically forbid teaching teens how to use protection and contraception in the very communities with the highest rates of STIs and pregnancy.

"Don't You Love Your Daughter?"

It was just before Christmas in 2009 when Arcadia Smith found herself at a Heartbeat and Care Net affiliate near her home in Mississippi. Smith was about a month pregnant. After years of struggling as a single parent, she had finally landed a managerial job at a doctor's office. She didn't want to end up homeless again or become too busy to help her seven-year-old daughter with homework.

Smith is not against all abortions but didn't want one for herself. She decided to place her baby for adoption, she says, to "give the baby to someone who wanted to cherish every moment—the first crawl, the first words."

At the center, Smith and her boyfriend met with a counselor from a third-party adoption agency that works with pregnancy centers. In the small house, Smith could hear other couples' conversations through the walls. "I poured my heart out," she said.

She remembers the counselor asking, "Don't you love your daughter? Don't you want to do for this one what you do for your first?"

"It's not that I don't like this baby—I'm just afraid for the baby," Smith recalls saying.

Smith says the counselor asked her boyfriend if he was willing to coparent. When he said he was, the counselor insisted they had no reason to consider adoption. "It shocked me," Smith says. "I was thinking, But adoption is what you do."

Smith questioned her boyfriend, saying he might not stick around, regardless of whether they shared a child. But the counselor insisted. "It seems like he wants to be there," she said, and Smith could always raise the child without him. "I'm a single mother myself. I know how it is," Smith remembers the counselor saying.

At the Heartbeat conference I attended, a workshop leader instructed pregnancy-center staff to offer their personal stories of hardship to encourage clients to follow their advice. Many pregnancy-center workers have told me their goal is for every woman to mother.

"I don't know what 'single mother' means to her," Smith told me later. "Maybe to her it means divorced with alimony, with grandparents around, but to me, being a single parent means doing everything. My mother passed away when I was eight. I don't have a safety net. People don't understand that to really invest in a child and be there to provide stability, I have to sacrifice every single thing."

With the adoption counselor and her boyfriend in agreement, Smith was outnumbered. "The counselor looked at me like there was something wrong with me. I was already putting the blame on myself for getting pregnant. There's so much emphasis on being a good mom. I felt like less of a woman. Maybe I was selfish, a bad person who should be ashamed of myself."

When I called representatives for both the pregnancy center and the adoption agency to discuss Smith's story, they each said their organization is a strong advocate for adoption and would never discourage a couple from making that choice. Smith never made adoption plans. And she didn't tell anyone else about her ambivalence toward her pregnancy. "I thought, If that's how an adoption counselor reacted, imagine what someone else would say about me not wanting a baby." She gave birth to a girl in the spring of 2010. Six months later, she and her boyfriend broke up. She "became numb" and "overwhelmed" with postpartum depression. After missing work, she lost her job. "Everything snowballed," she says. She sometimes looked at her baby daughter and thought, *It would be easier if she weren't here.* "It wasn't that I didn't love my baby," she says. "I just hated the situation."

Months later, she called the center. "Look, where are you when I don't have a job, I don't have a car?" she recalls asking. The woman who answered the phone was apologetic. She gave her the number for a counselor at a church who helped her access other services.

Smith is now a single parent of two. "People judge single mothers every step of the way," she says. "But how would they judge me if I exercised my other options, my rights? I could've had an abortion, given my daughter up for adoption, left her at a hospital." Whatever decision she made, Smith figures, the reaction would be the same. "I'd wear a label for the rest of my life."

Matter

This is the story of Dr. Sheik Humarr Khan and the fight he led to contain the Ebola epidemic as it spread across Sierra Leone in 2014. Working at a government hospital near the epicenter of the outbreak, Khan fell victim to the disease and was controversially denied a treatment that saved the lives of others. Despite his long experience as a journalist—his reporting on the al-Aqsa Intifada was nominated for an Ellie in 2003—Joshua Hammer writes that when he arrived in Sierra Leone in late 2014, he "had never faced anything so unsettling" as the fear he encountered there. Hammer's work—and his bravery—won Matter *the National Magazine Award for Reporting. Launched in 2012 with $140,000 raised on Kickstarter,* Matter *has already been nominated for five Ellies.*

Joshua Hammer

"My Nurses Are Dead, and I Don't Know If I'm Already Infected"

D
r. Sheik Humarr Khan, the head of the Kenema Government Hospital's Ebola ward, didn't want his head nurse moved into the main isolation unit. Ward A consisted of eight small rooms lining a dingy corridor of exposed wiring, peeling paint, and grimy cement floors. It was narrow and stiflingly hot, crowded with as many as thirty patients. Nurses squeezed between the beds, injecting antibiotics, emptying buckets of diarrhea, and hosing down vomit with chlorine. Some of the sick were delirious; others, catatonic, with a stony-eyed stare that usually signaled that death was imminent. All of them were hooked up to intravenous fluid bags; in a state of disorientation, some would rip the needles out of their arms, spraying their blood in all directions.

So Khan had bent the rules and moved the Ebola-stricken nurse to a private room in the observation wing, normally set aside for those awaiting their diagnostic test results. It was more comfortable and dignified—befitting the nurse's status, Khan thought, as the most beloved figure at the hospital. Khan and Mbalu Fonnie had been each other's family for much of the past decade. He called her "mom." She thought of him as her son, and she took maternal pride in his accomplishments. A round-faced man who had been born poor in a village near Freetown, Khan had become a hero in Kenema, a backwater town of 130,000. As the head of the Lassa fever ward, he had treated more cases of hemorrhagic fever than anyone else in the world, helping thousands of patients recover their health. He attended conferences from New Orleans to Nigeria, published studies in major medical journals, and was soon headed to Harvard on sabbatical to work at the cutting edge of tropical-disease research—mapping the virus genome. But now Khan was facing the greatest challenge of his life.

"We're working hard to help you," he said to Fonnie, his voice muffled behind a face mask. Like the attending nurses, Khan was clad in full protective gear—DuPont Tyvek hooded suit, two pairs of surgical gloves, Wellington boots, and an apron. "You have to hang in there." An attending nurse complained that the IV fluids weren't flowing into Fonnie's veins fast enough, so Khan retrieved a higher pole from which to hang the bag. He showed his chief nurse a get-well card sent by the U.S. ambassador, who had visited the hospital weeks earlier. "We are with you," it read. "Be strong." Then Khan turned away, struggling for composure.

The first Ebola cases in Sierra Leone had been diagnosed in late May, nearly two months before Fonnie's infection, in Koindu, one hundred miles north of Kenema. Since then the sick and the dying had been flowing into his hospital at an accelerating pace. The death toll had reached several hundred, though nobody knew the exact count; many were dying in isolated villages beyond the reach of health workers. Seventy people filled the wards at Kenema hospital, and more were arriving in ambulances or coming on foot every day. Khan felt let down by the Sierra Leone government, which had all but ignored the outbreak; the minister of health and other officials "were too frightened," says one U.S. doctor, to travel to Kenema. Khan was sending out e-mails to friends around the world, begging for equipment. Most of the staff had fled—Khan was the only local doctor left—and the handful who had remained behind had begun to die. Four nurses other than Fonnie and one lab technician lay gravely ill in the Ebola wards.

Nobody understood why so many nurses were getting infected. In the early days of the outbreak, Khan had introduced a rigorous decontamination procedure. After treating patients, staffers were thoroughly sprayed with a 30 percent chlorine solution. They would meticulously remove their personal protective equipment, or PPE—face shields, boots, and outer gloves—wash their hands with a 10 percent chlorine solution, a less abrasive but still effective mixture, and, after pulling off their second pair of gloves, receive a final squirt of Ebola-killing disinfectant. Still, they were falling ill. Some suspected that the problem was not the PPE-removal and cleaning-up process but the PPEs themselves. It was widely believed that Fonnie and three other nurses had picked up the virus at the same time in mid-July while helping another nurse, infected with Ebola, deliver her stillborn baby inside the isolation ward. The birth produced a massive amount of infected blood and other bodily fluids, and colleagues assumed that some viral particles had leaked through the PPEs.

Khan "was frustrated, distraught, and overwhelmed," says one Centers for Disease Control scientist. He spent much of his time trying to hold the hospital together. The facility was unguarded, and some patients, believing they weren't sick, wandered off, escaping into the streets to return home. Crowds had begun to gather outside the hospital gates, bewildered and angry by the deaths of so many people. None could believe that a disease could be killing their loved ones so fast; they assumed there had to be a plot behind it. One peaceful vigil for nurse Fonnie nearly turned violent when a rumor spread that she had died. "Let's storm the hospital," somebody yelled, and hundreds surged forward. After the outburst, they directed their rage at Khan. "The doctor is killing people, and these nurses are taking people's hearts," they cried. Khan had no choice but to address the crowd himself. He walked out of the hospital and assured them the rumor was false. "I'm putting my own life on the line," he told them. "My nurses are dead, and I don't know if I'm already infected or not."

Seeing Khan, exhausted and alone, the people quieted down and wandered back to their huts in the bush and jungle-covered hills.

$$\bullet \qquad \bullet \qquad \bullet$$

In October I flew on Brussels Airlines to Sierra Leone, a former British colony about the size of West Virginia, sandwiched between Liberia and Guinea on the tropical west coast of Africa. The Ebola outbreak was then in its sixth month, and it showed no signs of letting up. (By late December, the number of confirmed cases reached nearly seven thousand; more than two thousand people have died. Only neighboring Liberia has reported higher numbers.) The outbreak had swept across the country with terrifying force, leaving a trail of corpses and eerily empty villages. And yet Khan's story—a story that explains so much about the bravery of the first responders and how health officials, through ignorance, fear, and willful neglect, mishandled the situation—had gone largely unreported.

The plane was packed with returning Sierra Leoneans, Western doctors, and public health officials, and the atmosphere was hushed. I had covered more than a dozen wars, revolutions, and coups—including two trips to Sierra Leone in the midst of its devastating rebel war in the 1990s—but I had never faced anything so unsettling. On the ground, the fear was palpable. People had stopped shaking hands, and chlorinated water taps stood at the entrance to every building I entered. Outside Connaught Hospital, a crumbling facility in Central Freetown, I watched as a man stumbled out of a taxi, collapsed, and died in front of the entrance. Men in biohazard suits appeared moments later and sprayed down the vehicle; pedestrians hung back, horrified.

Khan knew the risks better than almost anyone else in the world. Born in Mahera, a village of muddy roads across an estuary from Freetown, to a schoolmaster, he and his nine brothers and sisters grew up under firm rules. The elder Khan was a "strict disciplinarian," recalls Humarr's older brother C. Ray, who used a switch on his children and insisted they be held back a year if they finished below the top five in their class. But the rules weren't without purpose. The Khans often offered to board poor children who lived too far away to walk to the school every day. "His father was intent on making sure that all kids could attend school," says one of Khan's close friends. "The mother would make clothes for all those needy families who didn't have any. Every week, they would invite some individual from the community to have dinner with them—someone very poor or someone with medical problems."

Khan, a bright boy with a mischievous streak, often tarried on the way to and from school to pluck mangoes from neighbors' gardens. By the time he was ten, he had started spending much of his time on weekends and after school down the street, wandering the grounds of Bai Bureh Memorial Hospital, a fifty-bed private clinic founded by a wealthy German French transplant and her husband, a Sierra Leonean obstetrician-gynecologist. The clinic drew expectant mothers and other patients from around the country—Siaka Stevens, Sierra Leone's president, came here to be treated for malaria. Some camped out overnight in the Khan family living room while awaiting treatment. "Squazu [Khan's nickname] wanted to know, 'Who is this person who is so important that people stay overnight to see him?'" remembered Khan's nephew "Alaska" Kargbo. Khan befriended the physicians' three children. As his friends played football, he was making toy stethoscopes out of string and a sink stopper and examining his brothers and sisters. "The surgeon became his role model," says Alaska. "He started asking the man's kids, when he was thirteen, fourteen, 'How do I become a doctor?' They told him, 'You have to study science.'"

At St. Francis secondary school—one of the best in the country for science—Khan led the debating team, read the news at assemblies, and tutored his schoolmates after hours in math, chemistry, and biology. He had so little money that his fellow students took turns buying him lunch at the "*kukeri*" shops that sold cheap meals of rice, cassava, and potatoes. His obsession with medicine was evident. One day he came across the report of a Western physician who had contracted Lassa fever and died. He told classmates: "I want to be that guy. I want to cure Lassa fever."

Khan graduated at the top of his class in 1993, and went on to medical school outside Freetown, where he started to date an attractive young nursing student named Assie. He had known Assie since junior high, but as the two grew closer, he fathered two children with two different women. "He was young, and he went out to sow his oats," says his brother C. Ray.

In 1991, a rebel movement called the Revolutionary United Front coalesced in the eastern corner of the country, near Liberia, vowing to bring down an authoritarian and corrupt government. The insurgents, many of them children, killed and hacked off the limbs of thousands of civilians. Like many, Khan fled to neighboring Guinea. In 1997, he made a perilous boat journey down the coast after leading student demonstrations against the military coup and eluding a warrant for his arrest. He remained in exile for months. After returning, he was again driven out when rebels marched into Freetown, killing and mutilating hundreds. In 1999, Khan and his whole family fled to Conakry, Guinea's capital, where his siblings—many of whom had already relocated to the United States—tried to persuade Khan to do the same. Khan was unmoved. "Everyone is saying Sierra Leone is lost," he told his family. "But I'm going back to Freetown." He caught a flight back days after British troops drove the rebels out of the capital and encouraged his nephew, who dreamed of moving to the United States, to join him. "He told me, 'America,

America, America. You're going to wash dishes, do odd jobs. You are wasting your time, Alaska. Come home.'" Alaska did as his uncle asked.

In the ruins of the capital, amid a traumatized population and a shattered infrastructure, Khan went to work. He practiced at a local government hospital and also became a visiting doctor in Kenema, a town 190 miles to the east. Since the 1970s, Kenema had maintained Sierra Leone's only treatment center for Lassa fever, one of the biggest killers in eastern Sierra Leone. Like Ebola, Lassa is transmitted by animals—rodents, in this case— and attacks almost every tissue in the human body, beginning with the sinus membrane, intestine, lungs, and urinary system, before devastating the vascular system. The end result is remarkably similar to Ebola: Internal bleeding and high fever kill up to 70 percent of Lassa patients who become sick enough to seek medical attention.

In 2004, the director of Kenema's Lassa fever program, Dr. Aniru Conteh, died after pricking himself with a needle while drawing blood from an infected patient. Khan saw an opportunity: he applied for the post and was quickly hired.

"I'm on my way to Kenema," he told his nephew. "I'm leaving tomorrow."

His family begged him not to take the job.

"But the last doctor died," Alaska replied. "Don't you know how dangerous it is?"

Khan was undaunted. "They need me there," he said.

•   •   •

The 190-mile stretch of highway between Freetown and Kenema has become one of the main transmission routes of the current Ebola outbreak. During the last week of October, when I made the journey in a four-wheel-drive vehicle with a driver and a translator, we were stopped en route at twenty "Ebola checkpoints," rudimentary roadblocks manned by police, soldiers, and government health workers. At each one, my translator and I were ordered out of the car for a temperature check and a hand washing at a chlorinated water tap. (For reasons that nobody understood, the driver was exempted from the ritual.)

Kenema, a decrepit tropical backwater, has been battered by the twin African scourges of war and disease. Smoke rose over jungle-covered hills in the distance, once a sanctuary for rebels. Just inside the front gate of Kenema Government Hospital, dozens of people sat listlessly on plastic chairs beneath a tarpaulin, possibly infected with Ebola, awaiting admission to a larger observation tent in the "red zone." I observed from about fifty feet away as a man collapsed beside the guard booth and lay face down in the gravel, his chest heaving. A small boy, probably his grandson, squatted beside him. "Can you hear me?" a Red Cross official asked, to no response.

When Khan arrived in Kenema in 2005, driving a beat-up sedan, the hospital was in a far different state. Tulane University had recently set up a state-of-the-art lab to test for Lassa fever, which meant that samples no longer had to be sent overseas. Researchers could diagnose the illness on the spot and get patients started on the right treatment. (A major scientific study had found that treating Lassa fever victims with the antiviral drug Ribavirin during the first week of symptoms pushed the cure rate to 95 percent.) Khan worked closely with the lab, which grew viral proteins from a single strand of RNA and cultured human antibodies. He also tended to patients and opened a private practice. "He liked to joke, and he was always advising you to further your education," says nurse Issa French. Khan often lingered with patients, asking about their families, their jobs, their aspirations; his enthusiasm struck his colleagues. "He always wanted to talk about his latest cases," said Robert Garry of Tulane University, who worked closely with Khan. "Poisonous-snake bites, vitamin deficiencies, seeing stuff that he had learned about in medical school [in clinical situations] fascinated him."

Kenema was still recovering from the rebel war, but Khan enjoyed the clean air and the slow pace. He found his way to The Capitol, a Lebanese-owned hotel and restaurant, which had hummus and tabbouleh on the menu, a murky swimming pool in the asphalt courtyard, and a flat-screen TV that played European football matches. After work he liked to sit in a wicker chair on the second-floor veranda, order a Maltina, and cheer on AC Milan, his favorite team. Peter Kaima, a bartender at The Capitol who would later become Khan's assistant, first met the doctor during the televised UEFA Champions League final in May 2005, shortly after his arrival in town. "When AC Milan scored a goal, he ran outside, took off his shirt, and was waving it and shouting in the street," Kaima recalls. "I asked people, 'Who is this man?' And somebody said, 'That man is a doctor.'"

A year after his arrival, Khan married Assie in a Freetown mosque, according to Muslim tradition (while Khan wasn't particularly religious, he did pray in mosque most Fridays). Khan's brothers and sisters used the occasion to pressure Humarr to make a fresh start. "I told him he should move to the U.S.A.," says his brother Sahid, who had settled in Philadelphia in 1992. "I wanted him to make more money. All he had to do was pass the U.S. medical boards." Assie wanted much the same: to begin a new life with her husband in England. Instead, the couple settled into a long-distance relationship. Assie visited Kenema once a year, staying for a month; Khan would stop in England on his way to occasional lectures and conferences in the United States.

The distance wore on the young couple. Peter Kaima remembered fierce arguments between them at Khan's bungalow in Kenema. "He would always say, 'I need to stay here and work with my people,'" Kaima recalls. Assie sent Humarr letters expressing her frustrations and, finally, asked him for a divorce.

"She wrote, 'It seems that you are married to your job. I cannot compete with it,'" says his older brother Alhajie.

Without Assie, Khan devoted himself further to his work. His efforts were recognized in 2013 when Kenema was included in a newly established, international consortium of medical schools and labs focusing on hemorrhagic fevers. The group won two multi-million-dollar grants from the National Institutes of Health, money that would allow Khan and his team to focus on sequencing the genetic code of a broad range of infectious tropical diseases, including Ebola—an essential step in the development of diagnostics and vaccines. In early May 2014, Khan met with Garry of Tulane University, Dr. Pardis Sabeti of Harvard University, and other members of the consortium outside Lagos to inaugurate a $10 million initiative. Khan was buoyant. The U.S. Navy had recently approved funding for a new Lassa fever ward at Kenema Government Hospital to replace the sweltering concrete shed with a new, forty-eight-bed ward—doubling capacity. In the evenings, Sabeti, Garry, Khan, and other members of the consortium would gather in a hotel suite near the university, discussing their plans to train a new generation of African researchers and doctors. "He was always the last one to fall asleep," says Sabeti. "He wanted to talk all night about the things we could do together."

Amid the good cheer, however, came disturbing news. In March, Guinea had notified the World Health Organization that it had confirmed a number of cases of Ebola—the first time the virus had ever appeared in that part of the continent. Then, just as quickly, the disease appeared to recede. "We dodged a bullet," Garry thought. Still, he told Khan he should be prepared when he returned to Kenema. "It could be a month, a year, or two years," Garry said. "But Ebola is going to come."

Unbeknownst to the doctors, deep in the rolling hills and diamond mines of eastern Sierra Leone, in a district called Kailahun, a traditional village healer had begun claiming that she had the power to cure the mysterious disease. Dozens of the desperately sick traveled from Guinea through the bush to visit the medicine woman's home, where she reportedly treated them by applying herbal remedies, draping snakes over their bodies, and uttering incantations.

Within weeks, the healer herself became infected and died.

On May 23, a pregnant woman who had attended the healer's funeral arrived to Kenema hospital, suffering from a severe hemorrhagic fever. Nurses initially assumed that she had Lassa. But the head of the Kenema laboratory performed the diagnostic test and it turned up negative. Khan understood the implications immediately. "Okay," he said, "then she has got Ebola." On May 24, the lab director tested the sample of a desperately ill woman from Kailahun along with the pregnant woman's blood and that of another woman who knew the healer. All three proved positive for Ebola. On May 25, the World Health Organization was notified that Ebola had spread to Sierra Leone.

Khan advised the hospital nurses and doctors to brace themselves: About 80 people had attended the herbalist's funeral—a ritualistic practice that involved washing and dressing the corpse and crowding around to lay their hands on and kiss the body. At least fourteen funeral-goers were now sick. "He said to me and [fellow nurse] Alex Moigboi, 'You should tighten your belts, we are expecting two ambulances from Kailahun,'" recalls nurse John Tamba. Two days later, Garry of Tulane University came to Kenema, bearing nine trunks filled with gloves, gowns, and every possible brand of PPE that he could find. Nine hundred "changes" in all. But in the first weeks, the disease was little understood by the staff. Many nurses disregarded safety protocols and worked the ward wearing surgical gowns and old shoes that they had brought from home. People removed their vomit- and diarrhea- covered equipment without hosing it off, then washed their hands with a perfunctory splash of chlorine. "A lot of people at the hospital got sick right away," says nurse Issa French. "We learned that it was a different disease than anything we'd ever seen before."

Khan traveled to the epicenter of the outbreak in Kailahun to try to convey to village people the dangers of the disease. He took blood samples, held workshops for local health-care workers, and helped to evacuate the sick. Villagers, he found, were in denial, blaming the illness on the dead herbalist's snakes. They resisted going to the hospital. Local officials, fearing the spread of panic and unrest, weren't helping. On one occasion, a local chief spitefully seized Khan's government-issued four-wheel-drive Toyota and held it overnight, warning him to stay out of Kailahun. In Koindu, the home of the healer, the population put up roadblocks and threw stones, breaking the windshield of the four-wheel-drive vehicle. "There were rumors that we were coming to give them the disease. They said we would take people away and never come back," says Garry, who traveled to Koindu chiefdom in late May. "The attitude was, 'Leave us alone.'"

Even those close to Khan had a hard time understanding the infectious power of the virus. During one trip north, Khan was about to step into his Toyota Land Cruiser when he noticed a sick woman lying sprawled in the back.

"Who is this?" he asked his driver.

"This is my sister, Dr. Khan."

"Who put her in the car?"

"I did," his driver replied.

"You? My God. Just stay outside the car."

Days later, the driver died of Ebola. Khan never used the Land Cruiser again.

.   .   .

By early July, more than a month after Khan first recognized the virus, the outbreak had moved from Kailahun to Kenema district. Across the region, the disease was spreading uncontrolled, carried by truckers and farmers and motorcyclists on a network of roads that ran from bush to town to city. The World Health Organization responded to the crisis by delegating authority to its regional offices, which in turn deferred to the governments of West Africa. But officials in Freetown were in denial about the severity of the outbreak. They didn't declare a state of emergency until August. And even then, they faced an acute shortage of hospital beds, ambulances, burial teams, and investigators. Ambulance drivers often crammed sick people and uninfected relatives into same vehicle. When hospitals were full the sick were placed on home quarantines, and when food wasn't provided the sick would go to markets and spread the contagion. "We had no strategy, no laboratories, no observation centers. We were completely unprepared," said Victor Willoughby, a veteran Sierra Leone internist with whom Khan did his residency in the early 2000s. The wards at Kenema were overflowing.

"The situation was chaotic," recalls Will Pooley, a British nurse from King's College Hospital in London who arrived to work on the Ebola wards in early July. When he first met Khan, the doctor was huddled with a visiting CDC scientist in his office, a small, cluttered trailer beside the isolation wards, trying to work out how many members of the nursing staff had died—between ten and fifteen, at that point. Khan shook Pooley's hand warmly, trying to make him feel welcome. Khan, Pooley says, was "the general," poised, in command, and working hard to hold things together.

Each morning from that point on, Pooley donned his protective suit and crossed a barrier of orange plastic mesh into the red zone. He started his rounds in the "Annex," a large white canvas tent filled with those awaiting their diagnostic results; some were already near death by the time they arrived at the hospital. Pooley frequently found corpses sprawled in the toilets, lying in pools of contaminated blood from the IV lines that they had ripped out of their arms during the night. One morning he walked into the ward and saw a naked male adult lying dead on the floor, and a "sweet-looking" naked toddler sitting in his blood. Somehow, the toddler survived.

Confirmed Ebola cases were remanded to Ward A, the former Lassa fever unit. One CDC official recalls following Khan inside, stepping over corpses in body bags lying on the walkway before the entrance. Within five minutes of entering the ward, he says, the oppressive heat and humidity in the windowless unit caused his plastic visor to steam up. He groped his way forward, banging into cots, too frightened to adjust the eyewear and risk exposing his skin to viral particles. Khan, he noticed with alarm, lifted his goggles from his face several times to defog them.

Just outside the entrance of Ward A stood a small shed where corpses were stacked like cordwood; the bodies often spilled over and lay scattered on the walkway. One day, trying to identify patients who had died overnight, Pooley unzipped a body bag and came face to face with a corpse wearing a protective suit—"masks, goggles, the full gear," he says. "I was wearing my suit, this guy was looking back at me, and it was as if I was looking into a mirror." (Ambulance attendants sometimes put infected Ebola patients into PPEs before transporting them to the hospital in a misguided attempt to protect themselves; the patients often died of heat stroke.)

After a few days working in the red zone, sometimes alongside Khan, Pooley calculated his chance of catching Ebola at 50 percent. If he got it, he figured that he stood a one-in-two chance of surviving. "I was thinking, 'How can I exit this situation without being a complete disgrace?'" he remembers. "Weeks went by, and then it wasn't possible to leave . . . I didn't want to look like a coward."

•   •   •

By July, Ebola was raging across three West African countries—Guinea, Sierra Leone, and Liberia, infecting more than eight hundred people and killing more than half of them. From Kenema, the virus made its way toward Freetown. On June 20, Doctors Without Borders declared the outbreak "totally out of control," and one week later the organization opened an Ebola treatment center at the epicenter in Kailahun—the first international medical organization to open a facility there. On July 17, the number of cases in Sierra Leone reached 442, surpassing the total in Liberia and Guinea. More than half of those had died. Every week, as many as seventy suspected Ebola patients were pouring into Kenema Goverment Hospital. Khan was working fourteen-hour days, too preoccupied now to unwind in the evenings at The Capitol, where crowds gathered to watch the World Cup in Brazil.

"I don't have any time for the World Cup anymore, Alaska," he told his nephew. "I'm either in the ward or the lab."

"Why can't you just leave Kenema?"

Khan laughed ruefully. "At a time when the whole country is looking to me, is it the time to run away here?" Khan replied. "Do you know what you were telling me to do? Abandon my profession." He optimistically told his nephew that he had just discharged forty-five people that day.

"I want to come to Kenema, to see you," Alaska told him.

"No. You have to stay away from here."

"I'm really worried about you."

"Don't worry about me," Khan said. "I am well protected." To reassure him, he sent a photograph taken in the Ebola ward showing Khan and two colleagues covered head to foot in their PPEs. Scrawled on the apron of the man standing to Khan's left was the name "Alex Moigboi." The nurse, Khan's closest friend at the hospital, would die a few days later of Ebola.

Khan was known to be meticulous about safeguards: He had even installed a mirror in his office in a small trailer beside the red zone, to check for tiny holes in his protective suit before entering the isolation ward. By now the staff had become well acquainted with their enemy. He and his colleagues knew that one tiny slip-up, one tear in the PPE, could have lethal consequences.

But Khan was overwhelmed with work, fatigued, and stressed. "He was animated, he was go-go-go, but he was also distraught. He was worried about the survival of the whole program," recalls a CDC scientist who spent several days with Khan and his staff in mid-July.

Nurse John Tamba believes he can pinpoint the precise moment when Khan dropped his guard. It was about five p.m. at the end of a long mid-July day. Khan and Alex Moigboi left Ward A and walked together, in their protective suits, to the decontamination area. Staff members sprayed each man down with a 30 percent chlorine spray. Their PPEs were bagged and removed for disposal.

As they stood together in their civvies in the low-risk zone, Moigboi confided to the doctor that he was not feeling well. Khan immediately began an examination. He reached for Moigboi's eyes, looking at his pupils. "He touched his skin," recalls Tamba. Perhaps, Tamba speculates, it was a momentary lapse of attention, or maybe he was in denial, unable to accept the possibility that his favorite nurse had contracted the disease. Whatever the case, Khan assured Moigboi that he was suffering from malaria, and advised him to have his blood tested. "We will prove that it's nothing to worry about," Khan said.

The following day, Moigboi's blood results came back positive for Ebola, and he was taken by ambulance to Kenema Government Hospital. Khan was devastated; he was also concerned for himself. "He remembered that he had touched Alex's bare skin," says nurse Issa French. It's not clear that the contact with Moigboi was responsible for what happened next—Khan had possibly exposed himself to Ebola infection several times inside Ward A when he removed his goggles—but at least three Ebola unit nurses witnessed the moment, and they all cited it when trying to explain the events that followed.

On July 19, Alex Moigboi died in Ward B, delirious and incoherent in his final hours. That evening, Khan returned home despondent—and more tired than usual. He had the chills, and he was running a slight fever. He told his assistant, Peter Kaima, that he was worried. "Doc," said Kaima, "you're under a lot of stress. Your staff is dead. Maybe you're traumatized. Don't think about something that is not inside you. Try to calm yourself down." The next morning the fever had abated, and Khan returned to the hospital for a day on the ward. That evening he addressed an audience at the Kenema community center. Sunday brought a setback: he awoke with a fever, too sick to work.

"Don't come closer by me, don't touch me," he warned Kaima that evening.

Khan went to the hospital on Monday for a blood test. The result came back a few hours later: negative. That day, Mbalu Fonnie, his beloved head nurse, died. "He called me in a dull voice, and he said, 'Alaska, Nurse Fonnie is dead. She was like my mom,'" recalls Khan's nephew. The next day, with Khan still ill, the laboratory ran the diagnostic test again. At two that afternoon the district medical officer and other officials arrived at Khan's home.

"You should go outside," they told Kaima.

Hovering in the doorway, Kaima watched a slumped-over Khan receive the news: the Ebola test had come back positive.

·   ·   ·

Medical officials were immediately concerned about how Kenema's patients and staff would receive the results. "If people know you are sick," the chief medical officer told Khan, "everyone will panic, they will leave Kenema." The officer made it clear that the best choice would be for Khan to go to the Doctors Without Borders center seventy-five miles to the north in Kailahun. Khan acquiesced.

After a five-hour ambulance ride, in heavy rains and over a rutted dirt and mud track, Khan was received by physicians in protective gear. "I can walk inside myself," he told them. They led him across a barrier of orange plastic mesh and into the isolation zone: six white tents, each one containing eight "cholera cots," military-style beds with holes cut out for defecation. The doctors immediately placed Khan on a standard regimen of oral treatments—paracetamol for pain relief, antibiotics for diarrhea, and rehydration salts. Doctors Without Borders seldom use intravenous fluids with Ebola, believing that the risks of death from bleeding are greater than the potential benefits.

Almost as soon as Khan entered isolation, a debate began about how to save him—one that would be steeped in agonized second-guessing and lingering controversy. On July 22, Sierra Leone's government sent an e-mail to medical experts around the world seeking information about a drug or a vaccine that might help. The appeal prompted a round of conference calls involving the World Health Organization, the U.S. Centers for Disease Control and Prevention, the Public Health Agency of Canada, the U.S. Army, and Doctors Without Borders. The discussion focused on ZMapp—an experimental vaccine manufactured from mouse-human antibodies grown in tobacco plants. The vaccine, which had cured 100 percent of eighteen rhesus monkeys that had been given Ebola in a lab, had never been tested on a human. But three vials of it were being stored in a battery-powered freezer in the isolation ward just steps from Khan. They had been left there in June by a researcher at the Public Health agency of Canada's research facility in Winnipeg as a way to test the vaccine's durability in tropical environments.

The drugs were a gift. "Everyone was on board for giving it to him, and I got off the phone thinking, 'He's got it,'" says one medical officer who participated in a conference call. There was some trepidation about giving Khan a drug that had never been tested on humans, but almost everybody, it seemed, believed that the potential benefits outweighed the risks. "Everybody agreed that it made sense that a very informed and important person, who had treated more patients with hemorrhagic fever than anyone else in the world, should be given the experimental drug," says the medical officer. But the final decision was left to Khan's primary caretakers: Doctors Without Borders and the World Health Organization.

"At the end they got cold feet," says the medical officer. "The thinking was, 'He's such a high profile individual. If we do it and we screw up we'll be in big trouble.' I think they should have gone forward. Khan would have wanted it. The family would have wanted it. But they panicked. It was a very hard decision that nobody wants to make, and you have to respect them for it, whether it is your choice or not your choice."

On July 25, the international groups finally informed Khan that they had decided against treating him with ZMapp. (Khan was made aware of the debate but was never asked for his opinion.)

Yet there was another potential way to save Khan's life. While the ZMapp debate intensified, Sierra Leone's government contacted an air-ambulance service to arrange for an evacuation to a better-equipped hospital in Western Europe or the United States. A jet reportedly owned by International SOS, founded by two French doctors in the 1980s, landed at Lungi Airport outside Freetown. Equipped with a single-person isolation unit, the jet sat on the runway while the minister of health, Miatta Kargbo, frantically contacted counterparts in Germany, Switzerland, and the United States, trying to arrange Khan's transfer. (International SOS would not comment on whether its plane was involved in the attempted rescue operation.) According to C. Ray Khan, who was in daily communication with Kargbo, Western governments all rejected the minister's pleas—none were apparently prepared to deal with the backlash from allowing an Ebola-infected patient into the country—but finally one country, possibly Germany, agreed to take him in.

No one had ever before attempted to air evacuate an Ebola patient. Doctors pondered whether they could treat Khan, who was vomiting and had diarrhea, in a small space without becoming infected themselves, and whether Khan could withstand the stress of being shuttled by ambulance to Lungi Airport and then put on a plane.

Conditions had to be perfect. Several times a day, the Doctors Without Borders physicians measured Khan's white blood cell count, relaying the numbers to Kargbo. The count dropped sharply and then rose but, according to the version of events that Khan's brother received in daily conversations with the minister of health, always remained too low to move him.

Khan's symptoms fluctuated accordingly. For the first three days in Kailahun, he was conversant and able to move with relative ease. He would spend much of the morning and afternoon—when the heat and humidity built up to uncomfortable levels inside the isolation tent—in a small cordoned-off outdoor area, sitting and chatting with visitors across the orange-mesh barrier. "I was there every day, bringing him coconut water, a new charger for his cell phone, corn porridge for breakfast," Kaima says. "Then Dr. Khan didn't come outside for two days. He was not eating anymore." A World Health Organization physician working with Doctors Without Borders told Kaima on the fifth day that Khan's condition had suddenly gone critical. The doctor helped Khan outdoors that afternoon. Khan looked frail, with a hollow-eyed stare, but he could still sit up.

"Doc, I know you are a fighter, you have to win this," Kaima said.

"Peter," Khan replied, weakly. "You don't know what I'm going through. This is not easy for me."

On July 28, Mohamed Sankoh-Yela, a nurse from the Kenema Government Hospital who had tested positive for Ebola the previous day, arrived for treatment in Kailahun. "Dr. Khan was not very strong, and he had frequent diarrhea," Sankoh-Yela remembers. Still, he was able to sit up in bed and make small talk. He did not seem, the Ebola-stricken nurse recalls, as if he were anywhere near the point of death. At Tulane University, Garry had been receiving regular updates from colleagues in Kailahun. "We heard that he was feeling okay, he was doing fine," Garry says. "We thought he had entered a critical period where if he makes it through the next few days he'd be out of danger."

On July 29, the health minister called C. Ray Khan with good news: His brother's white blood cell count had risen overnight, and he was nearing the level considered safe for air evacuation. But while his body was fighting the virus, he was now unable to stand without help, and he had near-constant bloody diarrhea. "He asked me to help him change his Pampers," recalls Sankoh-Yela, "then he asked me to take him out for fresh air." Sankoh-Yela, with the help of doctors, lay Khan down on pillows in the outdoor area in front of the tent. Around two p.m., Khan asked Sankoh-Yela to prop him up in a seated position. "Dr. Khan, I am tired, I am also sick, I think I must leave you now," Sankoh-Yela told him.

"Yela, are you leaving me?' Khan asked.

"Yes, I am running away from you now, I need to rest," he said and returned to the ward.

Minutes later, lying in his bed, Sankoh-Yela heard a shout from outside. It was another nurse from Kenema, holding vigil for Khan.

A few minutes later, C. Ray Khan received another call from the minister of health. "Your brother passed away," she told him. "We have to let the plane go."

·   ·   ·

Khan was a test case. Every high-profile instance of infection that came after him went completely differently. In late July, Dr. Kent Brantly, an American physician-missionary in Monrovia, Liberia, fell sick with Ebola and, as Khan lay dying, the National

Institutes of Health arranged a shipment of the three vials of ZMapp from Kailahun to his treatment center. As Brantly rested in quarantine, nine days after showing the first symptoms, a single dose was injected into his bloodstream. Within an hour, Brantly's breathing improved and a rash that had covered his body faded. Hours later he boarded a Phoenix Air Gulfstream jet contracted by the U.S. State Department and fitted with an "aero-medical biological containment system," a collapsible plastic tent designed to house a single patient. From his isolation room at Emory University Hospital in Georgia, Brantly told the assembled media that "God leads to unexpected places."

Brantly's colleague in Liberia, Nancy Writebol, contracted Ebola around the same time. She received the last two vials of the drug from Kailahun, and, on August 6, she was able to board the same Phoenix air ambulance and return to the United States, where she quickly recovered. During the same frantic period, the Spanish government sent a specially equipped Airbus A310 medical jet to Liberia to evacuate an infected missionary, Father Miguel Pajares, to Madrid. Pajares was also given ZMapp, but he died in a hospital a week after his evacuation, one of two Ebola patients treated with ZMapp who did not survive. (The other was a Liberian doctor.)

The fifth Ebola patient to be treated with ZMapp was Will Pooley, the British nurse at the Ebola ward in Kenema. The 50–50 odds of contracting the virus he had given himself did not work out in his favor. He believes he got the virus from an eighteen-month-old infant whose parents had died of the disease but who had initially tested negative; the nurse had begun changing its diapers, and the child developed Ebola symptoms while Pooley was caring for it.

"I thought I would go to Kailahun, and that scared me, because Khan had died there," Pooley recounted one evening over a beer in a bar in Freetown. "But it also occurred to me that I wouldn't have to go on the ward at Kenema." Instead Pooley traveled in an ambulance with a police escort to Lungi Airport, where he was put on a Royal Air Force air ambulance to London, and was given one of the world's last remaining doses of ZMapp. "I had a really high fever and the shits, and then I started to recover," he says. When we met, Pooley had been back in Sierra Leone for a week; he was working in the "suspect ward" at Connaught Hospital in Freetown, treating sick patients who were waiting for the results of their Ebola tests. The difference this time was that Pooley had almost certainly developed an immunity to the virus because of his previous exposure. "The doctors aren't 100 percent sure, but it's probable," he says. Pooley believes that ZMapp cured him, and probably could have cured Khan as well. Medical experts aren't so sure. "If the question is, 'Did ZMapp do this?' The answer is that we just don't know," says Anthony Fauci, director of the National Institute of Allergy and Infectious Disease. "People who are in much less sophisticated medical-care conditions in West Africa are recovering 50 percent of the time."

In the aftermath of Khan's death, many of those involved in the decision making have been reluctant to talk about what they know. "Unfortunately I cannot comment on this matter at this time. Is that okay?" Miatta Kargbo repeated robotically at least fifteen times when I pressed her on the phone after she had been fired from her post as Sierra Leone's minister of health. Doctors Without Borders, invoking patient-doctor privilege, refused to answer any questions about Khan's condition while in their care, or even to explain why a patient who is walking and talking can, as Khan did, rapidly deteriorate and die. (Studies have attributed sudden death to shock and organ failure caused by fluid loss, and a sudden onset of arrhythmia.) According to Doctors Without Borders, the determining factor in denying Khan ZMapp was "clinical"—the belief that Khan's condition had deteriorated to the point that ZMapp probably could not have helped him. But that doesn't explain why Khan was up and about, talking coherently and eating well for his first few days in the treatment center.

Doctors Without Borders also denied that it played any role in the "management" of the plan to evacuate Khan or the final decision to abort the flight. This contradicted what C. Ray Khan had been told by the minister of health. "Things aren't adding up," he said in a phone conversation from Mahera. "Somebody isn't telling us the truth." Khan's brother Alhajie remains angry that an African was denied treatment with the experimental drug while two white Americans became the first to be given ZMapp, and distrusts Doctors Without Borders's account of what happened. The decision, he says, "looks political." One medical professional who was involved in the conference calls told me that Doctors Without Borders "was being very paternalistic," entirely cutting Khan out of the decision-making process. "It's not that they didn't want to do what was best for Khan," the medical professional says, but the organization allowed the perception to take root that "it was about color."

.   .   .

Khan was buried in a hastily dug grave in a weedy field behind the Kenema Government Hospital, next to the new, unfinished Lassa fever research center. The minister of health attended the ceremony, but many other government officials were afraid to come, and Khan's immediate family stayed away. "He died like a brave soldier defending his country," I was told by Victor Willoughby, Khan's mentor, who himself died of Ebola in December. During my visit to Kenema, a nurse from the Ebola unit took me behind the compound to show me the grave. It was a desolate place, a slab of marble-tiled concrete standing alone in a field of dirt and weeds. There were no markings on the tomb, which was already crumbling, and the only indication of who was buried there were three black flags drooping from wooden posts, left by different departments at the hospital. "The district health-management team extend their condolence to the family and friends of Sheik Humarr Khan," one read, "who suddenly left us when we needed him most."

On my last afternoon in Sierra Leone, I took the ferry to meet Khan's family in Mahera, where the doctor's love of medicine had first taken hold. I was met by his brother C. Ray, and together we drove to a low-slung yellow house a few blocks from the sea. The family's ninety-eight-year-old patriarch sat on the porch, draped in a brown traditional gown and Muslim skullcap, still as a statue, acknowledging my presence with a trembling lip. His wife, who is eighty-six, sat beside him, clad in a richly patterned peacock-blue gown and maroon headscarf. She shook my hand and managed a soft "hello." I tried to engage them in conversation but made little headway, except when C. Ray prodded his mother about the corporal punishment that she had sometimes meted out to young Humarr when he misbehaved.

"I whipped him six times with a small, thin cane on his butt," she said.

"It was more like twelve times," C. Ray interjected.

The old woman nodded. "He was a very nice boy," she murmured. "A quiet boy."

C. Ray brought out a folder filled with family photographs— a portrait of his grandfather in the British colonial police force in the early 1930s, Khan posing in front of his car a decade ago: with a grin so wide he seems to be laughing at a joke between him and the photographer. After a time, I excused myself to catch my flight home to Europe, and the elder Khan finally mumbled something. "My father wants to pray for you," C. Ray said. Khan raised his hands and chanted a prayer in Arabic in a raspy whisper, which C. Ray translated: "Take this son of America home, safely. Guide him well."

As we walked to my taxi, C. Ray gazed at me intently. "When the minister of health called me about my brother, and told me that he had passed away, I said to myself, 'Oh, wait a minute, how am I going to tell my parents?'" He had decided to take them into their bedroom, where he asked them to sit down. "I have some bad news for you about your son," he said. "Do you remember that you didn't want him to go work in the Lassa fever program because of what had happened to the other doctor? Okay, well, he got sick from Ebola, and he died.'"

C. Ray braced himself for the worst. He had expected that his mother and father would collapse. He imagined having to call an ambulance and rushing with them to the hospital emergency room. Instead, they sat perfectly still, saying nothing. Then they raised their hands together toward the ceiling and began to pray.

"Thank you for what you've done for Humarr. For what you've done for us," they said. "You are the only one who gives life and takes life, so who are we to cry?"

C. Ray was flabbergasted.

His father looked at him: "Nobody cries in this house," he said. "We should all give thanks to God."

New York Times Magazine

FINALIST—REPORTING

In the last five years the United States has deported hundreds of thousands undocumented aliens. Even at a time when immigration is the subject of red-hot argument, their fate still has the power to shock. "Purgatory" describes the experience of Kelvin Villanueva, who was sent back to Honduras—where gang-related violence is commonplace—after being stopped near his home in Kansas City for a broken taillight. The Ellie judges described this story as "thoroughly original" and praised Luke Mogelson for his "resourceful and at times dangerous fact-gathering." Mogelson's article "The Dream Boat" won the National Magazine Award for Reporting for the New York Times Magazine in 2014. Another of his stories, "The River Martyrs," was a finalist in Reporting the same year. His first collection of fiction, These Heroic, Happy Dead, was published in April 2016.

Luke Mogelson

Purgatory

K elvin Villanueva was almost home one night last June when a policeman stopped him for a broken taillight. From his truck, he could see his longtime girlfriend, Suelen Bueno, waiting for him behind the glass door of their apartment. She often did that when he worked late. Villanueva supervised a small team of Hondurans—like him, undocumented migrants—who did finish carpentry on construction projects throughout Kansas City. It was normal for them to put in twelve-to-fourteen-hour days. During his fifteen years in the United States, he had never been pulled over. Still, Bueno worried. The threat of deportation did not subside with time. You just had more to lose.

Before Bueno reached them, the officer had arrested Villanueva. After being transferred to Immigration and Customs Enforcement, he spent the next four months circuiting a nexus of prisons and detention centers. Mostly, he was in a Missouri county jail that held Americans accused of felonies. Fights frequently broke out between the black and Latino inmates. Villanueva kept to himself, rarely leaving his bunk, passing the weeks by reading and drawing. He called Bueno and their children every day. When they met seven years earlier, at an adult-league soccer game, Bueno already had a young son and daughter; she and Villanueva had since had another one of each together.

Villanueva didn't differentiate. He'd always treated Bueno's first two children as his own. Now, when the kids asked when he would be back, Villanueva told them, "Soon."

Bueno, who was also undocumented, could not visit Villanueva during his incarceration. Instead, she borrowed enough money to hire an immigration lawyer, who filed an asylum claim on Villanueva's behalf. Before his hearing with an immigration judge, Villanueva was interviewed by an asylum officer, whose job it was to determine whether he possessed a "credible fear" of persecution in Honduras—would he be at risk of harm because of his race, religion, social group, or politics? The officer's analysis would inform the judge's decision on whether to suspend or proceed with Villanueva's deportation. When Villanueva spoke with the officer—from prison, by telephone, via a translator—she began by asking him why he came to the United States in the first place.

"To live and work," Villanueva told her, "because in my country it is very difficult."

"Difficult" might have been an understatement. Honduras is among the poorest and most violent countries in Latin America, and Villanueva's hometown, San Pedro Sula, has ranked as the city with the highest homicide rate in the world for the last four years. (In 2014, 1,319 of its 769,025 residents were murdered.) Much of the bloodshed is gang-related. During the 1980s, waves of refugees fled civil conflicts in El Salvador, Guatemala, and Nicaragua, many settling in Los Angeles, where street gangs were proliferating. Among Central Americans, two dominant organizations established a vicious rivalry: the Mara Salvatrucha, or MS-13, and the 18th Street Gang. When tough-on-crime legislation during the 1990s generated mass deportations, thousands of California gang members were sent back to developing countries ill equipped to receive them. In feeble, corrupt states like Honduras, the MS-13 and the 18th Street Gang flourished, brokering alliances not only with politicians, prison authorities, and the police but also with Mexican and South American drug cartels. The narcotics trade fueled the war between the two groups with unprecedented access to weaponry and cash. In San Pedro Sula, as in many other places throughout the region, resources plus impunity equaled more murder, torture, and rape.

For Villanueva, whose father was an alcoholic and regularly beat his mother, the violence continued at home. After his mother absconded to a different town, Villanueva and his three younger siblings were raised by their grandmother, aunts, and uncles. These relatives were very religious—one uncle was the pastor of a small evangelical church, another directed its youth group—and very poor. To contribute, Villanueva dropped out of school when he was twelve and started working. When he was sixteen, an uncle who lived in Kansas City offered to lend him the money to pay a coyote, or guide, who could usher him across the United States border. He also promised Villanueva a job in a glass factory, fabricating window panes, when he arrived. Villanueva's family in San Pedro Sula encouraged him to go. Members of the 18th Street Gang had begun pressuring him to join their ranks, and on one occasion they had jumped him for refusing.

"How do you know they were from the 18th Street Gang?" the asylum officer asked during the interview, after Villanueva described the incident.

"They had tattoos with the number on their faces and hands," he said, "and the walls of their houses are marked with the number."

Villanueva later described the torture and murder of the uncle who directed the youth group at his family's church. In 2013, the uncle disappeared after complaining to the police about the 18th Street Gang harassing the group members. A few days later, his body turned up in the Chamelecón River covered with puncture wounds, which investigators deemed to have been inflicted by an ice pick.

"How do you know the gang is connected to the police?" the asylum officer asked.

"Everybody knows that in my country," Villanueva said.

"Your attorney submitted an article that indicates the police captured a leader of the 18th Street Gang," the officer pointed out. "If the gangs are working with the police, why would the police arrest their leaders?"

"They arrest people so the community thinks they're doing something. But then they're out of jail in a week or two."

"Why are they released after a week or two?"

"This is the question that all of the good people of Honduras ask."

"Is there anything else that you're afraid of in Honduras?"

"No. Just losing my life."

Although the officer found Villanueva credible, she did not consider him eligible for asylum; the immigration judge agreed. Villanueva was sent to Louisiana, where he was loaded onto a plane with more than a hundred other Hondurans. They wore manacles on their wrists and ankles, and their hands were shackled to chains around their waists. Armed guards accompanied them. Midway through the flight, bologna sandwiches and cookies were distributed. They were packaged individually, the sandwiches and cookies. Most of the handcuffed men and women found it easiest to tear the plastic with their teeth.

●   ●   ●

On the outskirts of San Pedro Sula, Ramón Villeda Morales International Airport receives planeloads of Hondurans like Villanueva several times a week. The deportees are unshackled and disembark on the tarmac. They are herded to a processing center, where their belongings are returned to them. Outside the center, family members and girlfriends loiter in the shade, expectantly watching the door. They perk up each time it opens and another deportee emerges. Taxi drivers offer special rates. Money changers wave stacks of Honduran lempiras, buying American dollars. People speak emotionally on phones.

Over the last five years, the United States has deported more than half a million Hondurans, Guatemalans, and Salvadorans, many of whom, like Villanueva, have had to leave their children behind. Although Immigration and Customs Enforcement, or ICE, says it exercises discretion to target lawbreakers for removal, a majority of Central American deportees have no criminal record. Among those who do, about half are guilty of either a traffic violation or an immigration-related crime—entering the country illegally, for instance. At Ramón Villeda Morales, most arrivals I met were captured while crossing the border. This meant they had recently endured two distinct but often, in their telling, equally arduous ordeals: their voyage through Mexico (sleeping in shelters; trekking through deserts; evading bandits, kidnappers and rapists) and ICE detention.

As soon as they enter the processing center, the deportees are given coffee and *baleadas*, a Honduran dish of tortillas and beans. The staff members call them "ma'am" and "sir," make jokes, say "please" and "thank you." It is as if the staff is trying to convince the deportees that they are not the people they've been treated as for the past several days or weeks or months. The deportees undergo brief interviews with interlocutors who are all volunteers. One day, I sat at a table beside Dennis Abraham, a thirty-year-old singer-carpenter with wide-open eyes and shoulder-length hair tied up in a samurai bun. Abraham wore a laminated ID card around his neck that featured his photo beneath a logo for the Geo Group, the international corporation that operates a facility in Texas where he himself was detained just two months ago. When new arrivals sat down across from him, Abraham showed them the ID and said, "I'm like you."

Abraham first left for the United States when he was sixteen, with his mother, Maria. For two months, they clung together to the tops of northbound freight trains. Then, while fording a deep section of the Rio Grande, they were separated by a swift current. Maria made it to the other side; Abraham, a weak swimmer, was carried downstream. Uncertain what to do, he turned himself in to the Mexican authorities. Back in Honduras, Abraham had no way to get in touch with Maria and no one to take care of him. He decided to try to find her. He was apprehended and deported from Mexico seven times attempting to make the trip. "The eighth time, they did this to me," Abraham said, holding out his forearms and showing me a latticework of scar tissue. While on the trains, he had fallen into the hands of the Zetas, one of the largest drug cartels in Mexico and among its most prolific practitioners of abduction and extortion. Disinclined to believe that Abraham had no one to contact for a ransom, his captors tied him up in a dark room, beat him, urinated on him, cut him with machetes, threatened to castrate him, and forced him to endure mock executions. In the end, they let him work off his debt, and for eight months, Abraham slept in the streets of their town, cleaning their cars.

This all happened almost a decade ago; since then, Abraham had reached the United States, found his mother, married an American, had two children, and been deported.

"I have no choice," he said, scrolling through pictures of his children on his phone. "I have to take the trains again."

I watched Abraham interview half a dozen deportees. What he said was true: They were like him. To a middle-aged farmer who had three daughters in the United States and was on his way to his mother's town, Abraham said, "Is there someone where you're going who might hurt you?"

"Yes," replied the farmer, removing his hat and rubbing his face with his hands. "But I have to risk it. I have nowhere else to go."

"So you're afraid to go there?"

"Yes."

"But you're going there?"

"Of course."

The farmer, like everyone else from the plane, looked both exhausted and disoriented. In general, I had the sense that the deportees were not entirely convinced by the staff's overt exhibitions of decency. A wariness lingered; the transition was too abrupt. Of course, there was an additional dissonance at play: deep relief at having been liberated from ICE custody and, simultaneously, deep dismay at being back in Honduras.

Later that day, in a *pulpería* across the road from the processing center, I met a man named Bayron Cardona, who was a nervous wreck. He told me that he and his wife, Belky, had managed to cross the Rio Grande but were so intimidated by the Border Patrol presence in Texas that they decided to reverse course and were arrested while trying to get back to Mexico. Cardona and Belky were recent college graduates, still in their twenties, and last year they opened a computer-repair shop in a building owned by Belky's father. Their neighborhood was entirely under the control of the MS-13; members of the gang soon confronted Cardona, demanding an *impuesto de guerra*, or war tax. *Impuestos de guerra* are a common source of revenue for gangs throughout Honduras, and in Cardona and Belky's area, every business paid. The amount the gang wanted far exceeded what Cardona could afford. When he failed to produce the money, the MS-13 threatened to kill him. Cardona and Belky went to the United States Embassy, applied for visas and were denied. Then they alerted the police—"our big error," Cardona told me. That same day, after the couple closed their shop, someone slid a piece of paper under the metal shutter, a printed letter that read in part: "We know everything you do. We can kill you in your house or when you're walking out of church. Call home to see what happens." Cardona and Belky called Belky's father, with whom they were living. Minutes earlier, he told them, two gunmen on motorcycles had driven by, shooting up the front porch with handguns.

A few weeks later, the couple climbed out of a small boat onto the banks of Texas. It was nighttime. There were bushes and then a road and then a fence and then a highway. Their coyote told them there was a gap in the fence that they should run for. Cardona and Belky hid in the bushes. White and green SUVs drove up and down the road; officers patrolled on foot with dogs. Others rode on horseback. A helicopter appeared and hovered low. The rotor wash from its roaring blades flattened the tall grass and exposed the migrants hiding there.

Through the rest of the night and all the next day, Cardona and Belky watched one migrant after another make a dash, get caught. Sometimes, as the migrants ran, the dogs latched onto their pant legs. They were sleep-deprived and dehydrated. Belky told Cardona she wanted to go back. They had Mexican visas; they would stay there or find another country to flee to. Cardona called the coyote and asked him to send a boat. He and Belky were down by the water, waiting to be collected, when a skiff motored up and flashed a spotlight on them. From the bank, an officer on horseback galloped over and told them not to move.

At a Border Patrol station in McAllen, Cardona and Belky were separated. Cardona was put in a cell with other men that was shockingly cold—a *hielera*, or icebox, as migrants call them. The men positioned a trash can under the ceiling vent to capture the frigid air; that way, huddled together, they could lie on the concrete floor. After two days, Cardona was transferred to a detention center, where he told an ICE official that he and his wife wanted to request asylum. The ICE official asked for Belky's name. The next day, she was deported. The next week, so was Cardona. When I met him at the airport in San Pedro Sula, he had not seen Belky since their apprehension.

A few days later, I visited the couple at Belky's father's house. I met Cardona at a nearby restaurant so he could guide my driver through his neighborhood. He was anxious and fidgety. His father-in-law had paid half the war tax that they owed the MS-13 and told the gang that he and Belky were in America; Cardona didn't know what would happen when the gang discovered they were back. He had changed the way he wore his hair, grown a beard and replaced his contacts with prescription glasses. We passed the building where his business used to be—it was now a barber shop. As we turned onto Cardona's street, an MS-13 look-out, a teenager in a tank top, eyeballed us as we drove by. We rolled the windows down, a rule throughout Honduras when entering gang territory.

Climbing the front steps of his house, Cardona pointed out the divots in the walls where the bullets from the drive-by had struck. He went inside and returned with the death-threat letter that was slid into his shop. His father-in-law had found a nine-millimeter shell, he told me, and probably still had it. I said that was fine, I didn't need to see the shell. Belky came out, and we sat in the driveway between two huge barking dogs tethered to short chains. One had a painful-looking knob protruding from its brow. Someone had hit it with a bat or a pipe, Cardona explained, while stealing their propane tanks.

Belky cried several times as she spoke. In McAllen, she told me, she was also put in a *hielera*. She was in it for three days, with many other women and young children, including a newborn and her mother, who had undergone a cesarean. The detainees were issued thin Mylar blankets for warmth; they all slept on the floor. There were no showers, and the only toilet had a camera aimed at it. Every twenty-four hours, each detainee was given two bologna sandwiches.

Belky said that when she told the guards she wished to claim asylum, they advised her that she did not have that right. "They make you sign all these documents in English," she said, "and we just don't know what we're signing."

Neither Cardona nor Belky believed that they could safely re-main in Honduras. But Belky, who had not left the house since she had arrived more than a week ago, was against returning to America. For her, more than anything, the whole experience had been profoundly humiliating. Before we said goodbye, she described being called into a room in McAllen where officers studied a bank of monitors showing video feed from cameras that surveilled a section of the border. "They laugh at us," she told me, her face compressed with resentment. "One officer was celebrating all the people they'd caught. They watch the people crossing—and they laugh at us."

I went back to visit Cardona and Belky a couple of weeks later. As we drove though their neighborhood, we passed a group of young men surrounding someone in a crouch. The men were knocking on the top of his head with their knuckles—not violently, but with odd restraint. This was the gang's way, I later learned, of issuing one of their own a symbolic reprimand, a warning.

Belky told me that she still had not set foot outside the house.

$$\cdot \qquad \cdot \qquad \cdot$$

When I spotted him at the airport, Villanueva was in the *pulpería*, sitting at a wooden table with a Pepsi. As he raised the bottle, I noticed a tattoo across his hand—the name "Haley." He wore a blue Kansas City Royals hat. At his feet was a gym bag.

After we spoke for a bit, I asked whether anyone was coming to get him.

Villanueva laughed self-consciously. "I don't think so," he admitted. He had loose curls, a sparse beard and a slight overbite that seemed to facilitate his tendency to mumble. I offered him a ride, and he accepted.

A striking characteristic of San Pedro Sula is the intimate proximity of ostentatious wealth and extreme poverty—a multistory mall with valet parking on one side of a river, squalid slums and jungle on the other. On our way to the place where Villanueva's family lived, we passed block after block of ornate adobe mansions ensconced behind tall walls. Atop the walls was razor wire; atop the wire, electric fencing. Men with rifles manned the gates.

"Look at that," Villanueva kept saying as we drove. He was deported once before, in 2008, and spent two weeks in San Pedro Sula before heading back to Kansas City; still, a lot had changed since then. We pulled onto a rocky side street that turned off the pavement into an undeveloped area, lushly overgrown. Here and there, shanties had been patched together using salvaged tin. Villanueva had arranged to stay with his aunt Marta in a one-room plywood structure that stood in an open field amid boulders, thick weeds, and mango trees. By the time he stepped out from the car, he was smiling again.

"Man," he said in English, looking around, shouldering his bag. "It's weird to be here, you know?"

I stopped by a few days later and found Villanueva sitting on a boulder, talking on a cell phone to his younger son. "No, my love, you can't come," he was saying. "Behave, OK? Don't fight with your sisters, understand?" When he hung up, Villanueva told me, "I don't know how to explain it to them."

"They don't know?"

He shook his head. "They think I'm on a job."

A sheet obstructing the entrance to Marta's shack was pulled back, and a young man with gelled hair and a tight T-shirt stepped out. It was Villanueva's younger brother, Oscar. After being arrested on a DUI charge, he had recently been deported as well. Back in Colorado, Oscar told me, he had a wife, a daughter, and a son. All of them were citizens.

While Villanueva had been surprisingly good-humored at the airport and remained so that day (sort of grinning at his situation even as he lamented it), Oscar was morose. He spoke so softly that I had to lean in to hear, and when I asked how his kids were holding up without him, he hung his head, sighed, "Those kids," and wept.

Altogether, five people were living in Marta's shack. Tacked-up bedding divided the sleeping area from the kitchen area. At night, Oscar and Villanueva laid a mattress on the floor. They rarely left the property. Neither had acclimated to the dangers of the city of their youth; the daily slaughter to which most of San Pedro Sula's residents were by now inured still distressed the brothers as it might a typical American. One morning when I invited them to breakfast, we encountered a taped-off crime scene a few blocks from their house. A body was sprawled face-down on the sidewalk, and there was another in the street. You could see solid pieces in the blood around their heads. Forensic experts in white coats placed numbered markers near the bullet casings—forty-seven of them, so far. The few people who had gathered looked mostly unimpressed. Many passers-by didn't bother stopping.

"It's been a long time since I've seen that," Villanueva said.

"Welcome to Honduras," Oscar said.

When I took them home several hours later, we passed the scene again. The crowd had dispersed, and the forensic experts were gone. The bodies, though, remained.

Nobody had covered them. Traffic carried on.

.　　　.　　　.

The contrast between the reality of San Pedro Sula and the insular world that Villanueva's family had created on their little side street struck me every time I visited. More than fifteen relatives occupied three different houses there. They often gathered in the evenings on an old musty couch and a few metal benches outside Marta's shack. A yellow school bus belonging to their church sat nearby—"God Bless Honduras" and "Never Give Up" colorfully decaled across the windshields. Children pushed one another around in mop buckets and on dollies over a square of cracked foundation in the grass. Usually, Villanueva's grandmother would be cooking *baleadas* or pots of rice and beans over a wood fire in an outdoor grill fashioned from a chunk of concrete. Dogs and kittens begged for scraps. Everyone was always laughing.

One night while chatting with Villanueva and Oscar, I heard a violinist playing a classical concerto I didn't know—I don't know any classical concertos—but whose beauty was astonishing. Villanueva led me past the bus and through the trees to a small house set back from the road. There, his twenty-two-year-old cousin stood on a dilapidated porch beneath a naked bulb, immersed in her performance. As she played—the composer, she told me later, was Mozart—her two younger sisters emerged from the house with their own violins.

One of them also played the keyboard in the family church's band. Some nights later, I went with Villanueva to a service. When it was over, another cousin took the worshipers home in the school bus. It was so crowded that many had to stand. As we left behind the heavily fortified entrances to private communities and continued into the ramshackle barrios where the congregation lived, there was a raucous, joyful energy. Each person who got off kissed or hugged every other passenger onboard. So incongruous, all that good will. It took a couple hours to circumnavigate the city, and during that time we passed two taped-off crime scenes, as well as an assault: about a dozen teenagers kicking someone on the sidewalk curled into a squirming ball.

Besides attending church, Villanueva had little else to do. Each day's main event was his afternoon phone call to Bueno and the kids. Neither he nor Bueno had told them yet that he'd been deported. Briana, who turned ten the day before Villanueva was flown back to Honduras, and Jesse, who was eight, were coping with his absence better than their younger siblings. Haley, who was four and whose name was tattooed across the back of Villanueva's hand, had always been the most attached to Villanueva. She used to wait up for him with Bueno whenever he worked late. Now Haley refused to go to sleep, determined to be awake if he returned. Villanueva's three-year-old son, Jordi, had grown un-characteristically introverted and lethargic, sleeping most of the day and rarely speaking.

Bueno, who had remained home with the children after she and Villanueva moved in together, had gone back to work, clean-ing an office building seven nights a week while her mother babysat. She returned to the apartment around two a.m., woke at seven to get the kids ready for school, picked up Haley at noon, made lunch for her and Jordi, met Briana and Jesse at the bus stop at four-thirty, cooked supper at six, and left for work again when her mother arrived at eight.

Villanueva was desperate to find out whether there was any possibility of reuniting with them legally. His first few days in Honduras, he seemed optimistic. The immigration attorney Bueno hired to help him with his asylum claim had filed a petition with the Board of Immigration Appeals. The petition was still pending, and after consulting with the attorney, Bueno believed that their odds were good. The appeals process was go-ing to cost them an additional $5,000, on top of the $4,750 Bueno had already paid and the $8,000 she still owed in monthly installments; if there was a decent chance, though, they would find the money.

That meant borrowing. The legal fees, along with the $1,000 phone bill Villanueva had racked up during his two months in the county jail ($1 per minute talking to Bueno and the children), had depleted all their savings. To pay the attorney, Bueno had taken out a series of loans from an informal moneylender, who charged 5 percent interest every week. Villanueva's employer, meanwhile, had stopped answering his phone. Earlier in the year, Villanueva's team had built out the kitchens of more than a hundred new apartment units in Kansas City's River Market neighborhood; the contractor still owed Villanueva $28,000 for the job. Before he was arrested, Villanueva had planned to use the payment to buy a neglected house at auction, fix it up in secret, take Bueno there when it was ready, and propose. Now he knew he'd never see the money. Although he filed taxes every year and reported to the IRS all the wages that he paid his team (the IRS doesn't investigate the citizenship of taxpayers), there was no recourse to collect the debt.

When Villanueva expressed to me his hopefulness about his asylum claim, I was dubious. He had already been deported, after all, and that decision is seldom rescinded. Later, with Villanueva in the room, I called his attorney in Kansas City and asked him myself what he thought was the likelihood that the Board of Immigration Appeals would both consider and grant the appeal. The attorney, Allan Bell, told me: "The direct answer to your question is the chances are slim. I did not say slim to none. The chances are slim. I'll use the word 'remote.'" I asked what other options there might be for Villanueva to return, and Bell asked to speak in a few days, with Bueno conferencing in.

In fact, there were no options. An estimated 4.5 million American-born children have undocumented mothers or fathers, and every year tens of thousands of them lose at least one parent to deportation. In November 2014, President Obama took executive action to institute a series of reforms that would have granted temporary work permits to some parents of United States citizens and residents. Texas and twenty-five other states promptly filed a lawsuit arguing that the order was unconstitutional, and a federal judge in Brownsville—a major crossing point for migrants and asylum seekers on the Texas border—issued an injunction against the programs. For now, citizens can petition for their parents to obtain green cards only after turning twenty-one. For Haley, the older of Villanueva's two biological children, that would be in seventeen years. Moreover, because Villanueva had been deported once before, he was subject to a pair of ten-year "time bars." This required him to spend a minimum of two decades outside the country, as punishment, before he could become eligible to apply for permission to reenter.

When Villanueva and Bueno next spoke to Bell, Bell asked that I not be present for the conversation. I obliged, but Villanueva recorded it. The tape is disturbing. Bell, now dim on the appeal, suggests that Villanueva seek something called humanitarian parole and offers to steer the process for $3,000. Although Villanueva and Bueno—leery of spending more money on a long shot—press him about the likelihood of success, Bell fails to give them a straight answer. (I later spoke with several other immigration attorneys, all of whom held that humanitarian parole—which typically provides a temporary visa valid for family emergencies—was not a viable option for Villanueva.) At one point, exasperated, Villanueva stops using his interpreter and tries to speak directly to Bell in English. "I want to make sure, because I don't want to spend more money, more time," he says. "Because I want to be with my family over there. You know? I want—"

"Well, I know. The whole thing is terrible, I couldn't agree with you more."

"Don't tell me that, man," Villanueva says, raising his voice. "I know it's terrible. I'm in Honduras right now, far away from my family."

"Right, right, right."

"What I want to know is something clear, man. Do you think it's possible we going to win this case, or are we going to lose it?"

"I personally think it's possible . . ." Bell trails off, seems to walk away, comes back and then says: "Now hold on, please, I have to explain something. Let me explain to everybody. I know none of you know this, and I'm sure none of you care—but the Kansas City Royals baseball team is playing the championship for the American League right now. It's a big thing here. I think Suelen knows. Am I correct, Suelen?"

After a pause, Bueno says, "Yes."

"It's on national television," Bell continues.

"I don't care about the Royals right now, man," Villanueva says, again in English. "I'm worried about my case, about my family."

"I'm here," Bell says. "I'm not going to the game because of you. I gave my tickets away so I could help you. It's on world television right now. The Kansas City Royals against the Houston team. But anyway, I'll help you, don't worry."

After the call, I took Villanueva out to lunch. He ate and spoke little. The resilient cheerfulness that I had marveled at was gone, and for the first time, it occurred to me that the difference between Villanueva and his brother Oscar might not be constitutional, after all. Maybe the only difference was that Oscar had been stuck in Honduras, away from his family, longer than Villanueva had.

I asked what he was thinking.

Villanueva looked up, shook his head and said, "I'm thinking I have to make the trip again."

.   .   .

The last time Villanueva made the trip, he very nearly died. In 2008, after his first deportation—he was arrested at a party where someone else was caught with cocaine—he spent a month riding the trains by himself through Mexico and then waded across the Rio Grande with a group of some twenty other migrants. In the middle of their second day of following a coyote through the Texas desert, a small plane buzzed overhead and the rev of four-wheelers approached. Everybody scattered. Villanueva found a narrow, dry arroyo and hid beneath a rocky outcrop. Five hours later, he climbed out and started walking. He walked through the night and in the morning fell asleep. Around noon, he was woken by the heat. He had no backpack or supplies. The coyote had told him to keep the sun on his left and the shadows on his right—when it got dark, Villanueva guessed which way was north. Five days after crossing the border, and his third day alone, half-starved and in dire need of water, he came upon a skeleton. It was small, probably an adolescent. The skull was clean bone. Several of its teeth had fallen out. Nearby lay a blue denim knapsack. Villanueva emptied it. Inside the knapsack was a bag of bread—black with mold—but also a can of beans and a can of peaches. Villanueva used a sharp stone to pierce a small gash in the can of peaches. He downed the sweet syrup and pried the can open and ate the sweet pieces. He chugged the beans.

The food gave him enough strength to walk the rest of the afternoon and most of the night. Still, the next day Villanueva knew he might not make it. He prayed for a patrol to find him, for an airplane or a helicopter. He was staggering forward weakly when he glimpsed a far-off, incandescent spray. He saw a truck and a man squatting near its bumper. The man wore a head shield—he was welding something to the metal. Villanueva squinted. It felt like a hallucination: the vivid, molten shower splashing off the frame.

"Help!" Villanueva screamed. "Help me!"

The coyote had warned that ranchers in this part of Texas sometimes shot migrants if they caught them on their land. Villanueva didn't care. He wanted food. He wanted water.

"Help me, please!"

The man continued welding. Eventually, it occurred to Villanueva that perhaps God didn't want the man to hear. Perhaps God wanted Villanueva to keep going.

Before night fell, he collapsed. He was lying in the hot dirt while the colors went out in the enormous sky, and he was thinking about the skeleton, its teeth, when he saw tracers streaming through the distant dark. He rose and stumbled toward them. They were the lights of tractor-trailers driving on a highway.

A wire fence ran parallel to the shoulder. He found a culvert and crawled through it to the other side. For the rest of the night, he stayed to the chaparral; the next morning, he detected a faint rhythmic pounding and recognized it as a jackhammer. The sound energized him with fresh hope. If there was a jackhammer, there was construction. If there was construction, there were migrants. A little while later, he found a team of Mexicans ripping up a driveway.

The Mexicans lived across the border but had special visas that permitted them to commute for work. They gave Villanueva some of the food they had brought for lunch. One let him borrow a cell phone. Villanueva called his cousin in Kansas, who offered to wire $500 to anyone willing to drive Villanueva to San Antonio. Most of the Mexicans were afraid to jeopardize their visas—but when the team quit for the day, a worker in his early thirties agreed to take him. He took Villanueva in his pickup to a Walmart, where he could retrieve the wired money. Villanueva's cousin had sent an extra $100 for Villanueva, and after bidding farewell to the Mexican, he bought new socks and underwear, a T-shirt, and a pair of pants. He went into the bathroom and washed his face and arms.

When Villanueva walked out of the store, the Mexican was waiting for him. "Come on, let me buy you a hamburger," he said.

The man took him to a McDonald's and ordered him a Big Mac. When they finished, he drove him to a motel and paid for two nights.

"Rest," he told Villanueva.

·   ·   ·

Since then, reaching the United States has become only more difficult. Last summer, while an exodus of Central Americans was overwhelming U.S. immigration facilities, the Mexican government began implementing a host of aggressive enforcement measures on its southern border. Many of the migrants leaving Central America were unaccompanied minors; while the United States is obligated to assess their eligibility for refugee protections, Mexico can simply bus them back. The crackdown has been a boon for ICE and the Border Patrol. So far this year, the number of Central American migrants apprehended in the United

States has fallen by half compared with last year. The number of Central American migrants apprehended in Mexico is on track to increase by 70 percent.

In Honduras, the buses from Mexico bearing adult deportees without children arrive at a processing center just across the Guatemalan border. The center occupies a scenic beachfront property seized in September from a drug trafficker. I spent several days there; nearly everyone I spoke to had been captured in the deep south of Mexico. A vast majority, traveling in passenger vans, had been intercepted at roadblocks manned by the federal police, army soldiers, and immigration agents.

Juveniles and families with children are sent to a different center, off the highway on the outskirts of San Pedro Sula. Unaccompanied deportees as young as eight have shown up there. One day, I met a mother who had left Honduras with her sixteen-year-old daughter after gang members tried to rape her in her school. Another woman on the same bus had left with her four-year-old son after her brother was murdered. All four were standing on the shoulder of the highway, waiting for taxis to take them back to the neighborhoods they had fled.

If Villanueva did go north, he would need to hire a coyote. You could not traverse Mexico without one now. These days, the reputable guides were charging $8,000, Honduras to Houston. They gave you three tries. If caught a third time, you lost your money.

Even if Villanueva managed to get through Mexico, he would face the prospect of felony charges, in addition to deportation, if he was arrested on the United States border. Although entering the country without documentation has always been a crime, as recently as a decade ago public attorneys rarely prosecuted migrants in federal court. That has changed. Today, illegal entry and reentry are the most-prosecuted federal offenses in the United States, and the Justice Department receives more cases from ICE than it does from the Federal Bureau of Investigation, the Drug Enforcement Administration, the Marshals Service, and the Bureau of Alcohol, Tobacco, Firearms and Explosives combined. Prison sentences for people with multiple illegal entries, like Villanueva, can last more than ten years.

Say, though, Villanueva made it to Kansas City. He would still spend the rest of his life there in danger. Because of the twenty-year time bar from his deportations, he would be ineligible for legal status even after Haley grew old enough to petition for him.

When I talked to Villanueva about this, he said it didn't matter: As soon as the kids were out of the house, he and Bueno would happily return to Honduras. They would buy some land, build a house. The kids could visit them during school holidays or vacations from work.

"I just need to raise them," Villanueva said.

•　　　•　　　•

A week or so after he got back, Villanueva went with Oscar to visit their mother, Francesca, who lived a couple of hours away, in her hometown, Toyos. In the last fifteen years, Villanueva had seen Francesca only once, in 2008. Neither he nor Oscar harbored any grudges toward her for leaving them when they were young. Growing up, they sometimes went to Toyos to escape the 18th Street Gang. Back then, Francesca lived in a shanty that she built herself from bamboo and cardboard boxes; she made a living washing clothes in a nearby river. With the money her children had sent back from Missouri, Francesca had since moved into a small block house with electricity and running water. When we arrived, she was standing at a portable camping stove, making chicken soup.

"My son!" Francesca gasped when she saw Villanueva.

"You look shorter," Villanueva laughed.

While the soup boiled, Villanueva sat with Francesca at the table, swiping through the pictures on his phone: Jesse at a lake where they liked to fish for bass, Briana making snow angels, Jordi and Haley riding bumper cars at a family entertainment center. Francesca observed the pictures mutely. She had never been to America, seen snow, or heard of a family entertainment center.

Oscar sat across the table, drawing designs on a white cloth Francesca had given him. Later, she would embroider the designs with colored thread. Oscar held up the cloth for her to see. Penciled vines and leaves curled around the edges, blooming into roses.

"Is it good?" he asked.

"It's good," Francesca said.

When I seconded her opinion, Oscar went into the bedroom and came back with a stack of envelopes. They were from his time in detention. On both sides of each envelope Oscar had drawn intricate images in ballpoint pen. He still had the pen. It was short and made from flexible rubber so as to preclude stabbing.

From one envelope, I withdrew a sheet of notebook paper with six verses handwritten in Spanish. It was a song Oscar had composed and sung over the phone to his son on his sixth birthday. The last verse read:

> Although you're young
> some day you will understand
> why I wasn't there
> on your special day.

Before we left Francesca's, I asked about a framed photograph on the wall. It showed Villanueva; Oscar; their brother, Henry; and their sister, Miriam, standing beside a skimpily ornamented Christmas tree, arms draped on one another. Their uncle had taken it in Kansas City in 2004, the only year all four siblings were in the United States together.

. . .

I recognized the same photograph a couple of weeks later, hanging in Villanueva's father's house. Although he lived a few short blocks away, Javier Villanueva had little to do with the rest of the family—he did not attend the church or share any of his relatives' evangelical fervor—and Villanueva had seen him only once since arriving in Honduras.

Javier's home was one in a crowded row precariously situated on a rocky river bank. It was somewhat bigger than Marta's plywood shack and marginally better appointed. There was a toilet rigged to plumbing rather than an outhouse—and a television. We found Javier watching a James Bond film dubbed in Spanish. He was skinny, in shorts and a tank top, with a mustache and the same curly black hair as Villanueva. He sat at a cluttered table, upon which numerous white mice scurried about. There were at least a dozen of them, and they appeared to be multiplying. I spotted a box with a hole in its lid through which opposing traffic issued and vanished.

"You still have the mice," Villanueva said with displeasure.

"We want to sell them," Javier explained.

"So why don't you?"

"We tried. Nobody will buy them."

Javier's girlfriend served up cups of Pepsi and *arroz con leche*. Three children, Villanueva's half-siblings, entered the room. He greeted them cordially, impersonally. I asked their ages, and the woman revealed that today one of the boys had turned ten.

"It's his birthday?" asked Javier, surprised. He laughed. "And his dad didn't even know!"

Javier offered Villanueva a cigarette, and the two of them went outside. It was the first cigarette I'd seen Villanueva smoke. When they came back, they were talking construction. Javier was a tiler by trade. Villanueva told him about some of the carpentry projects he had done in Kansas City. He took out his phone and showed him pictures of the cabinetry he installed in the River Market units.

Javier said nothing.

"Where can I get used lumber to leave Aunt Marta?" Villanueva asked him.

"I don't know."

"How much is half-inch plywood here?"

"I don't know, I need some too," Javier said. "I need to build a bathroom, but I don't have any money." An expectant silence followed, and when it became clear that Villanueva was not going to fill it with an offer of assistance, Javier said, "I'll buy cardboard instead."

Eventually, Villanueva stood to leave. He and Javier shook hands. Javier didn't ask how long Villanueva would be in town or whether he would see him again.

∙　　∙　　∙

Above all, what had caused Bueno to fall in love with Villanueva was his way with Jesse and Briana. From the moment they met at the soccer game, he seemed as enamored of her kids as he was of Bueno. It was Villanueva who, shortly after they started dating, realized that something wasn't right with Jesse. The boy was three and hardly talked. Bueno had told herself that he was just a little late, that some kids developed slower, that it was no big deal. Villanueva insisted on consulting a doctor. Jesse, it turned out, was almost deaf. They had him fit for hearing aids and enrolled him in speech therapy. Jesse quickly turned into a different person. He became loquacious, socialized more with other kids, excelled in his classes.

"Jesse and Briana don't know that he's not their real father," Bueno told me when I met with her in Kansas City a week after I left Honduras. We were sitting in the living room of their apartment. Briana and Jesse were at school; Haley and Jordi were asleep, sprawled in Bueno's lap. "We're not going to keep it a secret forever. I just want them to grow up a little more. I'm afraid to tell them, because they love him so much."

We spoke, then, about the other secret. Bueno still had not revealed to any of the children that Villanueva had been deported. "It's very difficult, because I don't know how to explain it to them," she said. "They've never been separated from him before. I don't know what to say. I just keep telling them that he's traveling for work, he'll be home soon."

Later, while stroking Haley's hair, Bueno said: "It's the hardest for her. She can't sleep at night without him."

Bueno's job cleaning the office building seven nights a week paid about $1,000 a month. A fifth of that she gave to the moneylender from whom she borrowed to pay the immigration attorney. The moneylender had the title to Bueno's car, and what would happen if she fell behind? How would she get Haley and Jordi to school? How would she get to work? Their most valuable possessions had been the power tools that Villanueva had accumulated, piecemeal, over the years: a table saw, a miter saw, half a dozen screw guns. Villanueva had explained to Bueno that it was an investment—this way, he and his team would be less dependent on the gringo contractors. Shortly after Villanueva was detained, however, the contractor for whom he used to work—the one who Villanueva claims owes him $28,000—came to the apartment and left with all the tools, telling Bueno they were his.

At four-thirty, she woke up Jordi and Haley, and the four of us walked down to the highway to meet Briana and Jesse where the school bus dropped them off.

I spotted an energetic, grinning boy with hearing aids running down the sidewalk. A girl in glasses trailed behind them, toting a violin case.

"You must be Briana," I said when she reached us.

"Why does he know our names?" Briana asked her mother.

"He's a friend of your dad's," Bueno said.

"Daddy!"

Briana regarded me anew, and I could see her formulating the question. I braced for it. Where is he? What happened to him? When is he coming home? Then she seemed to think better, and we walked the rest of the way back in silence.

The New Yorker

WINNER—FEATURE WRITING

History suggests that the Pacific Northwest is already overdue for an earthquake of staggering power. "By the time the shaking has ceased and the tsunami receded," writes Kathryn Schulz in "The Really Big One," "the region will be unrecognizable." FEMA estimates that at a minimum, close to 13,000 people will die, 27,000 will be injured, 1 million will be displaced, and millions more will need food and water. The judges who awarded The New Yorker *the National Magazine Award for Feature Writing for this story said that "in language of quiet beauty, Schulz leads us to contemplate unimaginable devastation—in the writer's own words, 'a parable for this age of ecological reckoning.'" Schulz joined* The New Yorker *as a staff writer in 2015. "The Really Big One" also won the 2016 Pulitzer Prize for Feature Writing.*

Kathryn Schulz

The Really Big One

When the 2011 earthquake and tsunami struck Tohoku, Japan, Chris Goldfinger was two hundred miles away, in the city of Kashiwa, at an international meeting on seismology. As the shaking started, everyone in the room began to laugh. Earthquakes are common in Japan—that one was the third of the week—and the participants were, after all, at a seismology conference. Then everyone in the room checked the time.

Seismologists know that how long an earthquake lasts is a decent proxy for its magnitude. The 1989 earthquake in Loma Prieta, California, which killed sixty-three people and caused six billion dollars' worth of damage, lasted about fifteen seconds and had a magnitude of 6.9. A thirty-second earthquake generally has a magnitude in the mid-sevens. A minute-long quake is in the high sevens, a two-minute quake has entered the eights, and a three-minute quake is in the high eights. By four minutes, an earthquake has hit magnitude 9.0.

When Goldfinger looked at his watch, it was quarter to three. The conference was wrapping up for the day. He was thinking about sushi. The speaker at the lectern was wondering if he should carry on with his talk. The earthquake was not particularly strong. Then it ticked past the sixty-second mark, making it longer than the others that week. The shaking intensified. The seats in the conference room were small plastic desks with wheels. Goldfinger, who is tall and solidly built, thought, *No way am I crouching under one of those for cover.* At a minute and a half, everyone in the room got up and went outside.

It was March. There was a chill in the air and snow flurries but no snow on the ground. Nor, from the feel of it, was there ground on the ground. The earth snapped and popped and rippled. It was, Goldfinger thought, like driving through rocky terrain in a vehicle with no shocks, if both the vehicle and the terrain were also on a raft in high seas. The quake passed the two-minute mark. The trees, still hung with the previous autumn's dead leaves, were making a strange rattling sound. The flagpole atop the building he and his colleagues had just vacated was whipping through an arc of forty degrees. The building itself was base-isolated, a seismic-safety technology in which the body of a structure rests on movable bearings rather than directly on its foundation. Goldfinger lurched over to take a look. The base was lurching, too, back and forth a foot at a time, digging a trench in the yard. He thought better of it, and lurched away. His watch swept past the three-minute mark and kept going.

Oh, shit, Goldfinger thought, although not in dread, at first: in amazement. For decades, seismologists had believed that Japan could not experience an earthquake stronger than magnitude 8.4. In 2005, however, at a conference in Hokudan, a Japanese geologist named Yasutaka Ikeda had argued that the nation should expect a magnitude 9.0 in the near future—with catastrophic consequences because Japan's famous earthquake-and-tsunami preparedness, including the height of its sea walls, was based on incorrect science. The presentation was met with polite applause and thereafter largely ignored. Now, Goldfinger realized as the shaking hit the four-minute mark, the planet was proving the Japanese Cassandra right.

For a moment, that was pretty cool: a real-time revolution in earthquake science. Almost immediately, though, it became extremely uncool because Goldfinger and every other seismologist standing outside in Kashiwa knew what was coming. One of them pulled out a cell phone and started streaming videos from the Japanese broadcasting station NHK, shot by helicopters that had flown out to sea soon after the shaking started. Thirty minutes after Goldfinger first stepped outside, he watched the tsunami roll in, in real time, on a two-inch screen.

In the end, the magnitude 9.0 Tohoku earthquake and subsequent tsunami killed more than 18,000 people, devastated northeast Japan, triggered the meltdown at the Fukushima power plant, and cost an estimated 220 billion dollars. The shaking earlier in the week turned out to be the foreshocks of the largest earthquake in the nation's recorded history. But for Chris Goldfinger, a paleoseismologist at Oregon State University and one of the world's leading experts on a little-known fault line, the main quake was itself a kind of foreshock: a preview of another earthquake still to come.

·   ·   ·

Most people in the United States know just one fault line by name: the San Andreas, which runs nearly the length of California and is perpetually rumored to be on the verge of unleashing "the big one." That rumor is misleading, no matter what the San Andreas ever does. Every fault line has an upper limit to its potency, determined by its length and width and by how far it can slip. For the San Andreas, one of the most extensively studied and best understood fault lines in the world, that upper limit is roughly an 8.2—a powerful earthquake but, because the Richter scale is logarithmic, only 6 percent as strong as the 2011 event in Japan.

Just north of the San Andreas, however, lies another fault line. Known as the Cascadia subduction zone, it runs for 700 miles off the coast of the Pacific Northwest, beginning near Cape Mendocino, California, continuing along Oregon and Washington, and terminating around Vancouver Island, Canada. The "Cascadia" part of its name comes from the Cascade Range, a chain of volcanic mountains that follow the same course a hundred or so miles inland. The "subduction zone" part refers to a region of the planet where one tectonic plate is sliding underneath (subducting) another. Tectonic plates are those slabs of mantle and crust that, in their epochs-long drift, rearrange the earth's continents and oceans. Most of the time, their movement is slow, harmless, and all but undetectable. Occasionally, at the borders where they meet, it is not.

Take your hands and hold them palms down, middle fingertips touching. Your right hand represents the North American tectonic plate, which bears on its back, among other things, our entire continent, from One World Trade Center to the Space Needle, in Seattle. Your left hand represents an oceanic plate called Juan de Fuca, 90,000 square miles in size. The place where they meet is the Cascadia subduction zone. Now slide your left hand under your right one. That is what the Juan de Fuca plate is doing: slipping steadily beneath North America. When you try it, your right hand will slide up your left arm, as if you were pushing up your sleeve. That is what North America is not doing. It is stuck, wedged tight against the surface of the other plate.

Without moving your hands, curl your right knuckles up, so that they point toward the ceiling. Under pressure from Juan de Fuca, the stuck edge of North America is bulging upward and compressing eastward, at the rate of, respectively, three to four millimeters and thirty to forty millimeters a year. It can do so for quite some time, because, as continent stuff goes, it is young, made of rock that is still relatively elastic. (Rocks, like us, get stiffer as they age.) But it cannot do so indefinitely. There is a backstop—the craton, that ancient unbudgeable mass at the center of the continent—and, sooner or later, North America will rebound like a spring. If, on that occasion, only the southern part of the Cascadia subduction zone gives way—your first two fingers, say—the magnitude of the resulting quake will be somewhere between 8.0 and 8.6. *That's* the big one. If the entire zone gives way at once, an event that seismologists call a full-margin rupture, the magnitude will be somewhere between 8.7 and 9.2. That's the very big one.

Flick your right fingers outward, forcefully, so that your hand flattens back down again. When the next very big earthquake hits, the northwest edge of the continent, from California to Canada and the continental shelf to the Cascades, will drop by as much as six feet and rebound thirty to a hundred feet to the west—losing, within minutes, all the elevation and compression it has gained over centuries. Some of that shift will take place beneath the ocean, displacing a colossal quantity of seawater. (Watch what your fingertips do when you flatten your hand.) The water will surge upward into a huge hill, then promptly collapse. One side will rush west, toward Japan. The other side will rush east, in a seven-hundred-mile liquid wall that will reach the Northwest coast, on average, fifteen minutes after the earthquake begins. By the time the shaking has ceased and the tsunami has receded, the region will be unrecognizable. Kenneth Murphy, who directs FEMA's Region X, the division responsible for Oregon, Washington, Idaho, and Alaska, says, "Our operating assumption is that everything west of Interstate 5 will be toast."

In the Pacific Northwest, the area of impact will cover some 140,000 square miles, including Seattle, Tacoma, Portland, Eugene, Salem (the capital city of Oregon), Olympia (the capital of Washington), and some seven million people. When the next full-margin rupture happens, that region will suffer the worst natural disaster in the history of North America. Roughly 3,000 people died in San Francisco's 1906 earthquake. Almost 2,000 died in Hurricane Katrina. Almost 300 died in Hurricane Sandy. FEMA projects that nearly 13,000 people will die in the Cascadia earthquake and tsunami. Another 27,000 will be injured, and the agency expects that it will need to provide shelter for a million displaced people and food and water for another two and a half million. "This is one time that I'm hoping all the science is wrong, and it won't happen for another thousand years," Murphy says.

In fact, the science is robust, and one of the chief scientists behind it is Chris Goldfinger. Thanks to work done by him and his colleagues, we now know that the odds of the big Cascadia earthquake happening in the next fifty years are roughly one in three. The odds of the very big one are roughly one in ten. Even those numbers do not fully reflect the danger—or, more to the point, how unprepared the Pacific Northwest is to face it. The truly worrisome figures in this story are these: Thirty years ago, no one knew that the Cascadia subduction zone had ever produced a major earthquake. Forty-five years ago, no one even knew it existed.

.   .   .

In May of 1804, Meriwether Lewis and William Clark, together with their Corps of Discovery, set off from St. Louis on America's first official cross-country expedition. Eighteen months later, they reached the Pacific Ocean and made camp near the present-day town of Astoria, Oregon. The United States was, at the time, twenty-nine years old. Canada was not yet a country. The continent's far expanses were so unknown to its white explorers that Thomas Jefferson, who commissioned the journey, thought that the men would come across woolly mammoths. Native Americans had lived in the Northwest for millennia, but they had no written language, and the many things to which the arriving Europeans subjected them did not include seismological inquiries. The newcomers took the land they encountered at face value, and at face value it was a find: vast, cheap, temperate, fertile, and, to all appearances, remarkably benign.

A century and a half elapsed before anyone had any inkling that the Pacific Northwest was not a quiet place but a place in a long period of quiet. It took another fifty years to uncover and interpret the region's seismic history. Geology, as even geologists will tell you, is not normally the sexiest of disciplines; it hunkers down with earthly stuff while the glory accrues to the human and the cosmic—to genetics, neuroscience, physics. But, sooner or later, every field has its field day, and the discovery of the Cascadia subduction zone stands as one of the greatest scientific detective stories of our time.

The first clue came from geography. Almost all of the world's most powerful earthquakes occur in the Ring of Fire, the volcanically and seismically volatile swath of the Pacific that runs from New Zealand up through Indonesia and Japan, across the ocean to Alaska, and down the west coast of the Americas to Chile. Japan, 2011, magnitude 9.0; Indonesia, 2004, magnitude 9.1; Alaska, 1964, magnitude 9.2; Chile, 1960, magnitude 9.5—not until the late 1960s, with the rise of the theory of plate tectonics, could geologists explain this pattern. The Ring of Fire, it turns out, is really a ring of subduction zones. Nearly all the earthquakes in the region are caused by continental plates getting stuck on oceanic plates—as North America is stuck on Juan de Fuca—and then getting abruptly unstuck. And nearly all the volcanoes are caused by the oceanic plates sliding deep beneath the continental ones, eventually reaching temperatures and pressures so extreme that they melt the rock above them.

The Pacific Northwest sits squarely within the Ring of Fire. Off its coast, an oceanic plate is slipping beneath a continental one. Inland, the Cascade volcanoes mark the line where, far below, the Juan de Fuca plate is heating up and melting everything above it. In other words, the Cascadia subduction zone has, as Goldfinger put it, "all the right anatomical parts." Yet not once in recorded history has it caused a major earthquake—or, for that matter, any quake to speak of. By contrast, other subduction zones produce major earthquakes occasionally and minor ones all the time: magnitude 5.0, magnitude 4.0, magnitude why are the neighbors moving their sofa at midnight. You can scarcely spend a week in Japan without feeling this sort of earthquake. You can spend a lifetime in many parts of the Northwest—several, in fact, if you had them to spend—and not feel so much as a quiver. The question facing geologists in the 1970s was whether the Cascadia subduction zone had ever broken its eerie silence.

In the late 1980s, Brian Atwater, a geologist with the United States Geological Survey, and a graduate student named David Yamaguchi found the answer and another major clue in the Cascadia puzzle. Their discovery is best illustrated in a place called the ghost forest, a grove of western red cedars on the banks of the Copalis River, near the Washington coast. When I paddled out to it last summer with Atwater and Yamaguchi, it was easy to see how it got its name. The cedars are spread out across a low salt marsh on a wide northern bend in the river, long dead but still standing. Leafless, branchless, barkless, they are reduced to their trunks and worn to a smooth silver-gray, as if they had always carried their own tombstones inside them.

What killed the trees in the ghost forest was saltwater. It had long been assumed that they died slowly as the sea level around them gradually rose and submerged their roots. But, by 1987, Atwater, who had found in soil layers evidence of sudden land subsidence along the Washington coast, suspected that that was backward—that the trees had died quickly when the ground beneath them plummeted. To find out, he teamed up with Yamaguchi, a specialist in dendrochronology, the study of growth-ring patterns in trees. Yamaguchi took samples of the cedars and found that they had died simultaneously: in tree after tree, the final rings dated to the summer of 1699. Since trees do not grow in the winter, he and Atwater concluded that sometime between August of 1699 and May of 1700 an earthquake had caused the land to drop and killed the cedars. That time frame predated by more than a hundred years the written history of the Pacific Northwest—and so, by rights, the detective story should have ended there.

But it did not. If you travel 5,000 miles due west from the ghost forest, you reach the northeast coast of Japan. As the events of 2011 made clear, that coast is vulnerable to tsunamis, and the Japanese have kept track of them since at least 599 AD. In that 1,400-year history, one incident has long stood out for its strangeness. On the eighth day of the twelfth month of the twelfth year of the Genroku era, a six-hundred-mile-long wave struck the coast, leveling homes, breaching a castle moat, and causing an accident at sea. The Japanese understood that tsunamis were the result of earthquakes, yet no one felt the ground shake before the Genroku event. The wave had no discernible origin. When scientists began studying it, they called it an orphan tsunami.

Finally, in a 1996 article in *Nature*, a seismologist named Kenji Satake and three colleagues, drawing on the work of Atwater and Yamaguchi, matched that orphan to its parent—and thereby filled in the blanks in the Cascadia story with uncanny specificity. At approximately nine o'clock at night on January 26, 1700, a magnitude 9.0 earthquake struck the Pacific Northwest, causing sudden land subsidence, drowning coastal forests, and, out in the ocean, lifting up a wave half the length of a continent. It took roughly fifteen minutes for the Eastern half of that wave to strike the Northwest coast. It took ten hours for the other half to cross the ocean. It reached Japan on January 27, 1700: by the local calendar, the eighth day of the twelfth month of the twelfth year of Genroku.

Once scientists had reconstructed the 1700 earthquake, certain previously overlooked accounts also came to seem like clues. In 1964, Chief Louis Nookmis, of the Huu-ay-aht First Nation, in British Columbia, told a story, passed down through seven generations, about the eradication of Vancouver Island's Pachena Bay people. "I think it was at nighttime that the land shook," Nookmis recalled. According to another tribal history, "They sank at once, were all drowned; not one survived." A hundred years earlier, Billy Balch, a leader of the Makah tribe, recounted a similar story. Before his own time, he said, all the water had receded from Washington State's Neah Bay, then suddenly poured back in, inundating the entire region. Those who survived later found canoes hanging from the trees. In a 2005 study, Ruth Ludwin, then a seismologist at the University of Washington, together with nine colleagues, collected and analyzed Native American reports of earthquakes and saltwater floods. Some of those reports contained enough information to estimate a date range for the events they described. On average, the midpoint of that range was 1701.

It does not speak well of European Americans that such stories counted as evidence for a proposition only after that proposition had been proved. Still, the reconstruction of the Cascadia earthquake of 1700 is one of those rare natural puzzles whose pieces fit together as tectonic plates do not: perfectly. It is wonderful science. It was wonderful *for* science. And it was terrible news for the millions of inhabitants of the Pacific Northwest. As Goldfinger put it, "In the late eighties and early nineties, the paradigm shifted to 'uh-oh.'"

Goldfinger told me this in his lab at Oregon State, a low prefab building that a passing English major might reasonably mistake for the maintenance department. Inside the lab is a walk-in freezer. Inside the freezer are floor-to-ceiling racks filled with cryptically labeled tubes, four inches in diameter and five feet long. Each tube contains a core sample of the seafloor. Each sample contains the history, written in seafloorese, of the past 10,000 years. During subduction-zone earthquakes, torrents of land rush off the continental slope, leaving a permanent deposit on the bottom of the ocean. By counting the number and the size of deposits in each sample, then comparing their extent and consistency along the length of the Cascadia subduction zone, Goldfinger and his colleagues were able to determine how much of the zone has ruptured, how often, and how drastically.

Thanks to that work, we now know that the Pacific Northwest has experienced forty-one subduction-zone earthquakes in the past 10,000 years. If you divide 10,000 by 41, you get 243, which is Cascadia's recurrence interval: the average amount of time that elapses between earthquakes. That time span is dangerous both because it is too long—long enough for us to unwittingly build an entire civilization on top of our continent's worst fault line— and because it is not long enough. Counting from the earthquake of 1700, we are now 315 years into a 243-year cycle.

It is possible to quibble with that number. Recurrence intervals are averages, and averages are tricky: ten is the average of nine and eleven but also of eighteen and two. It is not possible, however, to dispute the scale of the problem. The devastation in Japan in 2011 was the result of a discrepancy between what the best science predicted and what the region was prepared to withstand. The same will hold true in the Pacific Northwest—but here the discrepancy is enormous. "The science part is fun," Goldfinger says. "And I love doing it. But the gap between what we know and what we should do about it is getting bigger and bigger, and the action really needs to turn to responding. Otherwise, we're going to be hammered. I've been through one of these massive earthquakes in the most seismically prepared nation on earth. If that was Portland"—Goldfinger finished the sentence with a shake of his head before he finished it with words. "Let's just say I would rather not be here."

· · ·

The first sign that the Cascadia earthquake has begun will be a compressional wave, radiating outward from the fault line. Compressional waves are fast-moving, high-frequency waves, audible to dogs and certain other animals but experienced by humans only as a sudden jolt. They are not very harmful, but they are potentially very useful since they travel fast enough to be detected by sensors thirty to ninety seconds ahead of other seismic waves. That is enough time for earthquake early-warning systems, such as those in use throughout Japan, to automatically perform a variety of lifesaving functions: shutting down railways and power plants, opening elevators and firehouse doors, alerting hospitals to halt surgeries, and triggering alarms so that the general public can take cover. The Pacific Northwest has no early-warning system. When the Cascadia earthquake begins, there will be, instead, a cacophony of barking dogs and a long, suspended, what-was-that moment before the surface waves arrive. Surface waves are slower, lower-frequency waves that move the ground both up and down and side to side: the shaking, starting in earnest.

Soon after that shaking begins, the electrical grid will fail, likely everywhere west of the Cascades and possibly well beyond. If it happens at night, the ensuing catastrophe will unfold in darkness. In theory, those who are at home when it hits should be safest; it is easy and relatively inexpensive to seismically safeguard a private dwelling. But, lulled into nonchalance by their seemingly benign environment, most people in the Pacific Northwest have not done so. That nonchalance will shatter instantly. So will everything made of glass. Anything indoors and unsecured will lurch across the floor or come crashing down: bookshelves, lamps, computers, canisters of flour in the pantry. Refrigerators will walk out of kitchens, unplugging themselves and toppling over. Water heaters will fall and smash interior gas lines. Houses that are not bolted to their foundations will slide off—or, rather, they will stay put, obeying inertia, while the foundations, together with the rest of the Northwest, jolt westward. Unmoored on the undulating ground, the homes will begin to collapse.

Across the region, other, larger structures will also start to fail. Until 1974, the state of Oregon had no seismic code, and few places in the Pacific Northwest had one appropriate to a magnitude 9.0 earthquake until 1994. The vast majority of buildings in the region were constructed before then. Ian Madin, who directs the Oregon Department of Geology and Mineral Industries (DOGAMI), estimates that 75 percent of all structures in the state are not designed to withstand a major Cascadia quake. FEMA calculates that, across the region, something on the order of a million buildings—more than 3,000 of them schools—will collapse or be compromised in the earthquake. So will half of all highway bridges, fifteen of the seventeen bridges spanning Portland's two rivers, and two-thirds of railways and airports; also, one-third of all fire stations, half of all police stations, and two-thirds of all hospitals.

Certain disasters stem from many small problems conspiring to cause one very large problem. For want of a nail, the war was lost; for fifteen independently insignificant errors, the jetliner was lost. Subduction-zone earthquakes operate on the opposite principle: one enormous problem causes many other enormous problems. The shaking from the Cascadia quake will set off landslides throughout the region—up to 30,000 of them in Seattle alone, the city's emergency-management office estimates. It will also induce a process called liquefaction, whereby seemingly solid ground starts behaving like a liquid, to the detriment of anything on top of it. Fifteen percent of Seattle is built on liquefiable land, including seventeen day-care centers and the homes of some 34,500 people. So is Oregon's critical energy-infrastructure hub, a six-mile stretch of Portland through which flows 90 percent of the state's liquid fuel and which houses everything from electrical substations to natural-gas terminals. Together, the sloshing, sliding, and shaking will trigger fires, flooding, pipe failures, dam breaches, and hazardous-material spills. Any one of these second-order disasters could swamp the original earthquake in terms of cost, damage, or casualties—and one of them definitely will. Four to six minutes after the dogs start barking, the shaking will subside. For another few minutes, the region, upended, will continue to fall apart on its own. Then the wave will arrive, and the real destruction will begin.

Among natural disasters, tsunamis may be the closest to being completely unsurvivable. The only likely way to outlive one is not to be there when it happens: to steer clear of the vulnerable area in the first place or get yourself to high ground as fast as possible. For the 71,000 people who live in Cascadia's inundation zone, that will mean evacuating in the narrow window after one disaster ends and before another begins. They will be notified to do so only by the earthquake itself—"a vibrate-alert system," Kevin Cupples, the city planner for the town of Seaside, Oregon, jokes—and they are urged to leave on foot, since the earthquake will render roads impassable. Depending on location, they will have between ten and thirty minutes to get out. That time line does not allow for finding a flashlight, tending to an earthquake injury, hesitating amid the ruins of a home, searching for loved ones, or being a Good Samaritan. "When that tsunami is coming, you run," Jay Wilson, the chair of the Oregon Seismic Safety Policy Advisory Commission (OSSPAC), says. "You protect yourself, you don't turn around, you don't go back to save anybody. You run for your life."

The time to save people from a tsunami is before it happens, but the region has not yet taken serious steps toward doing so. Hotels and businesses are not required to post evacuation routes or to provide employees with evacuation training. In Oregon, it has been illegal since 1995 to build hospitals, schools, firehouses, and police stations in the inundation zone, but those which are already in it can stay, and any other new construction is permissible: energy facilities, hotels, retirement homes. In those cases, builders are required only to consult with DOGAMI about evacuation plans. "So you come in and sit down," Ian Madin says. "And I say, 'That's a stupid idea.' And you say, 'Thanks. Now we've consulted.'"

These lax safety policies guarantee that many people inside the inundation zone will not get out. Twenty-two percent of Oregon's coastal population is sixty-five or older. Twenty-nine percent of the state's population is disabled, and that figure rises in many coastal counties. "We can't save them," Kevin Cupples says. "I'm not going to sugarcoat it and say, 'Oh, yeah, we'll go around and check on the elderly.' No. We won't." Nor will anyone save the tourists. Washington State Park properties within the inundation zone see an average of 17,029 guests a day. Madin estimates that up to a 150,000 people visit Oregon's beaches on summer weekends. "Most of them won't have a clue as to how to evacuate," he says. "And the beaches are the hardest place to evacuate from."

Those who cannot get out of the inundation zone under their own power will quickly be overtaken by a greater one. A grown man is knocked over by ankle-deep water moving at 6.7 miles an hour. The tsunami will be moving more than twice that fast when it arrives. Its height will vary with the contours of the coast, from twenty feet to more than a hundred feet. It will not look like a Hokusai-style wave, rising up from the surface of the sea and breaking from above. It will look like the whole ocean, elevated, overtaking land. Nor will it be made only of water—not once it reaches the shore. It will be a five-story deluge of pickup trucks and doorframes and cinder blocks and fishing boats and utility poles and everything else that once constituted the coastal towns of the Pacific Northwest.

To see the full scale of the devastation when that tsunami recedes, you would need to be in the international space station. The inundation zone will be scoured of structures from California to Canada. The earthquake will have wrought its worst havoc west of the Cascades but caused damage as far away as Sacramento, California—as distant from the worst-hit areas as Fort Wayne, Indiana, is from New York. FEMA expects to coordinate search-and-rescue operations across 100,000 square miles and in the waters off 453 miles of coastline. As for casualties: the figures I cited earlier—27,000 injured, almost 13,000 dead—are based on the agency's official planning scenario, which has the earthquake striking at 9:41 AM on February sixth. If, instead, it strikes in the summer, when the beaches are full, those numbers could be off by a horrifying margin.

Wineglasses, antique vases, Humpty Dumpty, hip bones, hearts: what breaks quickly generally mends slowly, if at all. OSSPAC estimates that in the I-5 corridor it will take between one and three months after the earthquake to restore electricity, a month to a year to restore drinking water and sewer service, six months to a year to restore major highways, and eighteen months to restore health-care facilities. On the coast, those numbers go up. Whoever chooses or has no choice but to stay there will spend three to six months without electricity, one to three years without drinking water and sewage systems, and three or more years without hospitals. Those estimates do not apply to the tsunami-inundation zone, which will remain all but uninhabitable for years.

How much all this will cost is anyone's guess; FEMA puts every number on its relief-and-recovery plan except a price. But whatever the ultimate figure—and even though U.S. taxpayers will cover 75 to 100 percent of the damage, as happens in declared disasters—the economy of the Pacific Northwest will collapse. Crippled by a lack of basic services, businesses will fail or move away. Many residents will flee as well. OSSPAC predicts a mass-displacement event and a long-term population downturn. Chris Goldfinger didn't want to be there when it happened. But, by many metrics, it will be as bad or worse to be there afterward.

.   .   .

On the face of it, earthquakes seem to present us with problems of space: the way we live along fault lines, in brick buildings, in homes made valuable by their proximity to the sea. But, covertly, they also present us with problems of time. The earth is 4.5 billion years old, but we are a young species, relatively speaking, with an average individual allotment of three score years and ten. The brevity of our lives breeds a kind of temporal parochialism—an ignorance of or an indifference to those planetary gears that turn more slowly than our own.

This problem is bidirectional. The Cascadia subduction zone remained hidden from us for so long because we could not see deep enough into the past. It poses a danger to us today because we have not thought deeply enough about the future. That is no longer a problem of information; we now understand very well what the Cascadia fault line will someday do. Nor is it a problem of imagination. If you are so inclined, you can watch an earthquake destroy much of the West Coast this summer in Brad Peyton's *San Andreas* while, in neighboring theatres, the world threatens to succumb to Armageddon by other means: viruses, robots, resource scarcity, zombies, aliens, plague. As those movies attest, we excel at imagining future scenarios, including awful ones. But such apocalyptic visions are a form of escapism, not a moral summons, and still less a plan of action. Where we stumble is in conjuring up grim futures in a way that helps to avert them.

That problem is not specific to earthquakes, of course. The Cascadia situation, a calamity in its own right, is also a parable for this age of ecological reckoning, and the questions it raises are ones that we all now face. How should a society respond to a looming crisis of uncertain timing but of catastrophic proportions? How can it begin to right itself when its entire infrastructure and culture developed in a way that leaves it profoundly vulnerable to natural disaster?

The last person I met with in the Pacific Northwest was Doug Dougherty, the superintendent of schools for Seaside, which lies almost entirely within the tsunami-inundation zone. Of the four schools that Dougherty oversees, with a total student population of 1,600, one is relatively safe. The others sit five to fifteen feet above sea level. When the tsunami comes, they will be as much as forty-five feet below it.

In 2009, Dougherty told me, he found some land for sale outside the inundation zone, and proposed building a new K-12 campus there. Four years later, to foot the $128 million bill, the district put up a bond measure. The tax increase for residents amounted to $2.16 per thousand dollars of property value. The measure failed by 62 percent. Dougherty tried seeking help from Oregon's congressional delegation but came up empty. The state makes money available for seismic upgrades, but buildings within the inundation zone cannot apply. At present, all Dougherty can do is make sure that his students know how to evacuate.

Some of them, however, will not be able to do so. At an elementary school in the community of Gearhart, the children will be trapped. "They can't make it out from that school," Dougherty said. "They have no place to go." On one side lies the ocean; on the other, a wide, roadless bog. When the tsunami comes, the only place to go in Gearhart is a small ridge just behind the school. At its tallest, it is forty-five feet high—lower than the expected wave in a full-margin earthquake. For now, the route to the ridge is marked by signs that say "Temporary Tsunami Assembly Area." I asked Dougherty about the state's long-range plan. "There is no long-range plan," he said.

Dougherty's office is deep inside the inundation zone, a few blocks from the beach. All day long, just out of sight, the ocean rises up and collapses, spilling foamy overlapping ovals onto the shore. Eighty miles farther out, ten thousand feet below the surface of the sea, the hand of a geological clock is somewhere in its slow sweep. All across the region, seismologists are looking at their watches, wondering how long we have, and what we will do, before geological time catches up to our own.

The Marshall Project and *ProPublica*

FINALIST—FEATURE
WRITING

A victim nobody in Seattle believed, a serial rapist in Colorado, two detectives who finally connected the two cases— "An Unbelievable Story of Rape" makes for gripping reading on its own. But the story is also a thoughtful examination of our society's uneven response to sex crimes as well as an example of both successful policing and abuse of power. When reporters for the Marshall Project and ProPublica discovered they were working on the same story, the two nonprofit newsrooms agreed to collaborate. How T. Christian Miller and Ken Armstrong worked together to report "An Unbelievable Story of Rape" is carefully explained in an online postscript to the article. One of seven finalists for the 2016 National Magazine Award for Feature Writing, the story won the 2016 Pulitzer Prize for Explanatory Reporting.

Ken Armstrong and
T. Christian Miller

An Unbelievable Story of Rape

March 12, 2009. Lynnwood, Washington

No one came to court with her that day, except her public defender.

She was eighteen years old, charged with a gross misdemeanor, punishable by up to a year in jail.

Rarely do misdemeanors draw notice. Her case was one of 4,859 filed in 2008 in Lynnwood Municipal Court, a place where the judge says the goal is "to correct behavior—to make Lynnwood a better, safer, healthier place to live, work, shop and visit."

But her misdemeanor had made the news and made her an object of curiosity or, worse, scorn. It had cost her the newfound independence she was savoring after a life in foster homes. It had cost her sense of worth. Each ring of the phone seemed to announce another friendship lost. A friend from tenth grade called to ask: How could you lie about something like that? Marie—that's her middle name, Marie—didn't say anything. She just listened, then hung up. Even her foster parents now doubted her. She doubted herself, wondering if there was something in her that needed to be fixed.

She had reported being raped in her apartment by a man who had bound and gagged her. Then, confronted by police with inconsistencies in her story, she had conceded it might have been a dream. Then she admitted making the story up. One TV newscast announced, "A Western Washington woman has confessed that she cried wolf when it came to her rape she reported earlier this week." She had been charged with filing a false report, which is why she was here today, to accept or turn down a plea deal.

Her lawyer was surprised she had been charged. Her story hadn't hurt anyone—no suspects arrested or even questioned. His guess was, the police felt used. They don't appreciate having their time wasted.

The prosecution's offer was this: If she met certain conditions for the next year, the charge would be dropped. She would need to get mental-health counseling for her lying. She would need to go on supervised probation. She would need to keep straight, breaking no more laws. And she would have to pay $500 to cover the court's costs.

Marie wanted this behind her.

She took the deal.

January 5, 2011. Golden, Colorado

A little after one p.m. on a wintry day in January 2011, Detective Stacy Galbraith approached a long, anonymous row of apartment buildings that spilled up a low hill in a Denver suburb. Snow covered the ground in patches. It was blustery and biting cold. She was there to investigate a report of rape.

Galbraith spotted the victim standing in the thin sunlight outside her ground floor apartment. She was young, dressed in a brown, full-length coat. She clutched a bag of her belongings in one hand. She looked calm, unflustered. Galbraith introduced herself. Police technicians were swarming the apartment. Galbraith suggested that she and the victim escape the icy gusts in a nearby unmarked patrol car.

The woman told Galbraith she was twenty-six years old, an engineering student on winter break from a nearby college. She had been alone in her apartment the previous evening. After cooking green mung beans for dinner, she curled up in bed for a marathon of *Desperate Housewives* and *The Big Bang Theory* until drifting off. At around eight a.m., she was jolted awake by a man who had jumped on her back, pinning her to the bed. He wore a black mask that seemed more like a scarf fastened tight around his face. He gripped a silver and black gun. "Don't scream. Don't call or I'll shoot you," he told her.

He moved deliberately. He tied her hands loosely behind her. From a large black bag, he took out thigh-high stockings, clear plastic high heels with pink ribbons, lubrication, a box of moist towelettes and bottled water. Over the next four hours, he raped her repeatedly. He documented the assault with a digital camera and threatened to post the pictures online if she contacted the police. Afterward, he ordered her to brush her teeth and wash herself in the shower. By the time she exited the bathroom, he had gone. He had taken her sheets and bedding. She clearly remembered one physical detail about him: a dark mark on his left calf the size of an egg.

Galbraith listened to the woman with a sense of alarm. The attack was so heinous; the attacker, so practiced. There was no time to waste. Sitting close to her in the front seat of the car, Galbraith carefully brushed the woman's face with long cotton swabs to collect any DNA traces that might remain. Then she drove her to St. Anthony North Hospital. The woman underwent a special forensic examination to collect more DNA evidence. Before she left with a nurse, the woman warned Galbraith, "I think he's done this before."

Galbraith returned to the crime scene. A half-dozen officers and technicians were now at work. They were knocking on neighbors' doors, snapping photographs in the apartment, digging through garbage bins, swabbing the walls, the windows, everywhere for DNA. In the snow, they found a trail of footprints leading to and from the back of the apartment through an empty field. They spraypainted the prints fluorescent orange to make them stand out, then took pictures. It was not much. But something. One officer suggested a bathroom break. "Just keep working!" Galbraith insisted.

As she headed home that night, Galbraith's mind raced. "Who is this guy?" she asked herself. "How am I going to find him?" Galbraith often volunteered to take rape cases. She was a wife, a mother. She was good at empathizing with the victims, who were overwhelmingly women. Most had been assaulted by a boyfriend, an old flame, or someone they had met at a club. Those investigations often boiled down to an issue of consent. Had the woman said "yes"? They were tough for cops and prosecutors. Juries were hesitant to throw someone in prison when it was one person's word against another's. Rapes by strangers were uncommon—about 13 percent of cases. But there was still the issue of the woman's story. Was she telling the truth? Or fabricating a ruse to cover a sexual encounter gone wrong?

In that way, rape cases were unlike most other crimes. The credibility of the victim was often on trial as much as the guilt of the accused. And on the long, fraught trail between crime and conviction, the first triers of fact were the cops. An investigating officer had to figure out if the victim was telling the truth.

Galbraith had a simple rule: listen and verify. "A lot of times people say, 'Believe your victim, believe your victim,'" Galbraith said. "But I don't think that that's the right standpoint. I think it's listen to your victim. And then corroborate or refute based on how things go."

At home, her husband David had done the dishes and put the kids to bed. They sank down on separate couches in their living room. Galbraith recounted the day's events. The attacker had been cunning, attempting to erase any traces of DNA from the scene. Before he left, he showed the student how he broke in through a sliding glass door. He suggested she put a dowel into the bottom track to keep out future intruders. The victim had described him as a "gentleman," Galbraith said. "He's going to be hard to find," she thought.

David Galbraith was used to such bleak stories. They were both cops, after all. He worked in Westminster, some fifteen miles to the northeast. Golden and Westminster were middle-class bedroom towns wedged between Denver's downtown skyscrapers and the looming Rockies.

This time, though, there was something different. As David listened, he realized that the details of the case were unsettlingly familiar. He told his wife to call his department first thing in the morning.

"We have one just like that," he said.

Lynnwood, Washington

> She does not know if she attended kindergarten.
> She remembers being hungry and eating dog food.
> She reports entering foster care at age six or seven.

The report on Marie's life—written by a mental-health expert who interviewed her for five hours—is written with clinical detachment, describing her life before she entered foster care . . .

> She met her biological father only once.
> She reports not knowing much about her biological mother, who she said would often leave her in the care of boyfriends.
> She was sexually and physically abused.

. . . and after, with:

> adult caregivers and professionals coming in and then out of her life, some distressing or abusive experiences, and a general lack of permanency.

"I moved a lot when I was younger," Marie says in an interview. "I was in group homes, too. About two of those and probably ten or eleven foster homes."

"I was on like seven different drugs. And Zoloft is an adult drug—I was on that at eight."

Marie has two brothers and a sister on her mother's side. Sometimes she was placed in foster homes with her siblings. More often they were separated.

No one really explained why she was being moved or what was going on. She was just moved.

After Marie became a teenager, her years of upheaval appeared at an end. Her foster family was going to adopt her. "I really loved the family, and I made a lot of friends," Marie says.

The first day of the first year of high school fills many students with anxiety. Marie couldn't wait for it. She had gotten all the classes she wanted. She had a social circle. She felt like she belonged.

But on the first day, a support counselor came to the school and told Marie the family had lost its foster-care license. She couldn't live with them anymore. The counselor couldn't offer any more details.

"I pretty much just cried," Marie says. "I basically had twenty minutes to pack my stuff and go."

Until something more permanent could be found, Marie moved in with Shannon McQuery and her husband in Bellevue, a booming, high-tech suburb east of Seattle. Shannon, a real-estate agent and longtime foster mom, had met Marie through meetings for kids with troubled pasts and had sensed a kindred spirit.

Shannon and Marie were both "kind of goofy," Shannon says. "We could laugh at each other and make fun. We were a lot alike." Despite all Marie had been through, "she wasn't bitter," Shannon says. She kept in touch with previous foster families. She could carry on a conversation with adults. She didn't have to be pushed out the door to school.

But no matter her affection for Marie, Shannon knew they couldn't keep her because the foster child already in their home required so much care. "We were really sad that we weren't able to have her with us," Shannon says.

Marie left Shannon's home after a couple of weeks to move in with Peggy Cunningham, who worked as a children's advocate at a homeless shelter and lived in Lynnwood, a smaller suburb about fifteen miles north of Seattle. She was Peggy's first foster child.

"I was preparing for a baby. I had a crib—and they gave me a sixteen-year-old," Peggy says, with a laugh. "And it was fine. I have a background in mental health and I've been working with kids for a really long time. And I think the agency just thought, 'She can handle it.' So."

At first, Marie didn't want to live with Peggy. Marie was used to being around other kids. Peggy didn't have any. Marie liked dogs. Peggy had two cats. "Our personalities didn't match at first either," Marie says. "It was hard to get along. For me it seems like people read me differently than I see myself."

Peggy, who had received a file two to three inches thick documenting Marie's history, was surprised at how well she was coping. Marie was into boys, drawing, and music, be it rock, country, or Christian. "She was very bubbly and full of energy, but she also had her moments where she could be very intense," Peggy says. Like kids most everywhere, Marie wanted to fit in. She picked out a feminine white coat with a fur collar because she thought that's what girls were supposed to wear but then kept the coat in the closet when she realized it wasn't.

Recognizing that Marie's high school wasn't a great fit—"pretty cliquey," Peggy says—Peggy found an alternative school that was. Marie settled in. She remained close with Shannon, who would joke that she and Peggy were raising Marie together—Shannon the fun one (*let's go boating*), Peggy the disciplinarian (*be home by . . .*).

Through friends, Marie met Jordan Schweitzer, a high-school student working at a McDonald's. In time, they became boyfriend and girlfriend. "She was just a nice person to have around. She was always nice to talk to," Jordan says.

Marie figures her happiest years were when she was sixteen and seventeen, and the happiest day may have been one she spent with her best friend, another high-school student who was teaching Marie the fine points of camerawork.

"I would spend hours at the beach watching the sunset go down, and that was one of my favorite things. There was a particular photo that I really liked that she took. We went to the ocean, it was like seven o'clock at night, I don't know what we were thinking, I got in there and I jumped out and swung my hair back."

Instead of finishing high school, Marie went for her GED. She was seventeen, starting to stay out late, worrying Peggy, creating tension between the two. In the spring of 2008, Marie turned eighteen. She could have stayed with Peggy, provided she abided by certain rules. But Marie wanted to set out on her own.

Peggy, searching online, discovered a pilot program called Project Ladder. Launched the year before, the program was designed to help young adults who had grown up in foster care transition to living on their own. Case managers would show participants the dos and don'ts of shopping for groceries, handling a credit card, buying insurance. "The rules about life," Marie says. Best of all, Project Ladder provided subsidized housing, with each member getting a one-bedroom apartment.

"This was a godsend," Peggy says.

There were few slots, but Marie secured one. She was a little scared, but any trepidation was tempered by a sense of pride. She moved into the Alderbrooke Apartments, a woodsy complex that advertises proximity to a mall and views of the Cascades. She also landed her first job, offering food samples to customers at Costco. Six hours on her feet didn't bother her. She enjoyed chatting with people, free from pressure to sell.

So many kids, institutionalized, wound up on drugs or in jail. Marie had made it through.

"It was just nice to be on my own and not have all the rules that I had had being in foster care," Marie says. "It was just like, freedom.

"It was awesome."

January 6, 2011. Golden, Colorado

The morning after the rape in Golden, Galbraith hurried to work to follow up her husband's lead. At 9:07 a.m. she sent an e-mail to the Westminster Police Department. The subject line was pleading: "Sex Aslt Similars?"

Westminster detective Edna Hendershot had settled into her morning with her Starbucks usual: a venti, upside-down, skinny caramel macchiato. She read the e-mail and her mind shot back five months, to a crisp Tuesday in August 2010. She had responded to a report of a rape at a blue-collar apartment complex in the northwest corner of her city. A fifty-nine-year-old woman told her that she had been asleep in her home when a man jumped on her back. He wore a black mask. He tied her hands. He stole her pink Sony Cyber-shot camera and used it to take pictures of her. Afterward, he made her take a shower. He picked up a kitchen timer and set it to let her know when she could get out. "I guess you won't leave your windows open in the future," the man told the woman, who had recently been widowed.

There was more. Hendershot remembered that while investigating her case, an officer had alerted her to an incident in October 2009 in Aurora, a suburb on the other side of Denver. There, a sixty-five-year-old woman told police that she had been raped in her apartment by a man with a black scarf wrapped around his face. He tied her hands with a ribbon. He took pictures and threatened to post them on the Internet. During the attack, he knocked a yellow teddy bear off a desk in her bedroom. "You should get help," the woman, a house mother at a local fraternity, told the man. "It's too late for that," he replied.

Cops can be protective about their cases, fearing that information could be leaked that would jeopardize their investigations. They often don't know about, or fail to use, an FBI database created years ago to help catch repeat offenders. Between one-fourth to two-thirds of rapists are serial attackers, studies show.

But Hendershot right away recognized the potential in collaborating and in using every tool possible. "Two heads, three heads, four heads, sometimes are better than one, right?" she said. So did Galbraith. Her department was small—a little more than forty officers serving a town of about 20,000. It only made sense to join forces. "I have no qualms with asking for help," Galbraith said. "Let's do what we can do to catch him."

A week later, Galbraith, Hendershot, and Aurora detective Scott Burgess gathered around a conference table in the Westminster Police Department. They compared investigations. The descriptions of the attacker were similar. So, too, his methods. But there was a clincher: the woman in Galbraith's case had remained as focused as possible during her ordeal, memorizing details. She recalled the camera that the attacker had used to take photos. It was a pink Sony digital camera—a description that fit the model stolen from the apartment of the Westminster victim.

Galbraith and Hendershot hadn't known each other before the meeting. But the hunt for the rapist united them. As female cops, both women were members of a sorority within a fraternity. The average law-enforcement agency in America is about 13 percent female. Police ranks remain overwhelmingly male, often hierarchical and militaristic. But both women had found a place for themselves. They had moved up in the ranks.

The two bonded naturally. Both were outgoing. They cracked fast jokes and smiled fast smiles. Galbraith was younger. She crackled energy. She would move "a hundred miles an hour in one direction," a colleague said. Hendershot was more experienced. She'd worked more than one hundred rape cases in her career. Careful, diligent, exacting—she complemented Galbraith. "Sometimes going a hundred miles an hour, you miss some breadcrumbs," the same colleague noted.

Their initial attempts to identify the attacker faltered. Golden police obtained a surveillance tape showing the entrance to the apartment complex where Galbraith's victim had been attacked. A fellow detective sat through more than twelve hours of blurry footage. He laboriously counted 261 vehicles and people coming and going on the night of the incident. There was one possible lead. In the predawn hours, a white Mazda pickup truck appeared ten times. Maybe it was the attacker waiting for the woman to fall asleep? But efforts to identify the vehicle's owner failed. The license plate was unreadable.

As the weeks passed, the dead ends continued. Hendershot turned to the database meant to capture serial rapists by linking cases in different jurisdictions. It turned up only bad leads. Frustration grew. "Someone else is going to get hurt," Galbraith worried to herself.

By late January, the detectives decided they needed to broaden their scope. Hendershot asked one of her department's crime analysts to scour nearby agencies for similar crimes. The analyst turned up an incident in Lakewood, another Denver suburb, that occurred about a month before the rape in Westminster. At the time, police had labeled the case a burglary. But in fresh light, it appeared very much like a failed rape attempt, committed by an attacker who closely resembled the description of the rapist. The analyst shot Hendershot a message, "You need to come to talk to me right now."

The report detailed how a forty-six-year-old artist had been accosted in her home by a man with a knife. He wore a black mask. He tried to bind her wrists. But when the man looked away, the woman jumped out of her bedroom window. She broke three ribs and punctured a lung in the seven-foot fall to the ground, but managed to escape.

Investigators at the scene uncovered a few, tenuous pieces of evidence. Thundershowers had soaked the area before the attack. Police found shoe prints in the soft, damp soil outside the woman's bedroom. On a window, they found honeycomb marks.

Honeycomb marks. Hendershot seized on them. Westminster crime-scene investigators had discovered similar marks on the window of the victim's apartment. Hendershot asked for a comparison. The marks at the two crime scenes were the same. They also appeared similar to prints from a pair of Under Armour gloves that a Lakewood investigator, on a hunch, had discovered at a Dick's Sporting Goods.

Galbraith checked out the footprints left at the Lakewood scene. They matched the footprints in the snow outside her victim's apartment in Golden. She sent images of the shoe prints to crimeshoe.com, a website that promised to move an investigation "from an unidentified scene-of-crime shoeprint to detailed footwear information in one simple step." The site, now defunct, identified the prints as having been made by a pair of Adidas ZX 700 mesh shoes, available in stores after March 2005.

By the end of January 2011, the detectives had connected four rapes over a fifteen-month period across Denver's suburbs. The trail started in Aurora, east of Denver, on October 4, 2009, with the sixty-five-year-old woman. It picked up nine months later and twenty-two miles to the west, when the rapist attacked the artist in Lakewood. A month after that the fifty-nine-year-old widow was raped in Westminster, some ten miles to the north. And then, finally, in January 2011 came the attack on the twenty-six-year-old in Golden, about fifteen miles southwest of Westminster. If you drew a map, it was almost like the rapist was circling the compass points of Denver's suburbs.

Galbraith and Hendershot turned to DNA to identify the serial rapist. The detectives had thoroughly examined their crime scenes. Technicians had swabbed window panes, doorknobs, even toilet handles—anything that the attacker might have touched. But the man was familiar with the ways of law enforcement, perhaps even a cop. He knew to avoid leaving his DNA at the scene. He used wet wipes to clean up his ejaculate. He ordered the women to shower. He took their clothing and bedding with him when he left.

He had been punctilious. But not perfect. The attacker had left behind the tiniest traces of himself. The technicians recovered three samples of so-called touch DNA, as few as seven or eight cells of skin that can be analyzed with modern laboratory techniques.

One sample was collected from the kitchen timer in Westminster. A second came from the victim in Golden. And one came from the teddy bear in Aurora.

August 11, 2008. Lynnwood, Washington

A little before nine on a Monday morning, two Lynnwood police detectives responded to a report of rape at the Alderbrooke Apartments. A couple of other officers were already there, protecting the crime scene. A K-9 officer was outside, his dog trying to pick up a scent.

The detectives, Sgt. Jeffrey Mason and Jerry Rittgarn, found the victim, Marie, on a couch, in a blanket, crying off and on. She was accompanied by her foster mother, Peggy Cunningham, and by Wayne Nash, her case manager with Project Ladder.

Marie, who had turned eighteen three months before, told police she had been talking on the phone much of the night with her friend Jordan. After finally falling asleep, she was awakened by a man with a knife—and then tied up, blindfolded, gagged, and raped. The man wore a condom, she believed. As for what her attacker looked like, Marie could offer few details. White man, gray sweater. The attack seemed to last a long time, Marie told police, but she couldn't say for sure. It was all a blur.

Marie said that after the rapist left she had managed, with her feet, to retrieve some scissors from a cabinet's bottom drawer; she cut herself free then tried calling Jordan. When Jordan didn't answer, Marie called her foster mother, then her upstairs neighbor, who came down to Marie's apartment and called 911.

Mason, then thirty-nine, had spent his years mostly in patrol and narcotics. His longest law-enforcement stint had been with a small police department in Oregon, where he served for almost nine years and received a medal of valor. He was hired by Lynnwood in 2003 and served on a narcotics task force. He was promoted to sergeant—and transferred to the Criminal Investigations Division—six weeks before the report of Marie's assault. He had previously worked only one or two rape cases. But this investigation was his to lead.

Rittgarn had been with the department for eleven years, the last four as a detective. He had previously worked as a technician in the aerospace industry. Before that, he had served in the Marine Corps, specializing in helicopter avionics.

The Lynnwood Police Department had seventy-nine sworn officers, serving a city of about 34,000 people. In 2008, Marie's case was one of ten rape reports the department fielded; with so few, the Criminal Investigations Division didn't have a separate sex-crimes unit.

By the time Marie reported being assaulted, sex-crime specialists had developed protocols that recognized the challenges and sensitivity of investigating rape cases. These guidelines, available to all police departments, detailed common missteps.

Investigators, one guide advised, should not assume that a true victim will be hysterical rather than calm, able to show clear signs of physical injury, and certain of every detail. Some victims confuse fine points or even recant. Nor should police get lost in stereotypes—believing, for example, that an adult victim will be more believable than an adolescent.

Police should not interrogate victims or threaten to use a polygraph device. Lie-detector tests are especially unreliable with people who have been traumatized and can destroy the victim's trust in law enforcement. Many states bar police from using them with rape victims.

Police, walking around Marie's apartment, discovered that the rear sliding-glass door was unlocked and slightly ajar. It led to a back porch, with a wooden railing that was covered with dirt—except one part, about three feet wide, where it looked like maybe someone had brushed the surface while climbing over. On the bed officers found a shoestring—used, apparently, to bind Marie. On top of a computer monitor they found a second shoestring, tied to a pair of underwear, the apparent blindfold or gag. Both laces had come from Marie's black tennis shoes, in the living room. Next to the bed was a black-handled knife. Marie said the knife was hers—that it had come from the kitchen, and was what the rapist had used to threaten her. Police found Marie's purse on the bedroom floor, her wallet on the bed and her learner's permit, for some reason removed from her wallet, on a bedroom window sill.

Mason told Marie she needed to go to the hospital for a sexual-assault examination. After Marie left, accompanied by her foster mom and case manager, the detectives helped process the scene. Looking for a condom or its wrapper, Rittgarn checked the bathroom, trash cans, and a nearby hillside but came up empty. The dog, outside, had tracked to the south, toward an office building, but was unable to lead officers to anything that might identify the rapist.

At the hospital, medical staff collected more than a dozen swabs from Marie. Labs were taken for hepatitis, chlamydia, HIV. Marie received Zithromax and Suprax, for possible exposure to sexually transmitted diseases, and an emergency contraceptive pill.

The medical report noted abrasions to Marie's wrists and to her vagina. The bruising on her right wrist measured 6.5 centimeters, or about 2.5 inches, the one on her left, 7 centimeters.

During the exam, the medical report said, Marie was "alert and oriented, and in no acute distress."

On the day she reported being raped, Marie phoned Shannon, her former foster mom, after getting back from the hospital. "She called and said, 'I've been raped,'" Shannon says. "There was just no emotion. It was like she was telling me that she'd made a sandwich." That Marie wasn't hysterical, or even upset, made Shannon wonder if Marie was telling the truth.

The next day, when Shannon saw Marie at her apartment, her doubts intensified. In the kitchen, when Shannon walked in, Marie didn't meet her gaze. "That seemed very strange," Shannon says. "We would always hug and she would look you right in the eye." In the bedroom, Marie seemed casual, with nothing to suggest that something horrible had happened there. Outside, Marie "was on the grass, rolling around and giggling and laughing," Shannon says. And when the two went to buy new bedding—Marie's old bedding having been taken as evidence—Marie became furious when she couldn't find the same set. "Why would you want to have the same sheets and bedspread to look at every day when you'd been raped on this bed set?" Shannon thought to herself.

Peggy, too, was mystified by Marie's demeanor. When Marie called her on that first day, before the police arrived, "she was crying and I could barely hear her," Peggy says. "Her voice was like this little tiny voice, and I couldn't really tell. It didn't sound real to me. . . . It sounded like a lot of drama, too, in some ways." At the time, Peggy had new foster children—two sisters, both teenagers. Not long before, Marie had accompanied Peggy and the sisters and Peggy's boyfriend on a picnic. To Peggy's mind, Marie had spent the afternoon trying to get attention—so much so that Peggy now wondered if this was more of the same, only more desperate.

After rushing to the apartment that morning, Peggy found Marie on the floor, crying. "But it was so strange because I sat down next to her, and she was telling me what happened, and I got this—I'm a big *Law & Order* fan, and I just got this really weird feeling," Peggy says. "It was like, I felt like she was telling me the script of a *Law & Order* story." Part of it was what Marie was saying. Why would a rapist use shoelaces to tie her up? And part of it was how Marie was saying it: "She seemed so detached and removed emotionally."

The two women who had helped raise Marie talked on the phone. Peggy told Shannon she had doubts. Shannon said she did, too. Neither had known Marie to be a liar—to exaggerate, sure, to want attention, sure—but now, both knew they weren't alone in wondering if Marie had made this up.

On August 12, the day after Marie reported being raped, Sgt. Mason's telephone rang. The caller "related that [Marie] had a past history of trying to get attention and the person was questioning whether the 'rape' had occurred," Mason later wrote.

Mason's report didn't identify the caller—but the caller was Peggy.

She called police to share her concerns. Mason then came to her home and interviewed her in person. When she told police of her skepticism, she asked to be treated anonymously. "I didn't want it to get back to Marie," Peggy says. "I was trying to be a good citizen, actually. You know? I didn't want them to waste their resources on something that might be, you know, this personal drama going on."

In addition, Mason had received a tip that Marie was unhappy with her apartment. Maybe she was making up the rape to get moved to a new one.

On August 13, Marie met with Mason at the Lynnwood police station and turned in a written statement describing what happened. The statement was only one page. But to Mason, there was one critical passage. Marie wrote that the attacker said she could untie herself once he was gone:

> After he left I grabbed my phone (which was right next to my
> head) with my mouth and I tried to call Jordan back. He didn't
> answer so I called my foster mom. . . . She came right away. I
> got off the phone with her and tried to untie myself.

This didn't square with what Marie had previously told Mason.
Before, she told the detective she had tried calling Jordan after
cutting the laces. In this written statement, she described calling
him while still tied up.

Later that day, Mason talked to Rittgarn, his fellow detective,
and said that—based on Marie's inconsistencies and based on
what he had learned from Peggy and Jordan—he now believed
Marie had made up the story.

The fear of false rape accusations has a long history in the legal
system. In the 1600s, England's chief justice, Matthew Hale,
warned that rape "is an accusation easily to be made and hard
to be proved, and harder to be defended by the party accused."
Judges in the United States read the so-called Hale warning to
juries until the 1980s. But most recent research suggests that false
reporting is relatively rare. FBI figures show that police annually
declare around 5 percent of rape cases unfounded or baseless. Social scientists examining police records in detail and using meth-
odologically rigorous standards cite similar, single-digit rates.

The next morning, Mason went to Jordan's home to interview
him. Jordan told the detective that he and Marie had stopped
dating a couple months back but remained good friends. He said
nothing about doubting Marie's story, according to Mason's
written summary. But he did say Marie had told him: When she
tried calling him that morning, she had used her toes, because
she was tied up.

Later that day—August 14, three days after Marie reported being raped—Mason called Marie, to ask if they could meet. He said
he could come and pick her up to take her to the police station.

"Am I in trouble?" Marie asked the detective.

February 9, 2011. Westminster, Colorado

On February 9, 2011, more than a dozen cops and agents from the FBI and the Colorado Bureau of Investigation gathered in a briefing room at the Westminster police station to discuss the state of the investigation.

The news was not great. After a five-week crush, there were few leads and no suspects. The analysis of the touch DNA produced mixed results. The samples narrowed the field of suspects to males belonging to the same paternal family line. But there was not enough genetic material to identify a single individual. Thus the results couldn't be entered into the FBI's nationwide DNA database to check for a match to a suspect.

Galbraith was hopeful. At least it was concrete now. The same person was at work. "It's huge," she said. "But not enough."

As the meeting drew to a close, a young crime analyst from the Lakewood police department stood up. She had conducted a search for any reports of suspicious vehicles or prowlers within a quarter mile of the Lakewood victim's home for the previous six months. She had turned up something. But she didn't know if it was important.

Three weeks before the attempted rape in Lakewood, a woman had called police late in the evening to report a suspicious pickup truck parked on the street with a man inside. Police checked it out, but the man was gone. The officer filed a brief report on the vehicle. What had attracted the analyst's attention was the location of the pickup. It was parked half a block from the Lakewood victim's house, by an empty field adjacent to her backyard.

The pickup was a 1993 white Mazda.

It was registered to a Lakewood man named Marc Patrick O'Leary.

The investigation instantly turned urgent. Could the detectives connect O'Leary's Mazda with the blurry image of the white Mazda in the surveillance footage from Golden? Aaron Hassell, the detective on the Lakewood case, raced back to his office. Lakewood patrol cars had cameras that automatically took pictures of every license plate they passed. The result was a searchable database of thousands of tag numbers indexed by time and location. Hassell typed in the license plate number from the Lakewood report: 935VHX. He got a hit. A Lakewood patrol car had snapped a picture of O'Leary standing by his white Mazda in the driveway of his house—only two hours after the August attack on the widow in Westminster.

Hassell transmitted the image to Galbraith. Carefully, she compared O'Leary's white Mazda to the surveillance tape. One freeze frame showed that her white Mazda had a broken passenger side mirror. So, too, did O'Leary's truck. Both vehicles had ball hitches on the back. Both had smudges on the back in the same place—perhaps a bumper sticker that had been torn off.

"That's our guy," Galbraith said.

Hendershot discovered the Lakewood patrol car had snapped its picture as O'Leary was headed to a nearby branch of the Colorado Department of Motor Vehicles. DMV records showed O'Leary sat for a driver's license mugshot about four hours after the Westminster attack. The photo showed a six-foot-one man with hazel eyes. He was thirty-two years old and 220 pounds. He wore a white T-shirt. The physical description closely matched the descriptions provided by the victims. And the Westminster widow had told Hendershot that her attacker wore a white T-shirt during her assault.

Hendershot did not want to be too hasty. "I'm encouraged, I'm excited," she said. But "I haven't made my decision yet, that yay, we've got the guy." Over the next twenty-four hours, more than a dozen investigators threw their collective effort and experience into finding out everything possible about O'Leary. O'Leary had no criminal record. He was not a registered sex offender. He had served in the army. Galbraith and her husband David once again faced each other on the couches in their living room. They used laptops to search for any references to O'Leary, each using a different search engine. Before long, David stumbled onto something. O'Leary had purchased a pornography website in September 2008. They wondered whether it contained photos of his victims.

The investigators decided to try to get a sample of O'Leary's DNA. Though the degraded DNA lifted from the crime scenes could not definitively match O'Leary's DNA, it could show that a male from his family line had most likely committed the crime. If detectives could eliminate O'Leary's male relatives, they could place O'Leary at the scene of the crimes with a high degree of certainty. "We still have to make that definitive identification," Hendershot said.

On the morning of Friday, February 11, FBI agents were surveilling O'Leary's house. It was a small, single-story home with gray siding half a block from a gas station, an auto-body shop, and a *carniceria* in a beat-down neighborhood. A low chain-link fence surrounded it. Tall, winter-bare trees towered above the roof. Just after noon, the agents saw a woman and a man who looked like O'Leary leave. They tailed the pair to a nearby restaurant and watched them eat. When they finished, the agents raced in. They grabbed the drinking cups from the table. The rims would have traces of his DNA.

While the agents were following the man believed to be Marc O'Leary, another FBI agent knocked on the door of the home. He planned to install a surveillance camera nearby and wanted to make sure that nobody was around. Unexpectedly, a man came to the door. He looked like Marc O'Leary. Confused, the agent fell back on a practiced ruse. He told the man he was canvassing the neighborhood to warn of a burglar in the area. The man introduced himself. He was Marc O'Leary. His brother, Michael

O'Leary, had just left to get lunch with his girlfriend. O'Leary thanked the officer for the information and closed the door.

Michael's appearance was confounding. The investigators hadn't known that Michael lived with his brother. Or that he looked so similar. They decided to run Michael O'Leary's DNA, collected from the restaurant glass, against the DNA found at the crime scenes. Analysts at the Colorado Bureau of Investigation got the samples. Usually, a DNA analysis took months. But in this case, they worked through the night. By two p.m. on Saturday, they had a result. The DNA from the cup matched the DNA collected from the victims. An O'Leary man was responsible. But which one?

Galbraith ruled out the brothers' father—he was too old and lived in a different state. But investigators could not yet rule out Michael as a suspect. It was possible that Michael had committed the rapes. Or even that Michael and Marc had worked together. They needed more information.

Galbraith hastily typed up a search warrant to enter the brothers' home. It was dark outside when she finished. She called the judge who was on duty for the weekend. He insisted on a fax. Galbraith rushed to a Safeway near her house to send the warrant. The judge signed it at ten p.m. on Saturday.

She knew exactly what she was looking for. She trusted her victim's memory. The dark mark on his leg.

She emailed a crime analyst at another police department, "I so want to see this guy's leg! BAD."

August 14, 2008. Lynnwood, Washington

In Sgt. Mason's experience, when someone asked if they were in trouble, almost always, they were.

When Mason, accompanied by Detective Rittgarn, went to pick up Marie at about three-thirty p.m., they found her outside her apartment, sitting on the grass. The three went to the

Lynnwood police station, where the detectives escorted Marie to a conference room.

From what Mason wrote up later, he wasted little time confronting Marie, telling her there were inconsistencies between her statements and accounts from other witnesses. Marie said she didn't know of any discrepancies. But she went through the story again—only this time, saying she believed the rape had happened instead of saying it for certain. Tearfully, she described her past—all the foster parents, being raped when she was seven, getting her own place and feeling alone. Rittgarn told Marie that her story and the evidence didn't match. He said he believed she had made the story up—a spur-of-the-moment thing, not something planned out. He asked if there was really a rapist running around the neighborhood that the police should be looking for. "No," Marie told him, her voice soft, her eyes down.

"Based on her answers and body language it was apparent that [Marie] was lying about the rape," Rittgarn later wrote.

Without reading Marie her rights—*you have the right to an attorney, you have the right to remain silent*—the detectives asked Marie to write out the true story, admitting she had lied, admitting, in effect, that she had committed a crime. She agreed, so they left her alone for a few minutes. On the form she filled in her name, address and social security number, and then she wrote, in part:

> I was talking to Jordan on the phone that night about his day and just about anything. After I got off the phone with him, I started thinking about all things I was stressed out and I also was scared living on my own. When I went to sleep I dreamed that someone broke in and raped me.

When the detectives returned, they saw that Marie's new statement described the rape as a dream, not a lie.

Why didn't you write that you made the story up? Rittgarn asked.

Marie, crying, said she believed the rape really happened. She pounded the table and said she was "pretty positive."

Pretty positive or actually positive? Rittgarn asked.

Maybe the rape happened and I blacked it out, Marie said.

What do you think should happen to someone who would lie about something like this? Rittgarn asked Marie.

"I should get counseling," Marie said.

Mason returned to the evidence. He told Marie that her description of calling Jordan was different from what Jordan had reported.

Marie, her face in her hands, looked down. Then "her eyes darted back and forth as if she was thinking of a response."

The detectives doubled back to what she had said before—about being stressed, being lonely—and, eventually, Marie appeared to relax. She stopped crying. She even laughed a little. She apologized—and agreed to write another statement, leaving no doubt it was a lie.

> I have had a lot of stressful things going on and I wanted to hang out with someone and no one was able to so I made up this story and didn't expect it to go as far as it did. . . . I don't know why I couldn't have done something different. This was never meant to happen.

This statement appeared to satisfy the detectives. Rittgarn would later write, "Based on our interview with [Marie] and the inconsistencies found by Sgt. Mason in some of the statements we were confident that [Marie] was now telling us the truth that she had not been raped."

To Marie, it seemed the questioning had lasted for hours. She did what she always did when under stress. She flipped the switch, as she called it, suppressing all the feelings she didn't know what to do with. Before she confessed to making up the story, she couldn't look the two detectives, the two men, in the eye. Afterward, she could. Afterward, she smiled. She went into the bathroom and cleaned up. Flipping the switch was a relief— and it would let her leave.

The next day, Marie told Wayne Nash, her case manager at Project Ladder, that the police didn't believe her. Recognizing the jeopardy she was in, she said she wanted a lawyer.

The Project Ladder managers instead reached out to Sgt. Mason. He told them the evidence didn't support Marie's story, and that she had taken her story back.

But now, Marie wouldn't give. On August 18, one week after she reported being raped, she met with the two Project Ladder managers and insisted she had signed the recantation under duress. The three then went to the police station so Marie could recant her recantation—that is, tell detectives that she had been telling the truth the first time.

While the program managers waited outside, Marie met with Rittgarn and another officer.

Rittgarn asked Marie what was going on. Marie said she really had been raped—and began to cry, saying she was having visions of the man on top of her. She wanted to take a lie-detector test. Rittgarn told Marie that if she took the test and failed, she would be booked into jail. What's more, he would recommend that Project Ladder pull her housing assistance.

Marie backed down. The police officers walked her downstairs, where the Project Ladder representatives asked if she had been raped. Marie said no.

After leaving the police station, Marie learned that she still wasn't through. There was something else she had to do. The Project Ladder managers told Marie that if she wanted to stay in the program—if she wanted to keep her subsidized apartment— she would have to confess to someone else.

Later that day a meeting was called at the housing complex, with all of Marie's peers gathered in a circle. Marie, as directed, told her fellow participants in Project Ladder that she had lied about being raped. They didn't need to worry, she told the group. There was no one out there who had hurt her and no one who might hurt them next.

If there was sympathy in the room, Marie sensed it from only one person, the young woman to her right. The rest was awkward, excruciating silence.

After the meeting, Marie started walking to a friend's place. On her way, she crossed a bridge. She considered jumping. "Probably the only time I just wanted to die in my life," she says. She called a friend and said, "Please come get me before I do something stupid." Afterward, Marie hurled her phone over the side.

Later that month, there was a final surprise. Marie got a letter, notifying her that she was wanted in court. She had been charged with false reporting, punishable by up to a year in jail. The criminal citation was signed by Sgt. Mason. Afterward, the paperwork went to a small law firm that Lynnwood had hired to prosecute misdemeanors.

For Mason, his decision to file the citation required no complicated calculus. He was certain Marie had lied. The police had spent a lot of resources chasing that lie. The law said her lie was a crime. Really, it was as simple as that.

There are no firm statistics on how often police arrest women for making false rape reports nor on how often prosecutors take such cases to court. Nobody collects such data. But leading law-enforcement organizations urge caution in filing such charges. The International Association of Chiefs of Police and the FBI stress the need for a thorough investigation before discounting a report of rape. Cops must work as hard to prove a falsehood as they do to prove a truth.

In practice, many police departments will pursue charges against women only in extreme circumstances—say, in a highly public case where a suspect's reputation has suffered or where the police have expended considerable investigative resources. This reluctance stems from the belief that in rape cases, the biggest problem is not false reporting, but no reporting. Only about one-fifth to one-third of rapes get reported to police, national surveys show. One reason is that women fear police won't believe them.

Within days of reporting being raped, Marie had quit her job at Costco, unable to stand there, looking at people, lost in her head. Now, her losses mounted.

Project Ladder gave her a nine p.m. curfew and doubled the number of times she had to meet with staff.

The media wrote about Marie being charged, without identifying her. (The *Seattle Post-Intelligencer* headline read, "Police: Lynnwood rape report was a hoax.") Marie's best friend from high school—the one who had taught her photography and had taken that picture of her emerging from the surf—created a webpage that called Marie a liar, with a photo from Marie's Myspace page, with police reports, with Marie's full name. Alerted to the site, Marie went into a frenzy, trashing her apartment.

Marie stopped going to church. "I was mad at God," she says. She lost interest in photography. She feared going outdoors. "One night I did try to walk to the store by myself and felt like I hallucinated someone following me," she says. "It freaked me out. I didn't even get a half mile from my house. I ran home." At home she avoided the bedroom, choosing to sleep on the couch with the lights on.

"I went into this dark hole," she says.

Self-esteem gave way to self-loathing. She started smoking, drinking, gaining weight.

For Marie, this was a familiar drill, one she could trace to her years of being abused as a kid and to her years in foster care, bouncing from home to home and school to school. Shut down. Hold it in. Act like nothing bad had happened, like nothing ever affected her. Because she craved normalcy, she would bury the hurt.

Neither Peggy nor Shannon abandoned her, but things weren't the same. Marie knew that both had doubted her story even before the police had.

For Marie, Shannon's home had long provided an escape or respite. Marie and Shannon would walk in the woods or take out the boat then, at day's end, crash in Shannon's home. Now, fearful he could become the target of a wrongful accusation, Shannon's husband decided it would be best if Marie no longer spent the night. "When you become a foster parent, you're open to that," Shannon says.

It fell to Shannon to break the news. Delivering it crushed her. Receiving it crushed Marie.

In early October, less than two months after Marie was charged with false reporting, a sixty-three-year-old woman reported being raped inside her condominium in Kirkland, east of Seattle. The stranger wore gloves. He held a knife. He tied the woman up—with her own shoelaces. He took pictures and threatened to post them on the Internet. For the last two or three months, the woman told police, she felt as if someone had been following her.

Shannon saw an account of the attack on the television news and was taken aback. Her father had been the chief of police in Kent, south of Seattle. She grew up with police, trusted police, knew how the police worked. She went to her computer, looked up the number, and called—immediately—to alert police in Kirkland to Marie's story, to advise them of all the parallels.

Shannon called Marie and suggested she also contact the Kirkland police. Marie never did.

"I was just too scared," Marie says. She'd gone through so much already. She couldn't bring herself to meet with the police again and say anything more. But she did go online and look up what happened to the woman in Kirkland. When she read the story, she cried.

A Kirkland detective eventually called Shannon back. Based on Shannon's tip, Kirkland investigators had reached out to their Lynnwood counterparts and had been told the Lynnwood victim was no victim, the story had been made up.

One of the detectives working the Kirkland case was Audra Weber. She remembers calling the Lynnwood detectives twice and being told they didn't believe Marie's account. "I just kind of trusted their judgment, in terms of it's their case, they know the details and I don't," Weber says. But she remembers being "kind of shocked" to learn that they had charged Marie. She let it go and hung up, thinking, "OK, I hope that works out for you guys."

February 13, 2011. Lakewood, Colorado

At eight-fifteen a.m., Galbraith knocked on O'Leary's door.

"Police. Search warrant. Open the door," she shouted repeatedly. Seven cops stood behind her, pressed against the house, their guns drawn.

After a pause, O'Leary opened the door. He looked confused and shocked as he stepped out into the bright winter sun. Two dogs, a small pit bull and a shar-pei, tumbled out ahead of him. He wore a gray hoodie, baggy gray sweatpants, and gray slip-on houseshoes. He was alone.

Galbraith pulled him to the side and patted him down. When she got to his legs, she raised his pant leg to look.

There it was, on O'Leary's left calf: a dark birthmark the size of a large chicken egg.

It was him. He was the rapist. Galbraith flashed a quick thumbs up.

As an FBI agent confronted him, O'Leary immediately invoked his right to an attorney. Galbraith had maneuvered herself to stand behind O'Leary. At 8:35 a.m., she handcuffed him. "You're under arrest for burglary and sexual assault which occurred in the City of Golden on January 5, 2011," she told him. O'Leary was put in a patrol car and transported to the Jefferson County Jail.

She was wearing new boots that day. Whenever she looked at them in the future, she would remember catching O'Leary. For Galbraith, it was important to be the one who made the arrest. "I wanted to see the look on his face, I guess," she said. "And for him to know that we figured you out."

The search of the home validated the detectives' investigation. Investigators found a pair of Adidas ZX 700 shoes in O'Leary's closet. The treads matched the footprints in the snow in Golden and outside the window in Lakewood. They discovered a pair of Under Armour gloves with a honeycomb pattern. In the bathroom was a black headwrap, tied to serve as a mask.

"He was military—so he was very organized," Galbraith said. "This was the cleanest house I've ever searched. It was so organized, we were like, 'Oh, thank God.'"

The victims' accounts were also borne out. Most had described a white man with green or hazel eyes, about six feet tall, weighing about 200 pounds. They talked about being tied up. They mentioned that he had stolen their underwear. In O'Leary's house, investigators turned up a black Ruger .380-caliber pistol, a pink Sony Cyber-shot camera and a large backpack, along with wet wipes and lubrication. Hidden inside a piece of stereo equipment in his closet, detectives found a collection of women's underwear. Trophies.

That night, Hendershot drove to break the news to her victim, the fifty-nine-year-old widow in Westminster. The woman had lost her husband to cancer the previous year. She had no family nearby. She was still emerging from the mental and physical suffering she endured during the attack. Hendershot met her at a Denny's restaurant. She found her in a back corner, eating dinner alone.

"I walked in, and she was super happy to see me, and I told her. I mean, I get shiver bumps thinking about it, just even now,"

Hendershot said. "I told her, I said, 'It's over. It's over. We have him.'" By early March, a forensic computer specialist cracked into files that O'Leary had stored on his hard drive. He found a folder called "girls"—and pictures that O'Leary had taken of his victims in Golden and Westminster. Galbraith recognized them by sight. But then Galbraith stumbled across an image of a woman she didn't recognize. It was a young woman—far younger than the Colorado victims, perhaps a teenager. The pictures showed her looking terrified, bound and gagged on a bed. Galbraith felt sick. How would she identify her? How would she find justice for her?

After looking through the images, she found an answer. It was a picture of the woman's learner's permit, placed on her chest. It had her name. And it had her address.

Lynnwood, Washington.

August 11, 2008. Lynnwood, Washington

He arrived in the predawn hours, then waited outside her apartment, outside her bedroom, listening to her on the phone, waiting for her to fall asleep.

The night was dry, letting him settle in. The wall was thin, letting him hear her voice. A couple of times he left his position, for just a while, for fear of being spotted lingering.

He liked trees, for the cover they provided, and the Alderbrooke Apartments had plenty of them. Apartments didn't offer the privacy of a house, but still, there were advantages. All those windows, for one thing. And all those sliding glass doors—ridiculously easy to pick, when they weren't left unlocked, which so often they were.

She wasn't his type, not really. He'd realized that before while peeping into her bedroom. But he spent so much time hunting (that's what he called it, hunting), hundreds of hours, maybe even a thousand, that he conditioned himself to incorporate as many women as possible, young or old, into his fantasies.

That way his work wouldn't be wasted.

He had prowled before and broken into women's homes before, but following through was another matter. He had learned from past failures—one time, a guy walked in as he stood there, mask on, outside the bedroom door of the woman he planned to rape—so now, he did painstaking surveillance: peeking in windows, breaking in beforehand, gathering information. Years later, detectives would find notes on his cell phone from his surveillance of another target (his word) that detailed which room she was in and when, what lights were off or on, which windows and blinds were opened or closed, whether her boyfriend was there or gone. "BF in PJs, game over," he wrote in one night's entry.

He would rifle a target's personal documents. He would learn her date of birth and license plate number. He would watch her watching TV. And at the hunt's end, before he committed, he would take a final pass through the home, or what he called "precombat inspection," to make sure there weren't any weapons within the target's reach.

.   .   .

At a little before sunrise, he heard the phone conversation end. He waited a little longer, letting the silence stretch out, then climbed over the railing and slipped through the unlocked sliding glass door. For the next half hour or so, while she slept, he got ready while talking himself into following through.

He had first spotted her a couple of weeks before, through a window, while lurking outside her apartment. He had since broken into her place twice, both times through that same glass door.

He had a term for what he was about to do: "rape theater." Deviant fantasies had gripped him since he was a kid, way back to when he had seen Jabba the Hutt enslave and chain Princess

Leia. *Where do you go when you're five and already thinking about handcuffs?* he would ask himself. He was only eight the first time he broke into a home. It was such a rush. He had broken into more than a dozen homes since.

Now he was thirty, an army veteran—infantry, two tours in South Korea—who had enlisted in the reserves, only he hadn't appeared for duty in months.

In the kitchen, he went to the knife block and removed a black-handled blade from the top row, far left.

In the living room, he removed the laces from her black tennis shoes and put the shoes back. One detective later wrote in a report, "The shoes were lying next to each other near the end of the couch and the bedroom door, on the soles as if placed there (not disturbed)."

He was just being neat and orderly, the way he was with everything.

He threaded one of the shoelaces through a pair of underwear.

Then he walked to the bedroom.

Around seven a.m., he stood in her bedroom doorway, holding, at shoulder height, a knife in his left hand.

He watched as she awoke.

Turn away, he told Marie—and she did. Roll over onto your stomach, he told her. She did—and then he straddled her, putting the knife near her face.

Put your hands behind your back, he told her. She did. He bound her wrists and he covered her eyes. He stuffed cloth into her mouth to muffle any sound.

That was an interesting conversation you were having, he said, letting her know that he had been there, listening, waiting.

You should know better than to leave the door unlocked, he told her.

Roll back over, he told her—and she did, and then he raped her, and while he raped her he ran his gloved hands over her.

He put her learner's permit on her chest and took pictures of her.

When he was finished, he said that if she told the police, he would post the photos online so that her kids, when she had kids, could see them.

He took out the gag and removed the blindfold, telling her to avert her eyes and to keep her head in the pillow.

One of the last things he said was that he was sorry. He said he felt stupid, that it had looked better in his head.

He left the room, and walked to the front door, and he was gone.

Epilogue

O'Leary pleaded guilty to twenty-eight counts of rape and associated felonies in Colorado. On December 9, 2011, almost a year after his arrest, O'Leary was sentenced to 327½ years in prison for the Colorado attacks—the maximum allowed by law. He is currently housed in the Sterling Correctional Facility in the barren, remote northeastern corner of Colorado. He will never be released.

In an interview with police after his conviction, O'Leary recounted his attacks in detail. He described the feeling after raping one elderly victim. "It was like I'd just eaten Thanksgiving dinner," he said.

He let spill some lessons for law enforcement. He boasted of the countermeasures he'd taken to avoid getting caught. He knew that the army had a sample of his DNA. So he took steps to avoid leaving any traces of genetic material. He also realized police departments often did not communicate. So he deliberately committed each rape in a different jurisdiction.

The five other attacks—one in Washington, four in Colorado—all came after the attack on Marie.

"If Washington had just paid attention a little bit more, I probably would have been a person of interest earlier on," O'Leary said.

·   ·   ·

Working from Colorado, Galbraith not only linked O'Leary to the rape in Lynnwood, Washington but to the rape in nearby Kirkland. She made the connection by working with a Washington state criminal analyst to search a database for unsolved cases similar to O'Leary's crimes. She then found the Kirkland victim's name on O'Leary's computer, attached to an encrypted file.

O'Leary pleaded guilty in both of the Washington cases. In June 2012, he was sentenced to 40 years for the rape in Kirkland and to 28½ years for the rape of Marie in Lynnwood.

·   ·   ·

After O'Leary was linked to Marie's rape, Lynnwood police chief Steven Jensen requested an outside review of how his department had handled the investigation. In a report not previously made public, Sgt. Gregg Rinta, a sex-crimes supervisor with the Snohomish County Sheriff's Office, wrote that what happened was "nothing short of the victim being coerced into admitting that she lied about the rape."

That Marie recanted wasn't surprising, Rinta wrote, given the "bullying" and "hounding" she was subjected to. The detectives elevated "minor inconsistencies"—common among victims—into discrepancies while ignoring strong evidence the crime had occurred. As for threatening jail and a possible withdrawal of housing assistance if Marie failed a polygraph: "These statements are coercive, cruel, and unbelievably unprofessional," Rinta wrote. "I can't imagine ANY justification for making these statements."

Jensen also ordered an internal review, which was similarly damning. Mason's judgment was unduly swayed by Peggy's phone call. The detectives' second interview with Marie was "designed to elicit a confession of false reporting." The false-reporting charge arose from a "self-imposed rush."

Despite the reviews' tough language, no one in the Lynnwood Police Department was disciplined.

In a recent interview, Steve Rider, the current commander of Lynnwood's Criminal Investigations Division, called Marie's case a "major failing" that has left members of the department with a profound sense of regret: "Knowing that she went through that brutal attack—and then we told her she lied? That's awful. We all got into this job to help people, not to hurt them." Lynnwood sergeant Rodney Cohnheim said of Marie, "She was victimized twice."

Sgt. Mason is now back in narcotics, in charge of a task force. Interviewed in the same room where he had confronted Marie seven years before, he said: "It wasn't her job to try to convince me. In hindsight, it was my job to get to the bottom of it—and I didn't."

Marie's case led to changes in practices and culture, Rider said. Detectives receive additional training about rape victims. Rape victims get immediate assistance from advocates at a local health-care center. Investigators must have "definitive proof" of lying before doubting a rape report, and a charge of false reporting must now be reviewed with higher-ups. "We learned a great deal from this. And we don't want to see this happen to anybody ever again," Rider said.

Rittgarn, who left the Lynnwood Police Department before O'Leary's arrest, declined to be interviewed for this story. So did Zachor & Thomas, the law office that handled the prosecution of Marie on Lynnwood's behalf.

In 2008, Marie's case was one of four labeled unfounded by the Lynnwood police, according to statistics reported to the FBI.

In the five years from 2008 to 2012, the department determined that ten of forty-seven rapes reported to Lynnwood police were unfounded—21.3 percent. That's five times the national average of 4.3 percent for agencies covering similar-sized populations during that same period. Rider said his agency has become more cautious about labeling a case unfounded since Marie. "I would venture to say we investigate our cases a lot more vigorously than many departments do," he said. "Now, we're extra careful that we get the right closure on it."

.   .   .

Two and a half years after Marie was branded a liar, Lynnwood police found her, south of Seattle, and told her the news: Her rapist had been arrested in Colorado. They gave her an envelope with information on counseling for rape victims. They said her record would be expunged. And they handed her $500, a refund of her court costs. Marie broke down, experiencing, all at once, shock, relief and anger.

Afterward, Shannon took Marie for a walk in the woods, and told her, "I'm so sorry I doubted you." Marie forgave, immediately. Peggy, too, apologized. She now wishes she had never shared her doubts with police. "Because I feel that if I would have shut my mouth, they would have done their job," she says.

Marie sued the city and settled for $150,000. "A risk management decision was made," a lawyer for Lynnwood told the *Herald* in Everett, Washington.

Marie left the state, got a commercial driver's license, and took a job as a long-haul trucker. She married, and in October she and her husband had their second child. She asked that her current location not be disclosed.

Before leaving Washington to restart her life, Marie made an appointment to visit the Lynnwood police station. She went to a conference room and waited. Rittgarn had already left the department, but Mason came in, looking "like a lost little puppy," Marie says. "He was rubbing his head and literally looked like he was ashamed about what they had done." He told Marie he was sorry—"deeply sorry," Marie says. To Marie, he seemed sincere.

Recently, Marie was asked if she had considered not reporting the rape.

"No," she said. She wanted to be honest. She wanted to remember everything she could. She wanted to help the police.

"So nobody else would get hurt," she said. "They'd be out there searching for this person who had done this to me."

The Intercept

WINNER—COLUMNS AND
COMMENTARY

*Meet Barrett Brown: "Good
News!—The U.S. government
decided today that because I did
such a good job investigating the
cyber-industrial complex, they're
now going to send me to
investigate the prison-industrial
complex. For the next 35 months,
I'll be provided with free food,
clothes, and housing as I seek to
expose wrongdoing by Bureau of
Prisons officials." Inmate Brown
now writes a column for* The
Intercept, *an online publication
founded in 2014 by Glenn
Greenwald, Laura Poitras, and
Jeremy Scahill, investigative
journalists widely known for their
work with Edward Snowden.
The judges who awarded* The
Intercept *the National Magazine
Award for Columns and
Commentary described these three
columns as full of "irrepressible wit
and free-roaming erudition." Read
them. Want more? Go read Tim
Rogers's profile of Barrett Brown
from* D Magazine, *which won its
own Ellie and was published in*
The Best American Magazine
Writing 2012.

Barrett Brown

A Visit to the Sweat Lodge *and* Santa Muerte, Full of Grace *and* Stop Sending me Jonathan Franzen Novels

A Visit to the Sweat Lodge

Back in the go-go days of 2011 I got into some sort of post-modern running conflict with a certain declining superpower that shall remain nameless and shortly afterwards found myself in jail awaiting trial on seventeen federal criminal counts carrying a combined maximum sentence of 105 years in prison. Luckily I got off with just 63 months, which here in the Republic of Crazyland is actually not too bad of an outcome.

The surreal details of the case itself may be found in any number of mainstream and not-so-mainstream news articles, from which you will learn that I was the official spokesman for Anonymous, or perhaps the unofficial spokesman for Anonymous, or maybe simply the self-proclaimed spokesman for Anonymous, or alternatively the guy who denied being the spokesman for

Anonymous over and over again, sometimes on national television to no apparent effect.You'll also find that I was either a conventional journalist, an unconventional journalist, a satirist who despised all journalists, an activist, a whistleblower, a nihilistic and self-absorbed cyberpunk adventurer out to make a name for himself, or "an underground commander in a new kind of war," as NBC's Brian Williams put it, no doubt exaggerating.

According to the few FBI files that the bureau has thus far made public, I'm a militant anarchist revolutionary who once teamed up with Anonymous in an attempt to "overthrow the U.S. government," and on another, presumably separate occasion, I plotted unspecified "attacks" on the government of Bahrain, which, if true, would really seem to be between me and the king of Bahrain, would it not? There's also a book out there that claims I'm from Houston, whereas in fact I spit on Houston. As to the truth on these and other matters, I'm going to play coy for now, as whatever else I may be, I'm definitely something of a coquette. All you really need to know for the purposes of this column is that I'm some sort of eccentric writer who lives in a prison, and I may or may not have it out for the king of Bahrain.

Over the last couple of years of incarceration, I've had ever so many exciting adventures, some of which I've detailed in the prior incarnation of this column, "The Barrett Brown Review of Arts and Letters and Jail." I've watched two inmates get into a blood-spattered fight over the right to sell homemade pies from a particular table. I have participated in an unauthorized demonstration against an abusive guard and been thrown into the hole as a suspected instigator. I've shouted out comical revolutionary slogans while my Muslim cellmate flooded our tiny punishment cell in order to get back at the officers who'd taken his Ramadan meal during a search. I've found myself with nothing better to read than an autobiography by Wendy's Old-Fashioned Hamburgers founder Dave Thomas, and read it, and found it wanting.

I've stalked a fellow inmate who talks nonsense to himself all day due to having never come down after a PCP trip, suspecting that he might say something really weird that I could compare and contrast with the strange William Blake poems I'd been reading and thought this might be a funny idea for an article, and I was right, so do not ask me to apologize for this, for I shall not. I've been extracted from my cell by a dozen guards and shipped to another jail thirty miles away after the administration decided I was too much trouble. I've spent one whole year receiving sandwiches for dinner each night, but the joke's on them because I love sandwiches.

I've read through an entire sixteenth-century volume on alchemy out of pure spite. I've added the word "Story" to the end of every instance of prison graffiti reading "West Side" that I've come across thus far. I've conceived the idea of writing a sequel to the Ramayana but abandoned the project after determining that the world is not prepared for such a thing. I've been subjected to a gag order at the request of the prosecution on the grounds that the latest *Guardian* article I'd written from jail had been "critical of the government." I've learned all sorts of neat convict tricks like making dice out of toilet paper, popping locks on old cell doors, and appreciating mediocre rap. I've managed to refrain from getting any ironic prison tattoos and feel about 65 percent certain that I'll be able to hold out for the two years left in my sentence. And I've read Robert Caro's four-volume biography of Lyndon Johnson over the course of a month, in the process becoming something of a minor god, beyond good and evil, unfazed by man's wickedness.

After being sentenced last January I released a statement reading:

Good News!—The U.S. government decided today that because I did such a good job investigating the cyber-industrial complex, they're now going to send me to investigate the prison-industrial complex. For the next 35 months, I'll be provided with free food, clothes, and housing as I seek to expose wrongdoing by Bureau of Prisons officials and staff and otherwise report on news and culture in the world's greatest prison system. I want to thank the Department of Justice for having put so much time and energy into advocating on my behalf; rather than holding a grudge against me for the two years of work I put into in bringing attention to a DOJ-linked campaign to harass and discredit journalists like Glenn Greenwald, the agency instead labored tirelessly to ensure that I received this very prestigious assignment. Wish me luck!

In fact I had no intention of doing anything of the kind; it was merely the same manner of idle bluster that I've been putting out to the press for years now because I'm a braggart. Actually I was hoping to just sort of relax and maybe catch up on my plotting. But a month later, when I arrived at the Fort Worth Correctional Institution to serve the remainder of my sentence, the place turned out to be an unspoiled journalistic paradise of poorly concealed government corruption and ham-fisted cover-ups. Even so, I was still reluctant to grab at even this low-hanging fruit. I'd spent the eighteen months prior to my arrest overseeing a crowd-sourced investigation into that aforementioned "cyber-industrial complex," a subject which, although important, I also happen to find personally distasteful; the research end involved going through tens of thousands of e-mails stolen by Anonymous from the toy-fascist government desk-spies and jumped-up quasi-literate corporate technicians to whom the American "citizenry" have accidentally granted *jus primae noctis* over several Constitutional amendments. I hate all this computer shit and was actually a little relieved when the FBI finally took me down, thereby sparing me from the obligation to read another million words of e-Morlock jibber-jabber about Romas/COIN and Odyssey and persona management and whatever else the public is just going to end up ignoring until it's too late anyway.

So I was disinclined to sully the rest of my incarceration vacation by having to memorize a book of Bureau of Prisons policies and court rulings on due process rights for inmates to see which ones are being routinely violated by the prison administration, and then run around secretly interviewing inmates and getting copies of receipts and making Freedom of Information requests and all that. After all, there already exists here a clandestine network of inmates who do all of this and more and who routinely make significant discoveries ranging from procedural violations to outright criminal conduct by staff and administrators—and, naturally, all of these documented revelations are generally ignored by the incompetent regional reporters to whom the inmates occasionally send such materials. As I happen to know some of the 3 or 4 percent of U.S. journalists and editors who are capable of doing their jobs, I figured I'd just hook one of them up with the prisoner in question, hope that some instance of wrongdoing gets exposed in print, take more than my share of the credit, put out a victory statement reading, "No one imprisons Barrett Brown and gets away with it! Mwah ha ha!!" or something to that effect, and then spend the rest of my sentence doing whatever it is that I do for recreation.

In late March I put my awesome plan in motion, using the inmate e-mail system to follow up with a journalist I'd provided with contact info for one of the inmate researchers and reiterating that the fellow had documented evidence of corruption within the Bureau of Prisons. Then, an hour later, my e-mail was cut off. After a couple of days of inquiry I was pulled aside by the resident head of security, a D.C. liaison by the name of Terrance Moore, who told me he'd been the one to cut off my e-mail access, as I'd been "using it for the wrong thing," which he clarified to mean talking to the press. When I sought to challenge this plainly illegal move by turning in the BP-9 form to begin the Administrative Remedy process that inmates are required to exhaust before suing the federal official who's violated their right to due process under what's known as a Bivens claim, the prison's Administrative Remedy coordinator simply failed to log it into the system for over a month, finally doing so only after the matter had been brought to the attention of the press; finally, on June 4 he deigned to register receipt of the BP-9, thereby belatedly starting the clock on the twenty days the prison is allotted in which to address one's grievance—and then he failed to respond even by that illicitly extended deadline.

I've since learned that this sort of thing is common here and that in fact I was lucky to get my grievance officially acknowledged as received at all; I've seen copies of forms that have yet to be logged five months after being turned in to the unit staff. That would be problematic enough anywhere as it constitutes denial of access to the courts. But it's especially despicable at an institution like this, which includes a medical unit for inmates who require ongoing treatment—because to the extent that they don't actually receive that treatment, the only recourse is to pursue the Remedy process so that their complaints won't simply be tossed out of court on the grounds that they've "failed to exhaust" that process before going to the judge. I've included copies of the relevant documents in prior columns and will continue to provide updates as I take my case to the regional office, the national office, and finally to the courts, as of course it will be interesting to see whether or not the BOP takes due process seriously or, barring that, is at least willing to buy me off with a carton of Marlboros.

In the meantime, I continue to have neat adventures. Last month one of the American Indian inmates invited me to attend their weekly sweat lodge ceremony, which is held in a fenced-off area that each federal prison is required to provide for ritual use by the Natives. The next morning I showed up at the appointed time and, having determined that it wasn't an ambush, I began helping the twenty or so resident Indians break up tree branches for fire kindling, something I did very much with the air of a five-year-old who believes himself to be "helping Daddy." Next we built a large bonfire (I assisted by staying out the way and being good) by which to heat up several dozen large rocks that would be used for "the sweat." The fire-making process was expedited by strategically placed crumpled-up sheets of the Fort Worth *Star-Telegram*, which I gather is not a strictly traditional aspect of most shamanistic ceremonies. As if to acknowledge this, one of the Indians declared, "The one good thing the white man ever did was invent paper." Naturally all eyes were on me, and I knew that this might be my only chance to win them over. "We didn't invent it," I blurted out. "We just stole it from the Chinese." This produced appreciative chuckles all around. "I got a laugh out of the Indians!" I thought exultantly, my triumph so complete that I was unbothered by the fact that what I'd said wasn't really true.

By and by we crawled into the lodge, a wood-and-canvas structure with a dirt floor, in the middle of which had been dug a pit to hold the heated rocks that would be providing the extraordinary heat we would need to sweat out our sins. The flap was then closed from the outside, leaving us in perfect darkness, and thereafter began the first of the fifteen-minute "rounds" of the sweat ceremony, which consisted of all manner of tribal songs, entreaties to the spirits, and sometimes just discussions and announcements. At one point my sponsor, a Lakota, declared that although superficially white, I might nonetheless have an "Indian spirit." It was one of the nicest things anyone had ever said about me, this polite supposition that I might not really be descended from the fair-skinned race of marauding, treaty-breaking slavers whose *Novus Ordo Seclorum* had been built on a foundation of genocide. But insomuch as I'd spent the bulk of the ceremony not in prayer, but rather in a state of neurotic concern over whether or not my self-deprecating comment from an hour earlier about whites stealing paper could have perhaps been a bit more crisply phrased, I'm afraid my spirit would seem to be Anglo-Saxon after all.

Although undeniably majestic, the ceremony was also something of a disappointment. I had gone into the thing hoping that I might mysteriously know exactly what to do—how to pass the peace pipe and all that—and maybe even start singing old Cherokee songs that the eldest of those present would barely recall having heard from their own grandfathers. Stunned, the Indians would collectively intone, "He shall know your ways as if born to them," this being the ancient prophecy I had thereby fulfilled, and then I would unite the tribes under my banner and lead the foremost of their warriors on a jihad against our shared enemies, as Paul Muad'Dib did. Instead, the Indians had to remind me several times not to just stand up and start walking around during the ceremony.

I'm currently in the midst of another adventure, having been placed back in the hole two weeks ago after a suspicious incident in which staff singled me out for a search of my locker and found a cup of homemade alcohol, or "hooch." Next time, then, we'll take a look at life here in the Special Housing Unit, or SHU, as the hole is more formally known, and where I expect to spend some forty-five days. And when I get back, there better not be any more Republican presidential primary contenders. You don't need three dozen slightly different variations on right-Hegelian nationalist populism from which to choose. That's just excessive.

Santa Muerte, Full of Grace

Last time I mentioned that I'd been thrown into the hole, otherwise known as the Special Housing Unit (SHU), after a "random" breathalyzer test that I passed was nonetheless followed by a "random" targeted search of my locker, not unlike the "random" drug test for which I just happened to be selected out of 350 inmates in my unit a few months back, shortly after filing a complaint against prison officials regarding—wait for it—retaliation. In fairness, they did find a cup of homemade alcohol in my locker this time, the clever rascals, but I was only going to use it to drink a toast to the Bureau of Prisons and wish the agency luck in defending itself against the various lawsuits that have been filed against it lately. Also I wanted to look cool in front of the bigger kids.

Getting put back in Disciplinary Segregation was actually in some ways fortuitous as I'm now able to make a long-overdue inspection tour of this institution's Special Housing Unit. (I'm very much the Eleanor Roosevelt of the federal prison system.) The timing is grand, too, as the nation's tendency to keep prisoners in these sorts of twenty-three-hour-a-day lockdown settings for no good reason has come under a rare spate of scrutiny in recent months. But going to the hole isn't all champagne and roses. By policy, one doesn't receive one's property, including legal papers, until after two weeks of confinement. And by negligence, one is usually left without one's prescribed medications for at least three or four days. Bizarrely enough, there was also a shortage of the little pencils we're supposed to receive upon arrival, and so it took me a while to get one of my very own. And after over a month of confinement, despite countless requests to the ranking lieutenant, I've still yet to receive a high-end gaming laptop loaded with a Super Nintendo emulator, a complete set of Super Nintendo ROMs, and the latest stable release of Dwarf Fortress, although I guess I can see how this might be regarded as a not altogether reasonable demand.

But the most jarring aspect of going to the hole is always that period between arrival and the point at which one is able to get one's hands on a worthwhile book. Some previous occupant had left a couple of paperbacks in my cell, one of which was an early-nineties thriller called *The Mafia Candidate* in which a major presidential contender turns out to be a tool of the mafia and not of Northrop Grumman or Booz Allen Hamilton or Lockheed Martin or Bell Helicopter or Kellogg Brown & Root, like the more respectable candidates. As the story begins, an undercover FBI agent joins some suspected drug runners on a Caribbean yacht cruise in order to gather evidence, rather than simply lying to a grand jury to obtain a warrant like a real FBI agent would do. Alas, the narc's cover is blown and he's held at gunpoint by the mob henchmen. "If this were an Indiana Jones movie, he might throw himself to the floor and roll under the table while all these guys with cannons blazed away at each other," explains the author. "But this wasn't the movies and things like that didn't happen in real life. Or real death, either."

·　　·　　·

Proud though I was at having discovered the worst line ever written, I was now in full-on lit-crit final form blood frenzy battle mode, and so instead of resting on my snide and pompous laurels, I went ahead and picked up the other paperback. This was *Holiday in Death* by Nora Roberts, a contemptible writer who appears to have amassed an unwarranted fortune for herself and her foul publishers by catering to the gauche sexual fantasies of the American soccer mom, cursed among demographics. Having already written every possible combination of English words that can be jammed into a conventional 300-page romance novel and having thereby churned out some 900 trillion best-sellers, this arch-priestess of darkness next saw fit to concoct an entirely new genre, "futuristic romantic suspense," of which this *Holiday* title is listed as being just one of two dozen in a series.

The setting: New York, 2043. The hero: a female cop who just happens to be married to THE RICHEST MAN IN THE WORLD WHO IS ALSO RUGGEDLY HANDSOME. As the story begins, our pig protagonist is feeling sad because THE RICHEST MAN

IN THE WORLD WHO IS ALSO RUGGEDLY HANDSOME is on a business trip to space, presumably to attend the ribbon cutting for the Palantir-Pentagon Joint Orbital Omniscience Satellite Array or something of that nature. But then he picks up the space phone and makes a space call to tell his jack-booted thugget that he's coming home early because he just misses her so much. So he heads back to Earth, perhaps catching a space ride on one of Elon Musk's space yachts along with Palantir chief Peter Thiel and the biomechanical meta-clone of Admiral Poindexter that serves as Thiel's handler. (I should probably explain that I spent a pleasant afternoon creating a dystopian geopolitical backstory for Roberts' setting whereby the United States and its client states have fallen under the dual control of DARPA's Office of Perpetual Data Supremacy and the Shadow Council of Misguided Tech Billionaires. I wish I could say that this took a great deal of imagination.) When he gets home he takes his little cop wife by the hand, and what do you suppose he tells her? He tells her this: "The wanting of you never stops." Rather than do the only decent thing by shooting him in the back and casually tossing her taser next to the body in support of a falsified police report, this wanton cop-tart actually responds positively to her space husband's deranged and overwritten declaration of space lust. There follows what is likely intended to be a sex scene, though it's all rather abstract so they might just be doing tai chi in a humid room.

Among the various tacked-on elements by which Roberts occasionally sees fit to remind us that this is the future, a list of the contents of someone's apartment will usually include an "entertainment unit" or some such thing. Science fiction authors have been pulling this shit for literally eighty years now, sprinkling their projected futures with "comm units" and "food preparation units" and whatnot. It's time to accept that no one is ever going to market their consumer appliance as any sort of "unit." Things like that don't happen in real life. OR REAL DEATH, EITHER.

•　　　•　　　•

Anyhoo, I spent much of the first couple of days talking to my cellmate. (Note that a stint in the hole doesn't necessarily entail solitary confinement, which is not always viable due to over-crowding.) As far as SHU cellmates go, it would be hard to top the one with whom I was initially placed last time I was thrown into the hole a year ago, after allegedly inciting a demonstration: a white, red-bearded Texas Muslim with the words "Death Rain Upon My Enemies" tattooed across his back in Arabic, and who, when asked by a staff officer if he had anything to say to the disciplinary committee in his own defense, quoted Saddam Hussein's reply from his war crimes trial that he did not recognize the authority of their court, and who enjoyed not only gangsta rap and PCP but also the work of Phil Collins and, I swear to God, Oscar Wilde. I wrote two whole columns about this guy and was crestfallen when he was shipped off to the maximum-security prison which he has no doubt since claimed as a province of Islamic State. Indeed, the truly heartbreaking thing about federal prison is the absence of video cameras by which to fully document the almost supernaturally bizarre array of people that the FBI has managed to bring together.

To give you a better sense of this, my new cellmate here in the SHU snuck over to Dallas from Mexico when he was fifteen, became the leader of a gang, did a year in state prison for shooting another drug dealer with a shotgun, sometimes consulted a local television psychic called Indio Apache for intel by which to better plot his criminal strategy, and worships Santa Muerte, the skeletal narco-deity beloved throughout the Mexican underworld. He has three kids, is currently serving a fifteen-year sentence for conspiring to distribute methamphetamines, is listed on his indictment as having seven different aliases, and is, he tells me, "almost twenty years old." In the federal system, this qualifies him as a moderately interesting person. And, yes, here in

Texas dealing meth is fifteen times more serious than shooting someone with a shotgun.

Panchito Villa, as I'll call him, is actually a very good cellmate. For one thing, he gives me the bread from our food trays, which is a big deal here in the SHU where one can't get commissary, and particularly at this prison, where the rations have been inexplicably reduced over the last two years. Apparently his old boxing coach weaned him off bread products during training and the lesson stuck. Also he drew some very impressive decorations on our cell wall, including a life-size depiction of what would appear to be Princess Zelda wearing a handkerchief over her lower face gangster-style and sporting the tag "Vata Loca" tattooed above her eyes.

One morning, the two of us discussed the possibility that, this being Wednesday, which is hamburger day, our lunch might perhaps include potato wedges—a relatively beloved dish that the prison manages to provide once or twice a month—instead of the potato chips that it pawns off on us more often than not. Panchito knelt before the photograph of a robed skeleton that serves as a makeshift shrine to Santa Muerte and prayed to her on our behalf, asking that she intercede in this matter. An hour later, we received our hamburgers accompanied by potato wedges, and afterwards Panchito led me in a Spanish prayer of thanksgiving to our benefactress. The sad thing is that, given the alternative explanation is that the prison administration decided to feed us a sufficient lunch in accordance with the national standards, and given how rarely this actually ends up happening on any given day under the reign of our jerk-off warden, Rodney Chandler, and also taking into account what I've already documented in prior columns regarding this prison's ongoing failure to meet a whole range of such standards on everything from hygiene to due process, there's a better than even chance that it really was Santa Muerte who got us the fucking potato wedges.

On a day when we happened to receive cornbread with our dinner, Panchito handed it over to me as usual.

"Are you sure you don't want this?" I asked. "I think cornbread isn't as bad for you."

"I don't want to risk it," replied the shotgun-wielding child soldier who makes pacts with demons for potato wedges.

.   .   .

Shortly after arrival I received my incident report in which the "reporting officer" relates, with some apparent effort: "ON JUNE 17 2015 AT APPROXIMATE 8:35 PM DURING A RANDOM BREATHALYZER TEST I DECIDED TO SEARCH INMATES BROWN 45057-177 LOCKER AND FOUND A COFFEE MUG FULL OF PRISON MADE INTHOXICANT. OPERATION LT WAS INFORMED AND INMATE BROWN #45047-177 WAS ESCORTED BY THE COMPOUNP OFFICER TO THE SHU." How it was that the benighted man-child should have been taken by a sudden fancy to search, er, "INMATES BROWN #45047-177 LOCKER" in the midst of a "RANDOM BREATHALYZER TEST" that I passed is left to the imagination. Luckily I received a gratuitous confirmation that this account was nonsense a few days later, when a Special Investigations Service officer by the name of McClinton came by the hole to give me yet another drug test and to brag about how they knew the hooch was in my locker due to the informants they have watching me. That just leaves the mystery of how the reporting officer managed to render "compound" as "compounp." And if anyone out there is having trouble deciding on a name for their ska band, you could do worse than "PRISON MADE INTHOXICANT."

There've also been some exciting new developments in my ongoing quest to get the BOP to explain why its D.C. liaison, Terrance Moore, switched off my ability to e-mail the public an hour after I used it to contact a journalist about wrongdoing by bureau employees. Recall that the Administrative Remedy coordinator, a fellow named McKinney, fraudulently back-dated receipt of my original complaint about this to indicate that he received it on June 4, when in fact his office received it on April 30. Then, he failed to reply within the allotted twenty days of his make-believe date of receipt (and likewise missed his other self-declared deadline of June 29 for my second complaint regarding his failure to follow procedure on my first complaint, by golly!). According to the BOP's own guidelines, I'm permitted to take this failure to respond as a refusal of my claim, thereby finally allowing me to file a BP-10 form, which goes to the regional office. But—hark!—on June 30, McKinney belatedly filed for extensions on the illicit deadlines that he'd already missed, giving himself twenty more days to respond to *both* complaints. And then he missed his fake deadlines, too.

Meanwhile, the prison has failed to inform me immediately and in writing of the various media interview requests I've been receiving, as policy requires it to; actor and documentary filmmaker Alex Winter has even sent his latest application via certified mail, to no effect. It also turns out that I'm on the BOP's Central Inmate Monitoring system, billed in a BOP program statement as being used for prisoners who "present special needs for management," which is one way of putting it. Naturally, they've failed to "ensure that the affected inmate is notified in writing as promptly as possible of the classification and the basis for it," as is also required by policy. On a totally unrelated subject, I was sentenced recently to another thirty days in the hole beyond the month I'd already done, plus ninety days of phone, commissary, visiting and e-mail restriction, which will certainly teach me to break BOP rules without first getting a job with the BOP.

Luckily I've gotten lots of nifty books in the mail from supporters, including *The Muqaddimah*, the fourteenth-century scholar Ibn Khaldun's treatise on world history. Early on, Khaldun presents us with an example of an old story he deems unreliable: "Sea monsters prevented Alexander from building Alexandria. He took a wooden container in which a glass box was inserted, and dived in it to the bottom of the sea. Then he drew pictures of the devilish monsters he saw. He then had metal effigies of these animals made and set them opposite the place where building was going on. When the monsters came out and saw the effigies, they fled." Ibn Killjoy goes out of his way to discredit this charming tale: "Now, rulers would not take such a risk. Any ruler who would attempt such a thing would work his own undoing and provoke the outbreak of revolt against himself, and be replaced by the people with someone else. . . . Furthermore, the jinn are not known to have specific forms and effigies. They are able to take on various forms." Whatever, asshole.

Stop Sending Me Jonathan Franzen Novels

As I not only live in a federal prison but am also currently being held once again in a twenty-three-hour-a-day lockdown punishment cell due to my incorrigible behavior, I haven't been in a position to directly follow what I gather has been a very edifying net-driven controversy over Jonathan Franzen and his latest work, which really feels like another punishment in and of itself. Thankfully, though, I've received a couple of representative clippings in the mail, along with a copy of the book in question, *Purity*, which I've been asked to review.

Two things bear noting in the interest of full disclosure. First, this book revolves in part around the amoral antics of a character based rather closely on Julian Assange, while separately including references to Assange himself, most of them critical. I happen to have been an early and rabid partisan of Assange, and the two of us sometimes say nice things about each other in the press. Meanwhile, the criminal charges on which I've been imprisoned center on my fairly peripheral involvement in a 2011 raid by certain anarchist hackers of my acquaintance on the State Department–linked corporate espionage firm Stratfor, the stolen e-mails from which were provided to WikiLeaks. Second, and more to the point, I despise contemporary fiction almost as much as Jonathan Franzen despises women. In my view, the novel peaked with Dostoyevsky, and although I do admire, for instance, Lessing's *The Good Terrorist*, Eco's *Foucault's Pendulum*, and Burgess's *Earthly Powers*, you'll note that the most recent of these was published almost thirty years ago. Now, I don't doubt that some worthwhile works of "serious" fiction are still being put out now and again, but I wouldn't know how to go about finding them, as many of our nation's respectable outlets have apparently resorted to just hiring crazy people off the street to do their book reviews.

I have here, for instance, a copy of *Los Angeles Times* book critic David Ulin's recent review of *Purity*. This is just as well, as I needed a refresher on my Franzen lore, and Ulin opens with that very thing before promptly descending into some sort of fugue state. Naturally I was aware of the existence of *The Corrections*, which, Ulin reminds us, was "his masterful 2001 portrait of a Midwestern family," but I seem to have entirely missed the more recent *Freedom*, "a moving meditation on marriage and friendship." Nor was I aware that the author himself had reached the dual status of "both avatar and scapegoat." As Ulin explains, "By now, Franzen is often regarded less as writer than as cultural signifier, emblem of white male hegemony. That this has little if anything to do with the substance of his novels is (perhaps) the point and the tragedy; when it comes to Franzen, the writing is where we go last."

"Tragedy" may be a bit melodramatic in this instance (although it is indeed distressing to learn that the venerable old

White Male Hegemony is now being fronted by Jonathan Franzen; we seem to have taken something of a plunge since Winston Churchill). After all, Ulin himself here admits that "that depth, that texture," which is said to mark the characterization in *The Corrections*, "can be elusive in *Purity*, which is a more plotted novel, sometimes to its detriment." And plotting, he concedes, "has never been the author's strong suit." Perhaps there's a good reason why the writing is where we go last? But no—Ulin still maintains that our timely reading of this poorly plotted novel filled with low-resolution automatons is our only chance of averting tragedy because the writing itself is just that good. As proof, he actually cites the following snippet of monologue as delivered by a character named Tom:

> "Don't talk to me about hatred if you haven't been married," he tells us in the book's one extended first-person sequence. "Only love, only long empathy and identification and compassion, can root another person in your heart so deeply that there's no escaping your hatred of her, not ever; especially not when the thing you hate most about her is your capacity to be hurt by her."
>
> That's fierce writing, and it does what fiction is supposed to, forcing us to peel back the surfaces, to see how love can turn to desolation, how we are betrayed by what we believe. It is the most human of dilemmas, with which we must all come to terms.

Setting aside this sprinkling of third-tier lit-crit commonplaces that I blush even to reproduce, it's unclear to me exactly what "fierce" is supposed to mean in this context, although I can tell that the term is here being misapplied since it appears to be intended as a compliment. And though the passage itself isn't especially awful, it's alarming to be tasked with reading a 500-page tome in which that sort of overwrought prose is supposed to make up for bad plotting and notso-hotso characterization. It's also quite telling that Ulin manages to get his favorite passage wrong; the end of the selection actually reads, "her capacity to be hurt by you," not "your capacity to be hurt by her," and directly follows a key plot point that makes the distinction quite clear. But then, as the fellow said himself, the writing is where we go last. Shed we a tear for Franzen? Nay—shed we a tear for us all!

.   .   .

When I finally did get around to going to the writing last, I was relieved to find that *Purity* isn't a terrible book or even a very bad one. There is some clever use of language once in a while, yet Franzen resists the temptation to dip into the self-conscious attempts at "literary" phrasing that mark so much of his competition (our friend Ulin mentions that Franzen penned a 1996 *Harper's* essay on the state of fiction, inevitably titled "Perchance to Dream"; one might be better served in reading a piece *The Atlantic* ran a few years later, "A Reader's Manifesto," in which someone named B. R. Myers points out that a great portion of modern prose styling is conceptually fraudulent garbage). Characters will sometimes think clever thoughts or even say them out loud, but not so often that this becomes unseemly. Now and again we are even presented with snippets of real insight. One can see how Franzen could have written a much better book fifteen years ago.

But one can also see how that book might have been a fluke. In *Purity*, marriages fail one after another in excruciating fifty-page flashbacks. No one is particularly likable or even unlikable, though a few do manage to be insufferable. Toward the end we're treated to one great character, the cynical plutocrat dad of one of the dastardly feminists, but then he disappears from view and promptly dies. The megalomaniacal information activist is admirably complex, but as a megalomaniacal information activist myself, I found him unconvincing. The one murder that serves to kick off the plot is perpetuated against an otherwise minor off-screen character rather than one of the several main characters whom the reader might have much preferred to see murdered. Franzen is also rather hard on the ladies, whereas everyone would have been better served had he instead been harder on himself and maybe put out a better book.

It's worth reiterating, though, that this sort of subject matter is not my cup of tea to begin with, and I certainly don't want anyone to refrain from reading a novel that might interest them simply because I said mean things about it. If you're up for a "moving meditation on marriage and friendship," then you should probably read *Freedom* over and over again until your eyes bleed. If divorce and infidelity and guilt and trial separation is your thing, then you'd better get your ass over to the nearest book store and pick up a copy of *Purity.* You need not worry about what I think. But if you're curious anyway, what I think is that I hate you.

.　　　•　　　•　　　•

Just kidding. Ah, but there is indeed a major plot element interwoven into *Purity* that should be of interest to someone like me—that of Franzen's ersatz Assange, Andreas Wolf, and his leak-driven Sunshine Project. Let me put it this way. I was interested enough in WikiLeaks, state transparency, and emergent opposition networks to do five years in prison over such things, but I wasn't interested enough that I would have voluntarily plowed through 500 pages of badly plotted failed-marriage razzmatazz by an author who's long past his expiration date simply in order to learn what the Great King of the Honkies thinks about all this.

There are big ideas here, but none worth having, much less writing down. One big idea seems to be that Julian Assange has blood on his hands. Not even the Pentagon makes this charge anymore, but it's nonetheless raised almost in passing in an Oakland anarchist squat, of all places, by a transient Occupy activist, of all people, who proclaims: "But Wiki was dirty—people died because of Wiki," an assertion that goes unchallenged. To be sure, this is a bit character talking, rather than one of a handful of main characters whom we can be certain are speaking for Franzen when they start denouncing the Internet or women, but again, it sounds about as natural coming from a slum-dwelling anarcho-what-have-you as a declaration to the effect that the Multinational Imperialist State of Amerikkka must be brought to its knees by a reenergized Situationist International movement would sound coming from Mike Rogers. This, then, is the author speaking.

Not content to present discredited five-year-old anti-Assange Department of Defense talking points as if they were accepted facts even among Assange's own ideological constituents, Franzen has, again, also created this Andreas Wolf figure, unmistakably modeled on Assange—he's even escaped to a friendly South American country, as the real Assange is trying to do, and like Assange, he's in the habit of deploying a rather striking female emissary on secret missions around the world. And naturally, Franzen has made Wolf a near-sociopathic fraud, murderer, and cover-up artist who also has weird sexual hang-ups (although it's worth noting that most everyone in *Purity* has weird sexual hang-ups; one young lady can only achieve climax during a full moon, but then you know how feminists are). What's particularly interesting is the sort of cluttered presence of both the model of the real figure and the real figure himself, whereas generally a writer will content himself with one of the two. Do the inhabitants of this fictional world ever get suspicious, I wonder, concluding as they must that one of the two global celebrity leakers is clearly an unfair literary depiction of the other? Do they also notice that all of their mothers are psychotic and that their marriages tend to slowly collapse in the course of long, grueling flashbacks, and do they conclude that they're living in a Jonathan Franzen novel? This raises all manner of ethical questions that I will leave to others.

Rather than any measured objections to online activism as currently practiced or the social-networking culture, we're treated instead to a moving meditation on how the Internet is a totalitarian system comparable to East Germany under the Stasi or the Soviets under Stalin. The gurus of the information-technology field—the "New Regime," as Franzen calls them—are very much the natural heirs to the politburo. Oh, there are a few differences here and there, of course: "But Stalin himself hadn't needed to take so many risks, because terror worked better. Although to a man, the new revolutionaries all claimed to worship risk-taking—a relative term in my case, since the risk in question was of losing some venture capitalist's money, or worse of wasting a few parentally funded years, rather than, say, the risk of being shot or hanged—the most successful of them had instead followed Stalin's example."

So, at least in the sense that these wacky Internet people lack the moral authority conferred upon the Bolsheviks by virtue of risk, this, uh, otherwise useful comparison between the start-up crowd and the Stalinists does perhaps break down a little. But! But! It gathers new strength insomuch that "the most successful of them" often have recourse to terror, in this case the "terrors of technocracy," which consist of "the fear of unpopularity and uncoolness, the fear of missing out, the fear of being flamed or forgotten." So, there you go.

·　　　·　　　·

Just a page later, Franzen inexplicably switches gears and decides that the terrors of technology instead consist of "the algorithms that Facebook used to monetize its users' privacy and Twitter to manipulate memes that were supposedly self-generating. But smart people were actually far more terrified of the New Regime than of what the regime had persuaded less-smart people to be afraid of, the NSA, the CIA—it was straight from the totalitarian playbook, disavowing your own methods of terror by imputing them to your enemy and presenting yourself as the only defense against them." Setting aside the demonstrably false and frankly bizarre claim that recent concerns over the intelligence community's unprecedented capabilities stem merely from some sort of clever gambit by tech firm CEOs who must resort to falsely "imputing" such things rather than, say, from documented and ongoing revelations about those agencies, it's hard to see how Franzen can actually believe that the misuse of personal information by powerful corporations should logically preclude "smart people" from also fearing the NSA, as their "less-smart" counterparts have been "persuaded" to do. It's likewise difficult to see how Franzen can be entirely unaware of the contention that's been put forth over and over again by many of the very people who have made sacrifices to bring these matters to attention—that we are concerned with the *combination* of state and corporate power exercised in secret, drawing upon advanced and little-known information technology, wielded in such a way as to narrow further and further the potential for truly private life while also contaminating the very information flow that a citizenry requires if it is to survive above the level of a subject population, defended by an opaque protocol of deception and retaliation, and aided and abetted by a dysfunctional establishment culture that was unequipped to even discover the problem without a great deal of help from outside that establishment, which has nonetheless studiously refrained from learning any lessons from all of this.

There's an old joke which holds that in heaven, the cooks are French, the cops are English, and the engineers are German; whereas in hell, the cooks are English, the cops are German, and the engineers are French. We live in a sort of silly cultural hell where the columns are composed by Thomas Friedman, the novels are written by Jonathan Franzen, the debate is framed by CNN, and the fact-checking is done by no one. Franzen's nightmare—a new regime of technology and information activists that will challenge the senile culture of which he is so perfectly representative—is exactly what is needed.

ESPN the Magazine

FINALIST—COLUMNS AND
COMMENTARY

"A good columnist says things
that haven't been said," said the
Ellie judges about the three pieces
printed here. "Howard Bryant says
them in a way that won't be
forgotten. In prose that is as deft
and unflinching as it is concise,
Bryant shows us why sports offers
perhaps the best platform in
America for an honest discussion
about race." Bryant joined ESPN
in 2007 and now writes for
ESPN.com as well as ESPN the
Magazine. A regular Ellie finalist,
ESPN the Magazine has been
nominated in recent years in
categories ranging from Reporting
to Feature Photography. And it's
not just Ellie judges who have
been impressed. In an online poll
conducted by ASME in February,
readers voted the magazine's
2015 "Body Issue" their favorite
cover of the year.

Howard Bryant

Down for the Count *and* The King Has Spoken *and* The Power of Sight

Down for the Count

In post-Ferguson America, the language has sharpened as violence has increased. The vague "racism" succumbed to the stronger "white privilege," which has been radicalized into "white supremacy," a term not just relating to skinheads and lynching but to the daily condition whites enjoy of being the cultural default, the ones in charge, the ones always in the lead.

The white American boxer is dead as disco, yet the lead of director Antoine Fuqua's riveting, heartbreaking new film *Southpaw* is light-heavyweight champion Billy Hope, played by Jake Gyllenhaal. It's a historical incongruity that wafts like cigar smoke at ringside. The WBA, WBO, and WBC haven't had a white American light-heavyweight champion in the twenty-first century. The last white American IBF light-heavyweight champion was Bobby Czyz, nearly thirty years ago, in 1987. Yet after six *Rocky*s, *Raging Bull*, *Cinderella Man*, and *The Fighter*, the white boxer is one of Hollywood's enduring leading men.

Southpaw is hard and fantastic, a statement less about ethnicity than class. Hope was raised through foster care because he was born to an incarcerated mother. He and his wife (Rachel Mc-Adams) met as kids in an orphanage. He has self-destructive rage, but his path and pathologies are humanized. After a brutal fight, his ten-year-old daughter, Leila, receives a text from her mom that reads, "Daddy won." At home, little Leila counts the cuts on his battered face. He is a father. They are a family.

Still, despite the movie's excellence, Hope's whiteness is what the studio believed audiences needed to care about his story. (Kurt Sutter's screenplay was inspired by the life of Eminem, who was Fuqua's first choice for the lead.) Maybe it is because boxing stories are about underdogs, and the one place in America a black man is expected to be the favorite is in sports, especially in the ring. Maybe it is because with a black lead, a character with a dark and troubled backstory would only confirm white resentments and deep-seated fears of black masculinity, making it impossible to generate the necessary sympathy for the protagonist. "As a black man and director, I felt that," Fuqua says. "I don't know. Audiences will bring what they feel about black people to the film, and yeah, they can watch the news, see a black player failing and say, 'That's what they do.'"

There is another, simpler reality: Hollywood, like sports, measures its analytics, and the stars make movies happen, as Will Smith made *Ali* happen and Mark Wahlberg made *The Fighter* happen. In the case of *Southpaw*, a would-be Oscar contender with a modest budget, Fuqua made a black film that Hollywood seems to believe couldn't have a black lead, and even he, director of the brilliant *Training Day*, cannot always overcome these forces. "It's economics, really," Fuqua says. "It comes down to what the people with the money think they can sell. The thinking is, 'Why take a risk when you can do it with formula?'"

So as white American boxers face extinction, white movie stars are the wallpaper—the ones who save the day and kiss the girl, receive the humanizing roles, remain the default. This is the meaning of white supremacy: privilege so pervasive we rarely notice and hardly question its existence. "What it is like to be white is not to say, 'We have to level the playing field,' but to acknowledge that not only do white people own the playing field but they have so designated this plot of land as a playing field to begin with," author Fran Lebowitz wrote in 1997. "The advantage of being white is so extreme, so overwhelming, so immense, that to use the word 'advantage' at all is misleading since it implies a kind of parity that simply does not exist."

The privilege translates into the audience's caring about Hope, despite his flaws, and to caring about the black trainer who saves him (the tremendous Forest Whitaker, the conscience of the film), and to caring about the black boxing world where his rehabilitation begins. In *Southpaw*, the only white boxer in the entire film *is the lead*; everyone and everything else revolves around him, the cultural default at work. It's not easy to watch or to acknowledge. As Gyllenhaal says to McAdams when she predicts brain damage as the future cost of his fighting, "Why you gotta lay the truth right now?"

The King Has Spoken

In the first 239 days of 2015, 185 black men were murdered in the city of Baltimore. In post-Katrina New Orleans, FiveThirtyEight concluded, black residents are more likely to live in poverty than before the hurricane ten years ago. The *Washington Post* recently released data indicating that every nine days, on average, American police kill an unarmed black man. The Bureau of Labor Statistics reported a 9.1 percent black unemployment rate for July, nearly twice the rate of whites.

White America grows exasperated by the insistence that race still matters, but these facts are a neon sign pointing not at post-racialism but to an entrenched underclass. In Akron, Ohio, hometown of LeBron James, the black poverty rate is 28 percent, 12 points higher than the state average. To James, the numbers are not just a topic, ammunition for winning an argument, but statistical recognition of his life before fame. Days after the anniversary protests marking Michael Brown's death in Ferguson, Missouri, James partnered with the University of Akron and countered the numbers with other numbers, pledging $41 million to send as many as 2,000 at-risk Akron kids to college.

It was a massive initiative, a reminder that, in addition to protest and pressure, the rhetoric of pulling oneself up by one's bootstraps means nothing without boots. It was also something else: proof that James is the signature socially conscious athlete of his time. By this measure he need not aspire to be Michael Jordan. He's already run right past him.

James and Dwyane Wade organized the first athlete protest of the killing of Trayvon Martin. James used his power to rally players and challenge the NBA to be decisive on Donald Sterling. James wore an I CAN'T BREATHE shirt in warm-ups to show solidarity with young black men disposable to society because they lack his talent. Instead of blaming hip-hop or admonishing the less fortunate, he confronted the "dead or in jail" narrative that permeates black male life with a real program backed by real money. He wrote an enormous check as part of staring down a bitter truth: If "dead or in jail" is as good as it gets for black boys who don't have a blinding forty-yard dash time or a bull's-eye jumper, then at this late date in the American story, integration has been a colossal failure.

James does not live independent of his environment, and neither did Jordan. James is in the prime of his youth and earning power amid national protest and Black Lives Matter. His generation is not a new target of police brutality; it is the latest edition of the same old target. He grew up witnessing the collision between the progress of some and the dead ends for most of the kids who look like him, at a time when the term "postracial" sounds not only ridiculous but naive. America could not be more racial than it is right now.

Jordan, meanwhile, came of age during the most comprehensive wave of conservatism in the twentieth century, a political retrenchment that followed the sweeping social ambition of Lyndon Johnson. Jordan was fifteen when the Supreme Court struck down minority set-asides in the landmark *Bakke* case, limiting affirmative action, and eighteen when President Ronald Reagan fired 11,000 striking air traffic controllers. Jordan's 1980s were a market correction of the 1960s, not a time of protest or challenge but one of accumulating individual wealth while Great Society, labor union, and New Deal gains and attitudes were being scaled back. Jordan's time was when money was celebrated as the only measure. Greed is good.

The similarities between James and Jordan end when their shared no. 23 jersey rests on a hanger, for Jordan has never been known for a single courageous social act. While James attempts to bridge the powerless to a future, Jordan sued a defunct supermarket chain and won $8.9 million over an advertisement that reportedly yielded all of $4. (Jordan said he planned to donate the money to charity.)

James has accepted a challenge of his times so foreign to the 1980s, making him an heir not to Jordan but to the civil rights movement, to Jim Brown and Bill Russell, to the idea of the athlete as activist. Every day of his career has existed under the shadow of Jordan, but as citizen, LeBron does not look up to Michael. It should be the other way around.

The Power of Sight

A week after Flavia Pennetta engineered the Great Mic Drop of 2015 by winning a U.S. Open title that had been prematurely promised to Serena Williams, actress Viola Davis underscored the significance of what has been the Year of Serena, hoisting an Emmy for her role in the ABC series *How to Get Away with Murder*. The Emmys were first presented in 1949, the year Jackie Robinson won the National League MVP. Nearly seven decades later, after years of African Americans enduring insulting phrases such as "I don't see color," Davis finally became the first black woman to win an Emmy for best actress in a drama. Williams failed to reach the U.S. Open final, of course, losing in a seismic semifinal upset to Roberta Vinci, but Davis, in her historic moment, echoed the themes and grievances that the highly decorated Williams symbolized for women—and especially women of color—all summer. "In my mind," Davis said, quoting Harriet Tubman in her acceptance speech, "I see a line. And over that line I see green fields and lovely flowers and beautiful white women with their arms stretched out to me over that line. But I can't seem to get there nohow. I can't seem to get over that line. . . . The only thing that separates women of color from anyone else is opportunity."

The vitriol and passive aggressiveness directed at Williams for much of the year— whether on social media, from the Wimbledon crowd, or even from some peers (American Jamie Hampton looked small when she tweeted out "#forza #italiansonly" after Vinci beat Williams to set up an all-Italian final)—was often explained as a mere byproduct of the familiar favorite-underdog narrative, or of Williams's personality. Neither explanation felt honest, not at those decibel levels, especially at Wimbledon, when Williams's physique was critiqued so crudely that author J. K. Rowling took to social media in her defense.

Davis's rare victory might seem unrelated to Williams, who has won virtually every title her sport offers. The connection lies beneath the surface. Williams is no underdog, but so many of her most devoted followers certainly are. For them, her tennis is not about sport but about her existing as a counter to nonexistence, to the sixty-seven years of invisibility Davis's victory highlighted, to the invisibility that the visible—those who look the part and get the opportunities—often have the luxury of ignoring or dismissing. Serena exemplifies the black excellence that, as Davis pointed out, rarely receives an audition. African American women channel through her.

Williams was not only fighting Garbine Muguruza in the Wimbledon final and Maria Sharapova in the Australian Open final. She was also fighting for a feeling on the part of many of her supporters—the feeling that her victories, her presence, help stem the daily erasing, the smothering reality that black women really don't matter, cannot win, do not count in American culture. "You cannot win an Emmy for roles that are simply not there," Davis said. She could have been speaking of black female sports writers, whose voices were virtually nonexistent this summer, even though the season belonged to a black woman champion.

Serena always, and with particular urgency this year, represents actually counting, such a small yet critical thing.

The conversation of race in the United States has never been so much between black and white as between white and white, for the black demand of full citizenship has remained unchanged. For African Americans, Charleston and Sandra Bland connect to Serena Williams's being ridiculed for her muscular frame and to her making less endorsement money than Sharapova. They connect to Harvard-educated James Blake's being rousted in front of the Grand Hyatt by an undercover cop, and to a sixty-seven-year wait for a black woman to win a trophy for a TV drama.

Always convinced of their objectivity, too many white Americans denied the existence of the connective tissue, angry at the black response and uninterested in exploring its causes. They miss the significance of Serena. For her fans, often the unchosen, Serena's quest was deeply rooted in these themes of invisibility, of yearning to be attractive without ridicule, of the fight just to be seen. She ultimately did not lift the trophy, but across the country, in another industry, Davis did it for her.

Esquire

WINNER—ESSAYS AND CRITICISM

This is what it was like for Matthew Teague after his wife, Nicole, was driven mad by the cancer that was killing her: "I watched, speechless, as she pulled off the last of the gauze and made her way to the shower, dribbling stool and acid onto the floor." There to help him was his friend Dane Faucheux. "I had married into this situation, but how had he gotten here?" writes Teague. "Love is not a big-enough word. He stood and faced the reality of death for my sake." The Ellie judges used words like "brutal" and "graphic" for "The Friend" but also described it as "beautifully rendered." The Ellie won by "The Friend" was the seventeenth for Esquire *editor David Granger, who announced his departure from the magazine shortly before accepting the award for this extraordinary story.*

Matthew Teague

The Friend

Most of September 17, 2012, has evaporated from my mind. I still have a few memories. I have the way the surgeon's voice shook. I remember my wife calling my name while she was still under sedation. And I have an image of the hospital floor, up close. I remember white tile and a hope: *Maybe I will never have to get up. Maybe they will just let me die here.*

Nicole was thirty-four, and the doctor had been direct: "It's everywhere," he said. "Like somebody dipped a paintbrush in cancer and flicked it around her abdomen." I staggered down a hallway and then collapsed. I remember the tile, close to my face, and then watching it retreat as my best friend picked me up from the floor. His name is Dane Faucheux, and I remember noting, even in the midst of a mental fugue: *Dane's a lot stronger than I realized.*

I was in shock and stayed there a long time. We don't tell each other the truth about dying, as a people. Not real dying. Real dying, regular and mundane dying, is so hard and so ugly that it becomes the worst thing of all: It's grotesque. It's undignified. No one ever told me the truth about it, not once. When it happened to my beloved, I lost my footing in more than one way. The tiled floor of life—morals, ethics, even laws—became a shifting and relative thing. I smuggled drugs. Lied. Hid money from the IRS.

I think I've hung on to the sensation of the hospital floor and being lifted away from it because it captures everything that followed in the next two years. The shock of mortality. One man's collapse. And another man's refusal to let it happen.

.　　　.　　　.

Dane decided to move in around Christmas 2013, on the night our dog died.

Almost all of that year is lost to me. Nicole had ovarian cancer, which had metastasized to her stomach, and she endured a series of physical insults that, taken individually, would have been shattering; a single trip to the chemo ward, watching what looked like antifreeze flow into her veins while the nurses offered me cheese crackers, would have changed my life forever. Taken together, though, the surgeries and chemicals all form a smear that can't be taken apart and examined.

I do have a few recollections from that year, and Dane appears in each. For instance, when Nicole started finding hair on her pillow, I braced for her agony, because she was so young and so beautiful. But she asked me to meet her in the living room with a towel, scissors, and my beard trimmer.

She dragged a chair into the middle of the room and pulled her hair—long and dark and cascading—into a ponytail. "Go ahead," she said.

I sawed at it with the scissors until it came free in my hand. She looked up with wet eyes and smiled.

"I might as well rock this," she said. "Give me a Mohawk."

Afterward, we stepped into a bathroom so that she could look in a mirror. She was Creek Indian, and I had never seen her cheekbones so proud, her eyes so defiant.

I sent a photo of her to Dane, and a few minutes later he sent one back. He had carved a Mohawk of his own to match hers.

Nicole laughed. We had met Dane fifteen years earlier, when we all lived in New Orleans and they were in college together. Men trailed Nicole everywhere; in grocery stores men would follow her from produce to dairy and out into the parking lot. When she smiled, men imagined she needed them, and she smiled a lot. So I had developed a pitying skepticism of other men's motivations. But even when Dane didn't know I was watching, he averted his gaze from her body, and he accepted her smile as nothing more than a small gift. He offered us his friendship with such humility, such deference to our marriage, that I trusted him from the beginning. I'm not sure Nicole ever forgave us for both being men because over the years it allowed me to grow close to him in a way she never could.

His expressions of affection were, for her, tiny victories. So when she held up the photo of him with a Mohawk and laughed— "Look! Ha ha!"—I knew she meant it in the most competitive, gloating way possible.

In a season of butchery and wreckage and defeat, she had triumphed. I asked Dane later why he had done it. He didn't understand the question. "It was more fun than me just shaving my head bald," he said. It had never occurred to him to do nothing.

Later that year, I remember him standing sentry at the hospital. He had driven from New Orleans—we were living in a small town called Fairhope, Alabama—to stand guard for hours in the hallway outside Nicole's room so that she could sleep. One afternoon, a group of church ladies arrived. There is no force under heaven as mighty as a band of middle-aged Baptist ladies, and from inside the room we could hear Dane wage a battle of kind intentions.

"They are resting right now," he said. "I'm so sorry."

"Well, we came by to pray for them," one of the ladies said.

"Yes, ma'am," he said. "But I feel pretty sure God can hear you out here in the hall."

We spent that Christmas season in the hospital. Friends came and decorated the room, and our two little girls curled up against Nicole in her hospital bed while she read "'Twas the Night Before Christmas." We all tried to ignore the clear tube pumping feces up from her bowels and out her nose.

Dane had come to visit after Thanksgiving and never ended up returning home. He burned through his weeks of vacation time, visiting the hospital during the day and sleeping at our house each night.

The night after Christmas, our pug, Gracie, threw up something black and putrid on the floor at his feet. He put her in a basket with a blanket in his car and searched for an open animal clinic. When he found one, he explained our situation to the veterinarian, and after some testing she blurted, "I'm so sorry, but this dog has cancer and I think she's going to die. Actually, I know she is going to die." And then she burst into tears.

Dane called me. I sat in the blinking red and green lights of our hospital room, listened to the news, and offered, "Okay."

Gracie's death didn't move me. It annoyed me. She was forcing me to have a talk with my daughters that would link cancer and death, and I wasn't prepared yet.

Dane came to the hospital with a bottle of wine. We sat on the floor and drank amid the wrapping paper of the girls' Christmas presents.

"I think maybe I should just move in with you guys," he said. "Just to help out for a couple of months."

That meant leaving his job, his city, his friends, his apartment, his life.

"Okay," I said.

· · ·

We readied ourselves for the physical horrors of death. Nicole seemed especially practical about it. She told us, "Just don't let me stink."

She shed weight, but we expected that. Dane and I could hardly see it because we never left her. When visitors came, though, we could see it reflected in their faces or when her shirt slipped to the side, exposing her collarbone. It looked wrong, like something alien implanted under her skin.

The most obvious manifestation of her illness, aside from weight loss, were the wounds. After each surgery, her skin was slower to heal, and finally a surgeon asked me if I knew about wound packing.

"No," I said.

"You need to learn," he said.

Each night, Nicole would lie naked on the bed and, using tweezers, I would extract a piece of ribbon from the wounds in her abdomen, sometimes several feet long, which would uncoil in the air above her like a pus-covered tapeworm. Then I would repack new pieces of ribbon into the holes, folding them in, spiraling them inside her, while she wept and begged me to just skip it, please, this one time.

Please, Matt. Please.

Since we had met, when she was still a teenager, I had loved her with my whole self. Only now can I look back on the fullness of our affection; at the time I could see nothing but one wound at a time, a hole the size of a dime, into which I needed to pack a fistful of material. Love wasn't something I felt anymore. It was just something I did. When I finished, I would lie next to her and use sterile cotton balls to soak up her tears. When she finally slept, I would slip out of bed and go into our closet, the most isolated room in the house. Inside, I would wrap a blanket around my head, stuff it into my mouth, lie down and bury my head in a pile of dirty clothes, and scream.

Sometimes at night, Nicole would wake howling and sweating, with a twist in her bowels. I would call for Dane, waking him, and he would hold the back door open for me while I carried Nicole to the car. Then he would sit up with our girls until we came home. Sometimes hours later, sometimes weeks.

Eventually I started to notice something strange: little bits of half-digested food emerging from Nicole's wounds. I called her oncologist, who used a word I had never heard before: *fistulas*. When there's an infection or some other foreign thing in the body, the flesh works to eject it, forming tunnels to the surface. Her body no longer recognized food as useful and was now expelling it directly out the front of her abdomen, like a foreign substance.

Nicole tried to lift her head and look at her belly. "Does that smell like poop to you?"

"No, it's hard to . . ."

"Is there poop coming out my *front*? Tell me."

For months, we tried to catch it with everything from colostomy bags to special gauzes to cloth diapers, but the stomach acid would burn through any adhesive and eventually started eating her flesh. There was no stopping it. There were only more narcotics for the pain.

These physical horrors, though, were nothing compared to what would come.

I told our family counselor, Julia, I knew things would get worse. "If I have to put her in a backpack and carry her to the chemo ward, I'll do it if it means getting an extra day with her."

Julia is a kind woman, but honest. "Before this is over," she said, "you will long for it to end."

Never, I said.

•   •   •

For months after Dane moved in, Nicole couldn't eat much, so I fed her intravenously. I had no medical training, but it didn't require a doctor; it just required someone sterile and awake.

It's difficult to appreciate the sterility of a hospital or lab until you try to impose it at home. In the early months of 2014, Dane and I cleaned ceaselessly—the house, the children, me, the medical equipment, Nicole herself. Boiling, wiping, filtering. But human bodies defy sterility, with our holes and our sloughing and our fingernails and our wet places.

The machine that pumped the fluid into her veins would shriek any time it needed attention—if a tube kinked, or she rolled over on it, or it ran out of fluid, or any number of other possibilities occurred—which happened every few minutes. During those months, Nicole was drugged and mostly unconscious, and I lay awake listening to the IV pump. I turned its amber display to face the wall, but that didn't help; I lay there doing the math, calculating how many milliliters of fluid remained until she needed more. In those months, I may never have slept an unbroken hour.

One day Dane touched my arm and I cried out, unsure of who he was. "You need sleep," he said.

He started conspiring against me, or so I suspected. From outside the bedroom door, I would overhear him talking with Nicole about my exhausted mental state, which seemed absurd considering her condition. He started calling Julia, the counselor, behind my back. And he was making some sort of secretive arrangements with my other friends.

One morning he sat down with me. "We are going away for a couple of days," he said. "You and me."

"What? No."

We would drive up to the foothills of the Appalachians and spend a couple days hiking. Another friend of Nicole's had agreed to come sit with her, he said.

"No."

Julia felt it was for the best.

"*No.*"

It wasn't for me, he said. It would make me a better caregiver for Nicole. "And for your girls," he said.

I conceded. We spent the next couple days in a national forest, walking endless trails, crossing streams, climbing rock formations, mile after mile after mile. At the end of one trail, we found a waterfall and sat in the cool pool at its base, looking up at the cataract pouring down. My body was useless; I could feel my equilibrium shifting left and right, as though I were still hiking. But in my physical depletion, I discovered what Dane had known all along: My mind felt sharper and was more hopeful than it had been in months.

After a few minutes, we noticed movement at the top of the waterfall. A half dozen college-aged women had climbed onto rocks jutting from the top of the falls, and while we watched they started taking off their clothes. I blinked at Dane and we both burst out laughing.

"Dude. What is happening?"

"Don't question this, Matt. You need this."

The girls started leaping from the rock into the deepest water at its base, and then climbing up and jumping again. They looked like angels, perpetually falling to earth. They seemed impossibly joyful and healthy, and we could hear them laughing above the sound of the water. Finally Dane said, "Let's do it!" and took off his shirt.

"I can't do that, man."

"Why?"

I had no answer and every answer. I was married. My wife was dying. I knew that every moment of enjoyment in this forest would cost me later in guilt. And unlike Dane, I had not worked out in ages. No one wanted to see that. Instead I said, "We don't know how deep the water is."

I watched Dane climb up and chat with the girls on their rocks, all hugging themselves against a cool wind. Nicole's illness had cost Dane; at thirty-six, he had given up a management position and a girlfriend back in New Orleans. She could not grasp his devotion to Nicole and me—it is ungraspable—and their relationship had come undone. From her perspective, he must have seemed disloyal. He moved to the edge of the rocks to jump, and

I found myself on my feet, clapping and cheering and wishing the sun would stop setting, and these young women would never age or fall ill or die, and Dane could hang there in space for the rest of time, a portrait of readiness and compassion.

.   .   .

Nicole rallied. She started eating again. She had slept through the months of IV feeding and woke up pleasantly surprised that she could now fit into smaller clothes than ever before. She started entertaining visitors. People would drop in to see her and she would sit up, beaming. Chatting. Apologizing for the state of her dress, or the house, or her hair, which had started growing back. She would describe all the things she wanted to do, and people—wonderful, kind, well-intentioned people—would nod and encourage her and marvel at her bravery.

This happened again and again throughout 2014. She would disappear into herself, silent, sleeping, afloat on powerful drugs, and then she would awaken with a new item to cross off her list: She wanted to visit New York one last time. She wanted to be the grand marshal of a Mardi Gras parade. She wanted to jump into the downtown fountain with all our friends. We did it all. What her life lacked in length, it made up for in height.

Each time she went down, doctors and nurses offered dire timelines. Months to live. Weeks. Even days. Each time, she rose again. It was magnificent to behold. It also came with a hidden price.

Each time Nicole faded, Dane took over many domestic duties—washing clothes, cleaning, shopping, cooking. I took over the rest. I woke and dressed and fed the girls, Molly and Evangeline, who were ten and seven. I helped them with their homework. I scheduled dosages, ordered supplies, checked the mail, paid the bills. I juggled money because nobody would die if we didn't pay our taxes, so the hospitals and surgeons came first.

During those times, Nicole was adrift on an opiate sea. We kept so much liquid morphine in the house that the doctors warned us about burglars. Then she graduated to Dilaudid, which is seven times stronger than morphine and ran on a continuous pump around the clock, alongside a terrifyingly powerful drug called fentanyl. These potions interrupted the signals between her mind and body, along with everything else in the physical world; her hallucinations disturbed Dane and me and would have terrified the girls. So we had to start keeping them away from her.

One night, she called to me and said she needed help to the bathroom. I tried to help her sit up, but she said, "No, I'm a Barbie doll. I can only move one limb at a time." So I lifted her head and then her back, straightened her head, moved one leg off the bed and then the other, finally standing her up. I moved her left foot, then her right foot, and so on until we had completed the task. To this day, her lead nurse, a woman named Faith, saves a photo of one of Nicole's Dilaudid pumps, which she shows to other nurses. That one pump recorded more than twenty thousand milligrams poured into Nicole. "That's more Dilaudid than I and all the nurses I work with have ever given," she said. "Combined."

When she would emerge into one of her better periods, she would awaken, aghast at the way I was running the house. One morning, she staggered into the kitchen, shocking us all, and announced that she planned to make eggs for the girls. Where had I hidden the spatula? Why was there so little milk in the refrigerator? Was it spoiled? It didn't taste right. Nothing tasted right. "How am I supposed to leave in peace?" she asked me. "I can't die like this."

With each decline and rise, she became more manic. One morning early last summer, I found her standing over the stove with the gas wide open while she tried to teach Molly how to light it. She couldn't remember how. I moved to switch off the gas and Nicole glared. She was unrecognizable with hatred.

Molly saw it and winced.

"It's not your fault, baby," Nicole told her, leading her away. "It's not your fault. Daddy needs to fix the stove."

There was nothing I could say. Her impending death stripped our relationship of every external measure of fairness. I could offer no arguments; I could not say, "That's dangerous," or, "Please don't use the girls against me."

I could appeal to nothing, because nothing trumps dying.

• • •

Technology started to loom over our lives in a new way.

Dane continually found packages arriving on our front porch—packages of the most mundane items, like toilet paper or school notebooks—and assumed I was ordering them. Then medical supplies started to arrive. And clothing. Food. We discovered that Nicole was secretly ordering things online, clinging to her role as shopper.

"I am still a valid person," she seethed when I asked her about the packages. "I'm still part of this house."

I let it carry on a long time, in part because she couldn't keep track of her phone. She would call Dane and me to her bedside, enraged, to accuse us of stealing her phone as it sat on the pillow beside her head. Finally, when she tried to send money to someone in Iraq, I changed our accounts without telling her.

I found myself locked in a battle against a swelling horde of electronic opponents. When I discouraged Nicole from something—when I took away her car keys or access to our accounts or certain visiting hours—she would go to online cancer forums and write posts about my choices. Those forums are populated by people in similar awful situations who go online to hear *yes* in a world that is suddenly telling them *no*, and these people—this faceless mass of online handles—always told Nicole to keep fighting, that she could beat this, to just ignore my negativity.

Death is an invisible thing that can't be cursed at, or ignored, or denigrated. Each night, though, I lay down beside her, she would tear into me for hours, propelled by anger and fear and Dilaudid.

I started avoiding bedtime. I see now that, after fifteen years of marriage, this was my first step down a path that diverged from hers: hers toward death, mine toward a life afterward.

Dane and I stayed up late watching television every night. Without understanding why, we both became obsessed with zombie shows and movies. We spent every night—every night for an entire summer—watching the living dead shuffling eternally into frame just before being dispatched to the afterlife by some hero.

Afterward, we would sit in the dark for hours, sometimes in silence, but usually discussing the day's interactions with Nicole. I confessed to him one night that a dark fantasy had flickered through my mind earlier involving a spoon and mayonnaise.

He laughed. Nothing tasted right to Nicole anymore except mayonnaise. She ate so much of it that when Dane and I went to the grocery store, we would buy two jars at a time. She had a jar-a-day habit. On this particular day, she had asked me to make her a turkey sandwich, which I did and then brought into the bedroom. She took one bite and handed it back.

"Less turkey, more mayo," she said.

I remade it, spooning on double the mayonnaise.

"No," she said again, disgusted. "More mayo."

I heaped the stuff on this time. Great mounds of it.

When I handed it to her, she shook her head. "So you're trying to starve me," she said. "I guess I'm not dying fast enough."

Since the day of her diagnosis, everything in my life had revolved around this frail figure before me. Decisions and depression. Hopes and heartbreak. And now, for a sliver of a second, I pictured myself prying open her mouth and pouring a whole jar of mayonnaise down her throat.

When visitors came, Nicole could draw herself up and present a model of grace and fearlessness—the same for online forums and Facebook. Those sentiments were true—she carried herself with courage, and love, and poise—but when we were alone, she cut me without mercy.

In just a few words, Dane saved me.

He said, "She lashes out at you because she knows you'll stay."

And when I would deny her yet another delirious fantasy—of going someplace exotic when the bathroom would forevermore be the extent of her travels—he had a simple clarity that I assumed I had lost for good.

"Just tell her yes," he said.

·   ·   ·

A sort of delirium set in.

Dane had lived with us for almost a year now, lived in the shadow of death, and he and I found ourselves cracking jokes so dark, so morbid, that they defied explanation.

We made a pact: If he married someday or if I remarried and one of our wives was diagnosed with cancer, the other would show up at the hospital and slip a knife between his ribs. A mercy killing. We cried laughing, imagining the puzzlement of witnesses on the scene: "This guy just walked in and stabbed him. And what's really weird? The dead guy told him 'thank you.'"

We told stories about how we would both be old men, drooling and incontinent, and Nicole would shuffle in to demand a mayonnaise sandwich.

We laughed at our inept drug smuggling. I had heard weed could help counter the nausea from chemo, but medical marijuana is illegal in Alabama. So some friends offered to get us some. I told them to just leave it in their mailbox, where I could pick it up. "Just make sure to pick it up before noon," my friend said. "That's when the mailman comes." The next morning, I found the brick of weed in the right spot, wrapped in clear plastic, and on top of it, the day's mail.

Later, when we had to take away Nicole's phone—probably the most difficult decision of the entire ordeal—she started leaving us venomous, drug-addled handwritten notes. They were heartbreaking. But her creativity and determination in delivering them took on an artistry. We couldn't figure out how she was doing it.

"I got this on my pillow," Dane said one night. A crayon scrawl.

I showed him mine, a loopy screed about needing her phone. "I found it in the bathroom," I told him, "stuck on the wall opposite the toilet, at eye level when sitting."

In our heartache and exhaustion, we both started to giggle. "You know what she's doing, right?" Dane said.

"What?"

"She's texting us."

It got to where I started hiding from Nicole, unable to face the rage. Too cowardly to sit and bear it, I would curl in the fetal position on our porch swing, where she could not find me. Or I would retreat to one of the girls' bedrooms upstairs, where she could not follow. I stopped eating and drinking.

Dane appeared there one night with a plate of food and a bottle of water. He admonished me with profound compassion. "I'm going to let you stay like this for one more day," he said. "After that, you'll have to get up."

As he walked out the door, he stopped to complete his argument. "For your girls," he said.

Even in my spiral I could see that our daughters had fallen in love with Dane. They sensed in him a strength that I no longer had, and they confided in him.

Each night, he would sit alone on our porch after Nicole and I went to bed. He would read or call his friends back in New Orleans or count raccoons crossing under a streetlight. A few times Molly got up and went out to join him.

I watched them through a window. He would sit with her, rocking on the swing, and listen while she talked about bad dreams.

.   .   .

The dressing on Nicole's abdomen became a massive, complex thing that required specialist nurses to come in every couple days and assemble it as a team. Its purpose now was to keep her abdomen from coming apart altogether.

One day, immediately after the nurses left, Nicole started pulling apart the bandages. "I think I'd like to have myself a shower," she said.

I watched, speechless, as she pulled off the last of the gauze and made her way to the shower, dribbling stool and acid onto the floor as she walked. I just lay on the bed, unable to move.

A long while later she returned and lay beside me. She requested tape and gauze.

"Let me call the nurses," I said.

"No. I can do this myself."

As she unwound the tape, it stuck to her hands, to itself, to her belly. Her stomach belched up a geyser of yellow crap, which flowed down her sides onto the bed. Her hands stopped, and I looked up to her face. She had passed out.

I touched her cheek and her eyes fluttered open. She smiled. She seemed puzzled to find herself covered in hot excrement and tried with her bare hands to contain it. It smeared all over her torso, up her arms to her elbows, and all over the bed. I reached to help and she pushed me away.

Something in me broke. The remaining thread of the last fiber of the final cable holding me together just snapped, and I rolled off the bed. I didn't want her to see. I crawled into the bathroom and curled around the base of the toilet, shaking and weeping.

From the bedroom, I heard her call out, "Dane . . ." Her voice was diaphanous, like she was calling through silk. I heard Dane come to the door, and she told him I needed help. She had called him for me.

Dane opened the bathroom door and I cried out, "It's just shit everywhere, Dane." With vast discretion, he didn't try to pick me up from the floor this time. He just closed the door.

The nurses came and replaced Nicole's dressing. I don't remember how long I lay in the bathroom, but the light through the windows had shifted when I emerged.

Later, Nicole's lead nurse, Faith, sat down with me. "I see it now," she said. "She needs antipsychotics."

. . .

Haldol was designed as an antischizophrenic drug in the 1950s, at the peak of the mental-institution boom in America. It's a knockout drug. "Hound dog," the nurses called it.

According to Alabama law, licensed practical nurses, who were now staying at the house and watching Nicole around the clock, were not allowed to administer it. Registered nurses could, but they could come by only once a day.

There was a loophole in the law, though, they said: Someone else could administer it.

Me.

So while the nurses watched and advised me, I started giving my wife the injections that would, in a sense, finish her life. She drifted away on Haldol, an ocean measured in milliliters, no longer calling for food or water, which meant the volcano of her stomach stopped erupting. Her face relaxed. Her jaw drooped.

Her breathing slowed, and over the next few days it grew louder—loud enough to hear throughout the house. It sounded like someone slowly dragging a cello bow across her vocal cords.

I realized then that the last honest person to describe death may be whoever came up with "croaking."

The way dying looks, or so I expected, was like this: A small group of friends and family gather around the patient, watching as she draws and releases her final breath. People hold hands and exchange glances to acknowledge how profound the moment is just before a doctor checks for a pulse and announces, "It's done."

The way it actually happened was like this: There was medical equipment blocking the way to our bathroom, so on the morning of September 9, 2014, I went upstairs to shower. I had a head full of shampoo when I heard Dane call from the foot of the stairs. I couldn't make out what he said, so I rinsed off and stepped out of the shower. A few seconds later, as I tried to towel off, he called again: "Hurry."

I tried to pull jeans onto my wet legs as I stumbled down the stairs, and just before I made it to the bedroom I heard Nicole's rasping breath. I think I did, at least; I was trying to zip up my pants before entering the room, where Dane stood with two nurses. They stood looking at Nicole.

"What happened?" I said.

"That may have been the last one," Faith said. "Maybe. They're coming slow."

Nicole's pulse had faded days ago, to the point where no one could feel it. So we stood watching her for a couple minutes. She simply didn't breathe again. No spiritual release. No change in complexion. No shift in facial features. She just stopped.

It was a routine death in every sense. It was ordinary. Common. The only remarkable element was Dane. I had married into this situation, but how had he gotten here? *Love* is not a big-enough word. He stood and faced the reality of death for my sake. He is my friend.

.   .   .

The months after Nicole died stretched and shrank and stretched again, like taffy.

Grief hollowed me out, and I expected that. But underneath it I also felt a deep sense of relief, and even joy. For the first time in two years, I felt hope. I kept that a secret, though. People would stop me on the street to express their sorrow, and I would find myself stooping to match their emotional tone. "Oh, yes, it is so difficult, but we will make it somehow."

The truth was that, after two years of suffering, Nicole finally felt no more pain. After two years of horror, the girls and I felt like we had escaped something. Molly told me that, for the first time in as long as she could remember, she didn't dread hearing me call from the foot of the stairs because she knew I had no more bad news to deliver.

Dane helped the girls adjust to an endless life without their mother, but the days without Nicole were empty, and he wanted to find work. I told him there was no need. He could just live with us, and I would split my income with him. Forever if he wanted. We had survived an endless winter and entered into an existential springtime.

But Dane quietly descended into a depression of his own. He felt restless and started spending more time in his room. At one point, he visited a pet shop with a friend, and she alternated between picking up the puppies and kittens. "Don't you want to hold one?" she asked him.

"Nah," he said. He couldn't explain it, but he knew that if he held a small animal he would burst into tears.

In January of this year, four months after Nicole died, fourteen months after he abruptly left behind every single thing that makes up an adult life to put himself at the service of Nicole and me, he decided that he needed to move back to New Orleans and reclaim his own life.

In a most unexpected way, Dane's leaving hit me harder than Nicole's because I wasn't prepared for it. He didn't know how to tell me that he was leaving, so he just started packing up. He left one day when the girls were at school. On that day, he stopped as he climbed into his car. "I'll be back in a couple of weeks," he said. "It'll be weird, though, because you'll be married by then."

We both laughed. He pulled out of the driveway, and I just stood there in the yard for a long time, wondering what to do, my eyes all wet. Then, after a while, I turned and went back inside my empty house.

Poetry

*This essay was the centerpiece of a
Poetry issue that focused on . . .
well, let Tavi Gevinson explain (if
you don't know who Gevinson is,
she's the founder and editor of
Rookie, and if you don't know
what Rookie is, you're no
seventeen-year-old). So this is
what Gevinson, who edited this
special portfolio, said about it:
"What you have here are poems,
artwork, and essays . . . [about]
the fear so many of us have of
writing and reading poetry, which
is really a fear of seeming like an
angsty teen." And this is what the
Ellie judges said about "How It
Feels": "elegantly structured . . .
combines confessional memoir, art
criticism, literary analysis . . .
explores dark and disquieting
emotions." Got it now?*

Jenny Zhang

How It Feels

There was a girl in my middle school no one really liked. She told everyone her uncle had sexually abused her and that she had an older boyfriend who was a freshman at Yale, and yes, they did more than kiss. People said terrible things about her—that she was lying about her uncle, that she just wanted the attention, that her boyfriend was made up, that she had never seen a penis in her life, that the reason why she so frequently stared into space with her mouth hanging open was so she could remind everyone what her "blowjob face" looked like.

At the end of the year, she didn't come to school for a few days in a row. The rumor was that she tried to kill herself with a plastic spoon (the especially cruel said it was a plastic spork she got from the lunchroom). It was officially (unofficially?) the most hilarious and pathetic attempt at suicide anyone had ever heard of. I didn't find it funny, but I did rush home after hearing about it, grabbed a spoon from the kitchen, locked myself in my bedroom, and there, sitting on my bed, I pretended to slit my wrists with the spoon, pushing it against my vein. Is this at all meaningful? I wondered.

Remember in the teen flick *Heathers*, when Shannen Doherty's character, Heather 2.0, informs Winona Ryder's character, Veronica, that the school's numero uno loser Martha Dumptruck attempted suicide and failed? When even one's failure to live is a failure . . . is there anything more poetic?

In the movie, Heather rushes into Veronica's living room dur-ing "pâté hour" and announces gleefully, "Veronica, have you heard? We were doing Chinese at the food fair when it comes over the radio that Martha Dumptruck tried to buy the farm. She bellyflopped in front of a car wearing a suicide note."

"Is she dead?" Veronica asks, horrified.

"No, that's the punchline. She's alive and in stable condition. Just another case of a geek trying to imitate the popular people in the school and failing miserably."

•   •   •

Do popular kids write poetry? The popular kids in my high school were the cliché teen-movie jocks and cheerleaders who bitched and moaned through every poetry segment we did in English class. "This is just weird and makes no sense," was a con-stant refrain.

Or: "Yo, this person needs to chill out. It's just a tree/bird/building/urn/body of water. Like it's really not that big of a deal."

•   •   •

Darkness is acceptable and even attractive so long as there is a threshold that is not crossed. But most people I know who suffer, suffer relentlessly and unendingly no matter what sort of future is proposed ("it'll get better / it won't always be like this / you will start to heal / I know it's such a cliché but you really will come out of this stronger in the end").

•   •   •

Why is it so humiliating to go on and on about something that means a lot to you only to be told, "Wow, you spend *a lot* of time thinking about stuff, don't you?"

Or: "So, you're one of those people who analyzes everything, huh?"

Or: "That's kind of dark."

Or worse: "Um . . . OK."

. . .

My school's Martha Dumptruck frequently submitted poems to our literary journal, of which I was on the editorial board. I thought her poetry was terrible. I was so embarrassed for her. What I knew about poetry in high school was that it was both hard to understand and completely open to interpretation. I was told that a poem could really mean anything. Poems could have grammatical mistakes, they could give a fuck about narrative or the space-time continuum or reality as we knew it. Poetry was an attempt to dig into the buried stuff inside a person's psyche. It used dream logic instead of the logic of our waking lives. Poems were sputtered by demons not sprung out of morality. In other words, poems were *deep shit*, and they were also anything at all (this became clearer the further I strayed from my high school's poetry curriculum): a single word (lighght), symbols and signs (Hannah Weiner's code poems), phrases that a child learning to speak might say (a rose is a rose is a rose), words that have been uttered a zillion times (I love thee/you), a blank page, a collage, an erasure, a Google spam filter, whatever. But if that was the case, if poems could be anything at all, then why is the default to cringe whenever someone writes a poem about their feelings? Even worse if that someone is a teenager? Even worse if that someone is no longer a teenager but nonetheless thinks about themselves with the kind of intensity that is only acceptable between the ages of thirteen and nineteen?

. . .

Last year, someone commented on my Instagram that I had a responsibility to the young (mostly) women and men who were using the hashtag #noonecares. The comment was under a picture of me standing on the pier of the Williamsburg waterfront, days before I slipped into the kind of bland, unexciting-to-describe, low-grade depression that I mostly masked from my friends and family by not leaving my apartment and making excuses to duck out of every social obligation. It was several weeks of lying in bed, holding in my shit and piss for hours until I reached the tipping point (leakage happened occasionally) because I was too depressed to get out of bed—the thought of moving across the room and down the hallway to get to the bathroom seemed like a particular kind of hell that I could not agree to.

A few months later, when I was no longer in the I'd-rather-shit-my-pants-a-little-than-climb-out-of-bed phase of my depression, I became curious about what having little-to-no will to live looked like for other people. I browsed the hashtag I had used in the caption of my photo, "First taste of daylight in 72 hours #noonecares," and quickly spiraled into the territory of self-harm hashtags: from #noonecares to #noonecaresifidie, #wanttodie, #whatsthepoint, #depressed, #hurting, #help, #ihatemyself. I scrolled through the photos for as long as I could stomach it, which was not long as it was primarily pictures of slashed up arms, razors floating in the toilet with captions like, "the last of my stash . . . if I get 100 likes tonight, I'll flush them."

Why are some people's feelings so repellent and others so madly alluring? As a fourteen-year-old, I wanted to be someone who was destined to die beautifully like Shakespeare's Juliet—freshly fucked, dead before ever having the chance to know what it's like to despise the person you once loved. She died just as her love for Romeo was ascending, becoming heavenly. In the throes of love, infinity seemed like a good idea. Pain looked so good on her. It immortalized her. Juliet was my suicide idol—hers was a suicide to aspire to and I couldn't even get close. Like so many other fourteen-year-old girls, I was told that my problems were minor, my tragedies imaginary, and worst of all—I was told I hadn't lived enough to really want to die.

·   ·   ·

The failure to move someone with what you think is the tragedy of your existence. I don't know, or just another way of saying #noonecares.

·   ·   ·

That thing where we imagine what would happen if we died and our dead, needy souls could float above our own funeral, watching the people who didn't love us as we wanted to be loved, in attendance, weeping, blaming themselves for not having tried harder to save us, for not having been more generous, more attentive. Why does it give us such satisfaction to imagine them saying, "I should have been better to you. I should have never treated you this way."

When a young person dies, they are forever immortalized, forever grieved, but what happens when we are too old to die young? Or if we can't commit to dying a physical death but still want to reap the joys of being mourned, which I guess is just some way of saying: I need proof that my existence matters.

·   ·   ·

There was this other kid who was universally picked on in my high school. He had epilepsy and talked with his mouth a little crooked. The jocks (there were jocks) would purposefully bump into him in the hallway, knocking his books onto the ground and kicking them so he had to scramble to pick them all up again.

"We're just having some fun," they said whenever a teacher came out to investigate. No one really had the energy to stop the momentum of cruelty anyway. Then, during my senior year, it was announced over the loudspeaker that he had suffered a severe seizure in his sleep the night before and died.

Everything is embarrassing, everything seems like a facsimile of the real thing, whatever that might be, if it even exists. My whole high school went into mourning. I lost track of the red faces, the number of students who wanted to share their personal story of how he touched their lives, what a good person he was, how he represented the spirit of our school and our town. It was an exciting day ... to be so close to something so genuinely tragic, a rare instance where showing feelings in public was a good thing, as valuable as being an asshole had been the day before.

When someone dies, we go searching for poetry. When a new chapter of life starts or ends—graduations, weddings, inaugurations, funerals—we insist on poetry. The occasion for poetry is always a grand one, leaving us little people with our little lives bereft of elegies and love poems.

But I want elegies while I'm still alive, I want rhapsodies though I've never seen Mount Olympus. I want ballads, I want ugly, grating sounds, I want repetition, I want white space, I want juxtaposition and metaphor and meditation and ALL CAPS and erasure and blank verse and sonnets and even center-aligned italicized poems that rhyme, and most of all—feelings.

When I was a teenager, every little moment called for poetry. I mean, I'm still this way, except at my age it's considered inappropriate and embarrassing, if not downright creepy.

．　　　．　　　．

The first time I was exposed to Tracey Emin I was twenty-four and discussing misspellings and typos with my boyfriend at the time who had brought home a bunch of Tracey Emin art books from the library. Her work often contains "mistakes," like her monoprint that says, "RETIER SOFTLY" in little-kid chicken scratch above a drawing of a naked girl on her knees. We loved her sloppiness. We loved how little she seemed to process her emotions before turning them into art. "I'd rather eat processed food than have processed emotions," I wrote once in my notebook after reading a transcript of her film, *How It Feels*, where she describes in great detail the trauma of her first abortion: "I felt something slip and as it slipped I put my hand there and what I held between my thigh and the palm of my hand was a fetus, kind of mashed-up fetus . . ."

We loved the crudeness of her drawings and embroideries and monoprints and neons. I loved her self-absorption. I found it so incredibly generous—to be just as ugly as anyone but to emphasize that ugliness over and over again, to let yourself be the subject of your art and to take all the pummeling and the eye-rolling and the cruel remarks and the who cares? and the that's not art that's just a scorned woman unable to let go. Her pain was so alluring to me. I stared at the pictures of her depressed bed with the sheets all bunched up and stained with her bodily fluids and dried up menstrual blood and the psychic weight of psychic bedsores from not being able to lift oneself out of there. I had a bed too and it had been the site of my depression so many times in my life. I slept on my own dried blood as well and wore the same underwear so many days in a row that the discharge from my cunt had built up and become so thick that it essentially glued my pubic hair to my underwear and every time I had to pee and pull down my panties I would give myself like a little unintentional bikini wax.

My boyfriend and I were particularly enthralled with Tracey because at the time we were courting each other with misspellings and typos. It was the early years of auto-correct on phones. We both had flip-phones whose range of saved words were much more limited than iPhones now. "I miss you baby and my twat is still ringing" became "I miss you bikes and my twat is still ringing." "Come home and I'll make you ramen" became "Come home and I'll make you robb." "I will wait for you after class my pamplemousse" became "I will wait for you after class my samplenourse." "I miss you bikes" was mistyped one time as "I miss you bikers." "Bikers I'm preparing a very good robb for us" became "bikespspspspspspspspspsp I'm preparing a very good robb for us" because I accidentally hit the *s* key too long. We built our private little world through these mistakes, and like everyone else falling in love we tried to become one entity, impenetrable through our arsenal of inside jokes, through a language that other people could not understand or use.

·   ·   ·

The year I fell in love, I wrote a story about my relationship with my little brother and sent it to my mom. She wrote back:

> I just finished read whole story. It is very funny and touchable, plus nice pictures. you should e-mail this to Johnny too. I was laughed a lot. I wish I can translate this to Chinese. Maybe oneday I will.
>
> Love,
> Mom

I rarely have the impulse to correct someone's mistake, or misspelling, or mispronunciation, or misusage. Every time my mom speaks in English, she makes a mistake. She pronounces tissue "tee-shoe" and once, in the middle of the night, when she was sick with the flu she woke violently sneezing and asked my dad to get her a "tee-shoe," and so he got up and pulled a T-shirt from the drawer, thinking she was cold. Later, I tried to teach both of them how to "correctly" pronounce "tissue" and "T-shirt" and I truly, truly, truly felt like a scumbag.

•   •   •

But I have to get back to Tracey Emin and her misspellings and her intensity and her nakedness. I mean her literal nakedness and her emotional nakedness, both subject to such revulsion and praise and fascination and snap judgment and boredom and ugly patronizing and overt cringing. I look at the photo from her show *I've Got It All* where she's sitting on the floor, legs bent and spread, wearing chains around her neck and little messy braids tucked behind her ear. She's shoving bills and coins and miscellaneous bits of junky flotsam and jetsam. Her tits look unbelievably good and her legs look tired and she's looking down at all this garbage and bills and the moment captured is in a sense so completely trashy and gleeful and celebratory and excessive and weird, but in another sense, the photo is so much that it becomes a statement against allowing others to tell your story, against those who would insist on your victimhood. When I look at that photo, I don't pity her at all. I love her. She is the first poet I have loved.

And her scratched out poems are the greatest poems I know. One of her monoprints is a drawing of a naked girl standing in front of a nondescript black puddle, and next to it, the words:

PETHETIC
LITTLE
THING

Aren't we? At least those of us who still risk revealing ourselves in public?

In *How It Feels*, Tracey narrates through a voiceover her struggle to make art after her abortion:

Ah . . . I gave up painting, I gave up art, I gave up believing, I gave up faith. I had what I called my emotional suicide, I gave up a lot of friendships with people, I just gave up believing in life really and it's taken me years to actually start loving and believing again. I realized that there was a greater idea of creativity. Greater than anything I could make just with my mind or with my hands, I realized there was something . . . the essence of creativity, that moment of conception, the whole importance, the whole being of everything and I realized that if I was going to make art it couldn't be about . . . it couldn't be about a fuckin' picture. It couldn't be about something visual. It had to be about where it was really coming from and because of the abortion and because of conceiving, I had a greater understanding of where things really came from and where they actually ended up so I couldn't tolerate, or, or, err, I just felt it would be unforgivable of me to start making things, filling the world up with more crap. There's no reason for that. But if I couldn't fill the world up with someone which I could love for ever and ever and ever then there was no way I could fill the world up with just like menial things. That's art.

I guess that is what is so embarrassing about being a poet, that you might be filling the world up with more crap. That your pathetic little thing is not interesting to anyone but yourself.

When the warehouse that housed her piece *Everyone I Have Ever Slept with 1963–1995*—a tent with all the names of everyone she slept with embroidered on the inside—burned down, journalist Tom Lubbock wrote in *The Independent*,

But it's odd to hear talk about irreplaceable losses. Really? You'd have thought that, with the will and the funding, many of these works were perfectly replaceable. It wouldn't be very hard for Tracey Emin to re-stitch the names of *Every One I Have Ever Slept With* onto a little tent (it might need some updating since 1995).

If even internationally recognized artists can be invalidated with just one, "um . . . OK," then what about the rest of us? #noonecares

.   .   .

The quote I kept seeing again and again in all of these Instagram self-harm and suicide hashtags: "No one cares unless you're pretty or dying." But there were others as well:

I hope my last breath is a sigh of relief.
disgusted by my own self
I remember everything that you forgot
do you ever feel worthless
please please please let me die in my sleep
This is how you make me feel, like a black mass of nothing-
    ness, an ugly space filled with my own sadness
I fucked up I failed—it was my disaster—my choice—I just
    didn't expect to feel so bad—so foolish and so afraid of
    ever being touched.

All of these but especially the last one remind me of Tracey Emin's artwork. There's a part in her essay "You Left Me Breathing" where she writes about the dissolution of a relationship:

You left me—you left me breathing—just half alive—curled up like some small baby seal, clubbed half to death—you left me alone—you left me breathing—half alive—
    Half alive is not dead—stains on the shore, blood seeping into the water, but definitely not dead. I tried to think of and remember the times when I had cried, not just tears that ran down my cheeks, but the breathless sobs of overwrought, un-controllable emotion.

I don't know if we, as a culture, feel compelled to extend much sympathy to those who are half alive. Half alive is not dead.

.   .   .

In her neons, Tracey Emin takes a material that has long been associated with seediness to communicate some very adolescent feelings. Neon is cheesy, neon is tacky, neon hangs over love motels off the highway that charge by the hour, neon blinks in the part of town where the riffraff linger, where ne'er-do-wells pass each other on street corners, where people who might be there one day and dead the next hang out. Tracey's neons hang out in galleries, glow bright in Times Square, and they cycle through a moving range of teeny emotions, from the hopeful, *Fantastic to Feel Beautiful Again*, to the moody, *Sorry Flowers Die*, to the bratty, *PEOPLE LIKE YOU NEED TO FUCK PEOPLE LIKE ME*. Some of her neon messages are crossed out, *I KNOW I̶ ̶K̶N̶O̶W̶ I KNOW*, while others literally appear as indecipherable scribbles.

My favorite neon is the one that simply says:

Just Love me

.   .   .

Is there anything so inadequate as the words "I love you"? Is there anything so perfectly capable as "I love you"?

"O!" I said when my boss at my first real job working as an union organizer told me, "We don't do midriffs here." "O! Okay!" I said. "Don't get me wrong," she said, "you look great and you should show that off on your own time. But just as a rule, we don't do midriffs at work." "O!" I said when a boy I waited all year to meet again in Paris told me, "I want to elope with you," while we were on a train from Paris to Nice. We spent three days eating sandwiches from the garbage bins outside of cafes. We tried to go to an outdoor movie screening of *Terminator 3* on a cliff that overlooked the Mediterranean Sea, but it was twenty euros to enter and we were nineteen short, so he hoisted me up onto a tree—"O!" I said, "I'm gonna fall,"—and took off my underwear and scrunched it up into the pocket of my dress because I had an urinary tract infection and needed to pee every twenty minutes, my diseased urine dribbling through the leafy branches. "O!" I said, "I hope I don't accidentally pee on someone's head." Afterward we said goodbye in the doorway of the studio I was subletting in the Bastille—he was leaving to go back to Scotland and I was leaving to go back to the U.S.—and just as I was beginning to mourn what I had to leave behind, I heard a knock at the door and it was him again. "It would be easy to fall in love with someone like you . . . difficult in fact not to," he said, granting me my lifelong wish of being my own protagonist in a movie. "O . . ." I said, "I won't be able to forget you." "O!" I said when I saw my grandmother for the first time in three years, chilled by how old she looked this time, too old to dye her hair black like how she used to and how the hair dye she used was so cheap that it would run down her scalp and the little black drip marks would remain on her forehead for days. She was too old to curl her bangs by wrapping them around an empty can of Pepsi and then taking me and my brother out to the store to buy more with her Pepsi can roller on prominent display. O! I was mortified back then. "O!" I said when her nose started bleeding as soon as she saw my brother, and I noticed how small she was sitting in that wheelchair, how at every stage we occupy a different throne and hers now was that of a sick old person. "O!" I said, "you must," when she said she wanted to make one last trip to the United States to see us, even though I knew she would never make that trip. "O!" I said when she told me she likes to have conversations with me and my brother in her dreams. We come to her and we are just the age we were when she took care of us and lived with us in New York. "O! Yes, I remember," I say to every memory she details even though I do not remember any of it. "O!" I write in my poems sometimes with nothing to follow but it is wonderful to use that letter and that exclamation mark. It is wonderful to try and say anything.

O maybe no one really does care. Maybe it is humiliating to attempt anything.

I sincerely don't know why poetry can be mortifying but tattoos can be cool.

I think everyone wants to make something touchable, but most of us don't out of fear of being laughable. I'm not saying I'm fearless.

My mom used to ask her mom to touch her earlobes so she could fall asleep. When she immigrated to New York and could no longer fall asleep at her mother's house in Shanghai, she started asking me and my father. I remember one time I said, I don't get it, why do you like that? Let me show you, she said, and she rubbed my earlobes until I couldn't help but close my eyes. I started to see differently. I think we were spooning. Or I had my head in her lap and she was sitting upright against the bed. "Do you see how good it feels to be touched there?" she asked me. I did.

Permissions

Contributors

KEN ARMSTRONG is a staff writer at the Marshall Project, where he specializes in investigative reporting and narrative writing. His story "An Unbelievable Story of Rape," which was reported with T. Christian Miller, was awarded the Polk Award for Justice Reporting. A graduate of Purdue University, Armstrong lives in Seattle with his wife, Ramona Hattendorf, and their two children, Emmett and Meghan.

KEN BENSINGER is an investigative reporter based in Los Angeles for *BuzzFeed News*, where he has covered topics including the federal H-2 guest-worker program and insurance regulation of ride-hailing companies. Bensinger previously worked at the *Los Angeles Times*, where he primarily covered the auto industry. He has been honored with numerous journalism awards and has also worked at the *Wall Street Journal* and *SmartMoney* magazine. Bensinger is currently writing a book on the FIFA soccer scandal to be published by Simon & Schuster.

BARRETT BROWN is an imprisoned U.S. journalist and the founder of Project PM, a crowd-sourced investigation into the cyber-industrial complex. In 2012 the FBI raided his house; later that year Barrett was indicted on twelve federal charges relating to the 2011 Stratfor hack. The most controversial charge, linking to the hacked data, was dropped, but in 2015 Brown was sentenced to sixty-three months in prison. For more information about his case, and to contribute to his legal defense fund, please visit freebarrettbrown.org.

HOWARD BRYANT is a senior writer for ESPN.com and *ESPN the Magazine*. He has also served as the sports correspondent for National Public Radio's *Weekend Edition Saturday* since 2006. Before joining ESPN in 2007, Mr. Bryant spent two years at the

Washington Post. He has also worked at the *Bergen Record, Boston Herald,* the *Oakland Tribune,* and the *San Jose Mercury News.* A native of Boston, Bryant is the author of several books, including *Juicing the Game: Drugs, Power the Fight for the Soul of Major League Baseball; The Last Hero: A Life of Henry Aaron;* and *Shut Out: A Story of Race and Baseball in Boston.*

PAUL FORD is a writer, programmer, and cofounder of Postlight, a New York City agency that makes big, beautiful technology things like websites and apps. He has been an editor, essayist, novelist, and radio commentator for places like *Harper's Magazine, The New Republic,* and *All Things Considered* and is often found building content-management systems for fun. He has a column in *The New Republic* about databases called "Big Data." In addition to managing Postlight, he is writing a book about webpages for the publisher Farrar, Straus and Giroux, to be published in 2016.

JESSICA GARRISON is a reporter and editor for *BuzzFeed News* based in San Francisco. She joined *BuzzFeed News* in May 2014 after fourteen years at the *Los Angeles Times,* where she served as a reporter covering topics ranging from toxic waste to the fight for gay marriage in California.

JOSHUA HAMMER was born in New York and educated at Horace Mann School and Princeton University. In August 1988, he became a staff writer at *Newsweek,* covering business and the media and serving for several months as television critic. Four years later Hammer became Nairobi Bureau Chief, arriving in Africa during a time of war, genocide and revolution. He covered the unraveling of Somalia, the tragedy in Rwanda, South Africa's first democratic election and other compelling events during his four years on the continent. Since 2006, Hammer has been an independent journalist and author based with his family in Berlin. He contributes regularly to *Conde Nast Traveler, National Geographic, The New York Review of Books, Outside,* and *Smithsonian,* as well as the *New York Times.* His next book, *The Bad-Ass Librarians of Timbuktu: And Their Race to Save the World's Most Precious Manuscripts,* will be published by Simon & Schuster in April 2016.

ROGER HODGE is national editor of *The Intercept.* He is the author of *The Mendacity of Hope* and former editor of the *Oxford American* and *Harper's Magazine.* His new book, *Texas Blood,* is forthcoming from Knopf.

T. CHRISTIAN MILLER joined ProPublica in 2008 as a senior reporter. He spent the previous eleven years reporting for the *Los Angeles Times.* His work included coverage of the 2000 presidential campaign and three years as a bureau chief for the *Times,* responsible for ten countries in South and Central America. Earlier in his career he worked for the *San Francisco Chronicle* and the *St. Petersburg Times.* Miller has previously received the George Polk Award for Radio Reporting, the Dart Award for Coverage of Trauma, the Selden Ring Award for Investigative Reporting, the Investigative Reporters and Editors Award for Online Reporting, two Overseas Press Club awards, a Livingston Award for Young Journalists, the John B. Oakes Award for Distinguished Environmental Reporting, and a special certificate of recognition from the Daniel Pearl Awards for Outstanding International Investigative Reporting. In addition, Miller was given a yearlong Knight Fellowship in 2011 to study at Stanford University. Miller is the author of *Blood Money: Wasted Billions, Lost Lives, and Corporate Greed in Iraq.* He is currently based in Berkeley, California.

LUKE MOGELSON is the author of the short-story collection *These Heroic, Happy Dead.* He lives in Paris.

JEREMY SINGER-VINE is the data editor for the *BuzzFeed News* investigative unit and is based in New York. Singer-Vine's award-winning work has contributed to some of *BuzzFeed News*'s most impactful investigations, including the organization's investigation into the H-2 guest-worker program. Singer-Vine came to *BuzzFeed* from the *Wall Street Journal*, where he worked as a reporter and computer programmer. Singer-Vine is also the publisher of *Data Is Plural*, a weekly newsletter that highlights useful and curious datasets.

KATHRYN SCHULZ is a staff writer at *The New Yorker* and the author of *Being Wrong: Adventures in the Margin of Error*.

SHANE SMITH is the founder and CEO of Vice, the global youth media brand. One of the industry's most respected visionaries, Smith is also a critically acclaimed journalist and the host and executive producer for the Emmy-winning news series *Vice* on HBO. Under Smith's guidance, *Vice*, initially launched in 1994 as a punk magazine, has expanded and diversified to become the world's leading youth media company. Smith has reported from the world's most isolated and difficult places, including Afghanistan, Iran, Kashmir, Liberia, Greenland and North Korea. Smith has been awarded numerous journalism and media awards, including the 2014 Knight Innovation Award, two Environmental Media Awards, and the Frank Stanton Award for Excellence. *Vice* has also won scores of awards for its groundbreaking reporting, including an Emmy Award for Best Information Series or Special, two Peabody Awards, the PEN Center 2014 Award of Honor and the Television Academy Honors for Socially Conscious Programming. Smith graduated from Carleton University in Ottawa with a BA in English literature and political science.

MATTHEW TEAGUE writes from around the world for *The Atlantic* and *National Geographic* and covers the American South for the

Guardian. His work has been included in several anthologies, including *Best American Travel Writing*, *Best American Crime Writing*, *Best American Sports Writing*, and *Don't Quit Your Day Job: Acclaimed Authors and the Day Jobs They Quit.*

MEAGHAN WINTER is a freelance writer whose work has appeared in a range of publications, including *Bloomberg Businessweek*, *New York*, *The Believer* and *The Kenyon Review.* She reported on crisis pregnancy centers for *Cosmopolitan* in partnership with the Investigative Fund at the Nation Institute.

JENNY ZHANG is a poet and fiction and nonfiction writer based in New York. She is the author of the poetry collection *Dear Jenny, We Are All Find* and the nonfiction chapbook *Hags.* Her forthcoming collection of short stories will be published by Random House in 2017. She is a graduate of Stanford University and the Iowa Writers' Workshop.